ENGLISH CRICKET

ENGLISH CRICKET

The Game and its Players
through the Ages

CHRISTOPHER BROOKES

WEIDENFELD AND NICOLSON
LONDON

Weidenfeld and Nicolson
11 St John's Hill London sw11

isbn 0 297 77467 0

Printed in Great Britain by
Butler & Tanner Ltd, Frome and London

To my father and
the Gaieties Cricket Club

On doit des égards aux vivants ;
on ne doit aux morts que la vérité.

Voltaire

Contents

List of Illustrations   *xi*

Acknowledgements   *xiii*

1   Myths and Mysteries   *1*

2   Cricket: the Folk-Game   *9*

3   The Adoption of Cricket   *24*

4   'Gamesters, Jockeys and Cricket Players'   *34*

5   The Organization of Eighteenth-Century Cricket   *45*

6   The Early Years of the Marylebone Cricket Club   *67*

7   The Second Transformation   *81*

8   William Clarke and the Professional XIs, 1846–70   *101*

9   The County Championship, 1873–94   *120*

10   Amateurs and Professionals, 1873–1962   *138*

11   Three Generations of Post-War Cricketers   *155*

12   The Beginning or the End?   *187*

Notes   *191*

Bibliography   *199*

Index   *201*

Illustrations

1 John Frederick Sackville (*MCC*)
2 Sir Horatio Mann (*MCC*)
3 A scene during an early match (circa 1743) at the Artillery Ground (*MCC*)
4 A typical late-eighteenth-century cricket scene (*Mansell*)
5 The Laws of the Noble Game of Cricket (*MCC*)
6 Fuller Pilch (*MCC*)
7 A handkerchief showing William Clarke's All-England XI (*MCC*)
8 W. G. Grace (*Popperfoto*)
9 W. G. Grace – a stamp designed by Edward Ripley (*MCC*)
10 F. R. Spofforth in action for the Australians against Thornton's XI in 1878 (*Mary Evans*)
11 C. B. Fry batting for Sussex (*Mary Evans*)
12 Kerry Packer and Tony Greig (*Popperfoto*)

Acknowledgements

This book is based on research carried out during the preparation of my doctoral thesis. In the course of that research and the writing of this manuscript, I have received assistance from too many to mention here. But I would like to record my profound gratitude to the following persons: Professor Ilya Neustadt and Eric Dunning for their help and encouragement during the time I spent at Leicester University; Mr S. C. Griffith, former Secretary of the MCC, and all those connected with cricket who allowed me to interview them; Clive Senior, Harold Pinter and Christopher Falkus for their advice and assistance during the preparation of this book.

1 Myths and Mysteries

When Voltaire observed that 'our history is no more than accepted fiction', he might well have been referring to cricket. Accounts of its evolution from folk-game to modern sport have tended unfortunately to be based more on preconception and prejudice than fact. Considering the exalted position that cricket has occupied in the hearts and minds of millions of people in Britain and in the nations of the old Empire, the poverty of these histories is as surprising as it is distressing. Apart from such honourable exceptions as H. S. Altham, Neville Cardus and John Arlott, writers whose scholarship, insight and wit would grace any subject, the list of acknowledged 'authorities' on cricket's past has a depressingly long tail.

The general inadequacy of cricket's histories cannot be attributed to lack of effort. Far from it. So much has been written on the subject that the cynic could be forgiven for recalling the old story of the monkey with a typewriter and an infinite amount of time recreating the works of Shakespeare. If there is any truth in this quip, the definitive history of cricket must be imminent. Until such time as it appears, however, the works of a few outstanding writers will remain beleaguered on library shelves packed with the contributions of authors who had little understanding of the complexity of cricket's past, or of their own limitations.

While it is very easy to lament the obvious inadequacies of existing histories of the game, to fill the vacuum thus created is a much more demanding task. To avoid repeating the mistakes of previous writers, it is worth devoting a little time to considering why so many histories of cricket have been written, and why, in general, they have proved so unsuccessful. These questions may seem trivial, even irrelevant, at first sight, yet there have been strangely few attempts to explain the hold that cricket has maintained over writers of all colours and creeds during the past century. Neville Cardus probably came nearest to providing an answer when he noted that 'cricket somehow holds up the mirror to the English nature'.[1] This lead was taken up in a report, entitled 'The Cricket Industry', prepared by the research organization Political and Economic Planning Report in 1956. In answer to the question, 'What is cricket?', the authors of the report reached the following conclusion: 'It is a peculiarly English game: not suitable for export and found only in places where Englishmen have taken it. Cricket is an expression of the national character and, as such, inscrutable.'[2]

This inscrutability, real or imaginary, is undoubtedly what has endeared cricket to countless writers over the past one hundred years. In effect, it has given the game a double appeal. In addition to unravelling the intriguing complexity of cricket's past, many of the game's historians have taken the opportunity to explore the deeper recesses of the 'national character'.

So far, so good. The problems begin only when we consider the approach adopted by most of these authors. It is one thing for a novelist like Charles Dickens to idealize his descriptions of cricket matches and the characters that played in them. His account of the Homeric battle between Dingley Dell and the All-Muggletonians, for example, is memorable precisely for its wit and imagery. It is a very different matter when authors of supposedly factual histories of cricket adopt a similar approach. One basic prerequisite of any historian is that he bases his analyses and interpretations on facts. Unfortunately, very few of cricket's historians have succeeded in satisfying this requirement. In the great majority of cases, accounts of the game's past have been based on speculation and assumption, or, worse still, pure fantasy.

The task of writing a complete history of cricket has never been an easy one, and probably never will be. Not least of the difficulties that awaits those brave – or foolhardy – enough to try is the dearth of documentary evidence relating to the earliest forms of cricket. The reasons for this scarcity will be considered later; here we are only concerned with the surprising fact that so few 'experts' felt it to be a major obstacle to their attempts to solve the riddle of the game's ancestry. Why were these authors apparently so oblivious of the difficulties they faced? Why were they so anxious to trace cricket's origins?

The answer to the first of these questions is unfortunately quite simple. The writers in question were, for the most part, not representative of the best traditions of historical scholarship. To put it bluntly, they were amateurs. The second question, however, is more difficult. The first point to bear in mind is that most of the best-known accounts of cricket's ancestry were a product of the late nineteenth and early twentieth centuries. These were the years when the game's prestige as a social institution was at its highest. By the beginning of the present century, cricket had become as much a part of English life as Queen Victoria herself. It was the 'national' game. Moreover, it was no accident that during this period expressions like 'to play with a straight bat' and 'it's not cricket' became almost liturgical. The sentiments they echoed clearly reflected the upper-class values which, by this time, dominated the game. Ironically, it was this association with the élite that highlighted a problem which otherwise might have been conveniently ignored. At a time when breeding was still the basis of gentility, no-one could say with any certainty where or when cricket had been conceived, nor who the lucky parents were. Faced with such a damaging prospect, the *aficionados* of the day saw it as their duty to provide cricket with a respectable pedigree. This was the least that they could do for the 'national' game.

The search for the origins of cricket is a good example of the way powerful ideologies tend to spawn their own myths. Even though so few records of the earliest forms of the game had survived, several 'authorities' claimed to have found the key to cricket's birth and formative years. Predictably, their solutions are notable only for the lack of agreement they reveal. As Arthur Haygarth once remarked, 'there seem to be as many opinions as there are antiquarians'.[3]

The 'opinions' to which Haygarth alluded can be divided into two groups. The first include those explanations which sought to overcome the lack of information about the game's origins by making assertions about the innate capabilities of *homo sapiens*. Batting and bowling, for example, have often been described as expressions of innate drives. In Dr H. Squire's book, *Henfield Cricket and Its Sussex Cradle*, we find the following argument:

3

We need only to regard with perception the habits of some aboriginal race as yet uncontaminated by civilisation; or with a little more science and imagination, the behaviour of the developing baby who, as any medico will tell you, has already progressed through successive stages of evolution prior to birth. From both these authorities come irrefutable evidence that, closely related to the more generally recognised instincts, are two others – the Instinct to Throw and the Instinct to Hit. And herein we trace the remote origin of Cricket. Cricket satisfies, even for the most cultured of moderns, these age-old cravings, and who will venture to say that their inhibition would make the world a better place.[4]

The same approach is to be found in a series of articles, collectively entitled *Old English Cricket*, written by Percy Thomas under the pseudonym of H. P-T. For example, at one point Thomas argues,

Cricket will be born again as it was born first and has been born a thousand times since. Its only parents have been the human boy and the right implements to hand. Cricket was essentially a boy's game – the natural spirit of the young savage whose instinct it was to throw things with a club. Heaven help the race whose ancestors had not possessed and indulged this inclination. This is all the infant game was when it became Cricket, and it became Cricket as soon as that name was conferred on it and only by that fact.[5]

The distinctive feature of these passages is their reliance on the least sophisticated and most outdated forms of psychology and anthropology. Today, most sociologists and psychologists believe that the way in which men and women behave owes much more to the influence of the society and the groups in which they live than to any innate drives. Few would accept that instinct on its own is a sufficient explanation of human behaviour. Furthermore, there is little evidence to suggest that cricket ever possessed the universal appeal attributed to it in these passages. This type of assumption is typical of the chauvinism which pervaded much of the nineteenth- and early twentieth-century literature on cricket.

In the case of the passage from *Old English Cricket*, a further point needs to be emphasized. The idea that cricket became what it is when the name was conferred on it betrays a basic misunderstanding of the nature of traditional folk-games. Games of this type, examples of which were common in Europe, were a characteristic feature of medieval village life. Moreover, they were almost certainly the ancestral forms of our modern sports. Despite the social and historical importance of folk-games, however, the context and manner in which many of them were played remain something of a mystery. From the few records that have survived, it is clear that games like 'foteball', 'hurling', 'knappan', 'cat and dog', 'tip-cat' and 'trapball' lacked written rules and a central authority to standardize the way in which they were played. Bodies like the MCC, for example, did not come into existence until the eighteenth century.

As part of a traditional cultural heritage, folk-games were generally passed on from generation to generation by word of mouth. In these circumstances it is not at all surprising that each game tended to acquire a number of distinctive, local variations. The dimensions of the pitch (which often embraced entire fields), the size of the teams and the duration of the game often varied from village to village. The extent of these differences meant that, in many cases, the games could not be identified with as much certainty as their modern descendants. From contemporary descriptions, we can conclude that a game like football, for example, often combined features of what are now soccer, rugby, hockey, polo and wrestling. In fact, what was known as 'football' in one village could with relatively few modifications become 'hurling' in the next, 'camp-ball' in the next and so on. Thus, the game we now know as cricket need not necessarily have derived from games which were known by that name prior to the eighteenth century. Nor can we discount the possibility that our modern sport is a descendant of games which were known by names which bear no resemblance to the term 'cricket'.

Such was the credibility achieved by the nineteenth- and early twentieth-century accounts of cricket's origins that the misconceptions they embraced have never been seriously challenged. Even in the most recent histories of the game, one still finds examples of scientific concepts being used in a most unscientific fashion. In 1970, Major Rowland Bowen advanced the following intriguing argument:

Two hundred years later, the Irish were again found to have

a strong love for the game: there seems to have been some kind of affinity for it amongst what are loosely called the Celtic populations of the British Islands.

These Celtic populations are far larger than is generally realized: recent mapping of blood groups shows that large parts of England have a population of predominantly Celtic-type blood group and, most significantly, that there are even to this day large 'islands' of this blood group in Surrey and Hampshire.... These Celtic peoples are important because cricket, when it first reached English history, is located in and around what had been a very isolated part of the country, the Weald of Kent, Sussex, Surrey and Hampshire.[6]

Apart from the doubts surrounding the notion of 'Celtic blood groups', Major Bowen's argument contains one obvious flaw. If one accepts the existence of a special affinity between the 'Celtic populations of the British Islands' and cricket, it is difficult to see why cricket did not develop fastest and furthest in Wales, Scotland and Ireland. In fact, these are the areas where support for cricket has always been at its weakest.

The second of Haygarth's groups of 'opinions' contains those explanations which seek to trace a direct connection between the earliest forms of cricket and an even older game. In this context, 'stool-ball', 'tip-cat', 'cat and dog' and 'club-ball' have achieved fame as the 'acorn from which the mighty cricket oak has sprung'. Up to a point this argument seems to hold water. Each of these folk-games involved a stationary person striking a ball or a piece of wood, with another piece of wood, or bat, and, as in cricket, the object in these games was to score by running between two or more fixed points before a member of the opposing team could return the ball to any of these points. But impressive though these comparisons may seem, there is no firm evidence that cricket was descended *directly* from any *one* of these folk-games.

Looking at these attempted explanations, it is difficult to avoid reaching the conclusion that they serve only to emphasize the futility of trying to assemble a precise chronological account of cricket's origins. Unless new facts come to light, this must remain no more than a dream. The questions posed by cricket's evolution from a folk-game to a modern sport cannot be brought nearer solution until a fresh approach to the subject is adopted. If the study of the game is to embody more than a collection of dates, hearsay and a few witty anecdotes, its history has to be related to the history of the society in which it was nurtured. Cricket's evolution was not an isolated phenomenon, but part of a complex process in the course of which a whole range of games and pastimes emerged, and which was in itself closely related to basic changes in the structure of English society.

Though no single study can do justice to the richness of cricket's past, this book is an attempt to show the benefits of a different perspective on the game. The spotlight will be focussed throughout on the development of the game's organization and the careers of the players themselves. As the following chapters will show, the history of cricket falls into five distinct stages:

1 The age of the folk-game (pre-1660)
2 The era of the aristocracy and gentry (c. 1660–1830)
3 The end of patronage and the era of the professional elevens (c. 1830–1870)
4 The apogee of amateurism (c. 1870–1945)
5 The business years (post-1945)

Each of these stages covered a period in time when the game was dominated by a particular manner of playing and, in some cases, by a particular group of people. The dominant form was both the most technically advanced and the most highly organized cricket of the day. But this does not mean that it was the only form in existence at any one time, nor that it necessarily became extinct as soon as newer forms emerged. It merely ceased to be the dominant form. Moreover, at each stage in the game's history, composite forms of the game appear to have existed. 'Village' cricket is perhaps the best example of a composite form. Because they misunderstood the nature of folk-cricket, many writers have assumed that it was very similar, if not identical, to village cricket. But a closer examination of the typical village cricket of the eighteenth and nineteenth centuries shows that it was not a direct descendant of the folk-game, but a composite type – an amalgamation of characteristics from several stages in the evolution of cricket. In common with folk-cricket, village cricket was a traditional feature of rural life. But, unlike folk-cricket, it was dominated more often than not by the local magnate and his circle of friends. Not only did they pick many of the teams, but they also drew up the rules according to which the games were played.

Interesting though these composite forms of cricket may be, their existence has not been a profound influence on cricket's history. It is to the dominant forms of the game that one must look to find the source of the impetus behind its evolution from folk-game to modern sport. At each stage in cricket's history, a specific type of match and a particular batting or bowling technique has set the style and the standard for other matches and players first to emulate, and then to better. Thus, it is to these dominant forms that our attention must now turn.

2 Cricket: the Folk-Game

Most histories of cricket have been based on two fundamental misconceptions. They have assumed that the game has always been played in the same way, and that it has always possessed the exalted reputation that it acquired only towards the end of the eighteenth century. As a result, the stage in cricket's evolution when it existed only as folk-game has been largely neglected. Unfortunate though it may seem to those who find these mistaken beliefs totally acceptable, cricket, like all folk-games, was originally played by ordinary people, and rarely, if ever, by gentlemen. Sometimes children made up the nucleus of players, but on saint's days and other festivals entire communities would take part – women as well as men, the old as well as the young. In many cases, the opposite sides in a game were all the able-bodied inhabitants of neighbouring villages. Not surprisingly in view of the numbers involved and the absence of rules to control them, many of the ball-games of the Middle Ages were notable (or notorious) for their violence. Writing in 1583, one contemporary said of folk-football that,

It may rather be called a friendly kind of fight than a play or recreation. A bloody and murderous practise than a fellowly sport or pastime. For does not everyone lie in wait for his adversary seeking to overthrow him and to pick him on his nose, though it be on hard stones, in ditch and dale, in valley and hill or what place so ever it be, he cares not, so he may have him down. And he that can serve the most of this fashion, he is counted the only fellow and who but he. So that by this means, sometimes their necks are broken, sometimes their arms, sometimes one part thrust out of joint,

9

sometimes another, sometimes their noses gush out with blood, sometimes their eyes start out. But whosoever escapes away the best, goes not scot free, but is either sore wounded and bruised so he dies of it, or else escapes very hardly. And no wonder, for they have sleights to meet one between two, to dash him against the heart with their elbows, to hit him under the short ribs with their griped fists and with their knees, to catch him upon the hip and to pick him on his neck with a hundred such murdring devices, and hereof grows envy, malice, rancour doleur, hatred, displeasure, enmity and what not else. And sometimes fights, brawling, contention, quarrel picking, murder, homicide and great effusion of blood, as daily experience teaches.[1]

As late as the sixteenth and seventeenth centuries, the general character of the out-door games of ordinary people in England was essentially the same as of those found in Europe. Their precise form may have varied, but the manner of playing and the level of violence involved did not. In France, for example, the equivalent of football seems to have been a game called *la soule*. The most popular of the *jeux de force*, it was played with inflated bladders often encased in leather. Just as football was traditionally played on Shrove Tuesday, so Christmas Day was the occasion for games of *la soule*. However, the mere fact that many medieval English folk-games closely resembled games found in other parts of Europe at the same time does not mean that all folk-games diffused from a single centre. Games like 'football', 'hurling', 'stoolball', 'trap-ball' and 'cat and dog' were integral features of the indigenous folk-culture of Britain up to the seventeenth and even eighteenth centuries. They came into existence as part of a local cultural tradition and, in general, they survived as long as it did.[2]

Because any one folk-game was more than likely to exist in several different forms, and to go by a number of different names, and because, for the most part, the era of folk-games pre-dated the advent of the popular press, it is impossible to describe each game in detail. However, we do know enough about the manner in which they were played to outline three general types. The first, which included football, hurling and hand-ball, was characterized by the presence of a moving player who used his hands, feet or an implement such as a stick to control the ball. 'Points' were scored by throwing, kicking or hitting the ball into a 'goal', i.e. an object which had been selected as the 'aim' or 'goal' of the game. These were essentially team games, one group of individuals collectively facing another group. In the games which belonged to the second general type, such a 'goff', 'bandy' and 'pale-maille', the ball was struck by a stationary player away from his body with a club, mallet or some similar instrument. The object of these games was to project the ball either through the rings on the course, or into holes on it, in the smallest number of 'strokes' or 'shots'. Finally, they involved direct competition between individuals who took it in turns to hit the ball.

The games which belong to the third type, for example 'stool-ball', 'trap-ball', 'tip-cat' and 'cat and dog', bear the closest resemblance to what we now know as cricket. In *The Sports and Pastimes of the Peoples of England*, first published in 1801, Joseph Strutt compiled detailed descriptions of at least two games of this type. Stoolball, he tells us,

> consists in simply setting up a stool on the ground, and one of the players takes his place before, while his antagonist, standing at a distance tosses a ball with the intention of striking the stool, and this it is the business of the former to prevent by beating it away with the hand, reckoning one to a game for every stroke of the ball; if, on the contrary, it should be missed by the hand and touch the stool, the players exchange places. I believe the same also happens if the player who threw the ball can snatch and retain it when driven back, before it can reach the ground. The conqueror at this game is he who strikes the ball most times before it catches the stool. (p. 176)

In trap-ball, the 'bowler' was replaced by a crude catapult, or 'trap', which tossed the ball to 'a considerable height'. In addition, the striker used a bat, and the game required marked boundaries:

> It is usual in a game of 'trap-ball' when properly played to place two boundaries at a given distance from the trap, between which it is necessary for the ball to pass when it is struck by the batsman, for if a ball fall outside of either, he gives up the bat and is out; he is also out if he strikes the ball into the air and it is caught before it grounds, and again,

if the ball when returned by the opponents touches the trap, or arrests within one bat's length of it: on the contrary, if none of these things happen, every stroke counts for one towards the striker's game. (p. 168)

In tip-cat, a small piece of wood known as a 'cat' replaces the ball. Though Strutt's description of the two methods of playing this game is somewhat confusing, the basic structure of the game is clear enough.

A large ring is marked on the ground, in the middle of which the striker takes his station: his business is to beat the cat out of the ring. If he fails in so doing, he is out and another player takes his place; if he is successful, he judges with his eye the distance that the cat is driven from the centre of the ring, and calls for a number to be scored towards his game. If the number demanded be found upon measurement to exceed the same number of lengths of the bludgeon, he is out. On the contrary, if it is not, he obtains his call. The second method is to make four, six or eight holes in the ground in a circular direction, and as nearly as possible at equal distance from each other, and at every one is placed a player with his bludgeon. One of the opposite party who stands in the field, tosses the cat to the batsman who is nearest him, and every time the cat is struck the players are obliged to change their situation, and run from one hole to another in succession. If the cat be driven to any great distance, they continue to run in the same order and claim a score everytime they leave one hole and run to another: but if the cat is caught by their opponents and thrown between two of the holes before the player who has left one of them can reach the other, he is out. (p. 169)

The only other folk-game of this type that we know much about is cat and dog. The following description of the game is contained in John Jamieson's *Etymological Dictionary of the Scottish Language* (1808):

Cat and dog; the name of an ancient sport.

Three play at this game, two are provided with clubs. They cut two holes, each about a foot in diameter and seven inches in depth. The distance is about twenty-six feet. One stands at each hole with a club. The clubs are called dogs. A piece of wood about four inches long, and one inch in diameter, called a cat, is thrown from one hole to the other by a third person. The object is to prevent the cat from getting into the hole. Everytime that it enters the hole, he who has the club at the hole, loses the club, and he who has the cat gets possession both of the club and the hole while the former possessor is obliged to take charge of the cat. If the cat is struck, he who strikes it changes with the person who holds the other club: and as often as these positions are changed, one is counted in the game, by the other two who hold the clubs, and who are viewed as partners. This is not unlike the Stoolball described by Strutt (*Sports and Pastimes*, p. 176). But it more nearly resembles Club-ball, an ancient English game: *ibid.*, p. 183. It seems to be an early form of cricket. (pp. 78–9)

These descriptions indicate that the games which belonged to the third general type of folk-games were based on a stationary player striking a ball or piece of wood away from his person. The object of such games was to score by running between two or more fixed points. Finally, they were team games involving a particular type of co-operation. The sides took it in turns to bat and to bowl, but while the batting side played as individuals, their opponents played collectively.

Though stoolball, trap-ball, tip-cat and cat and dog belonged to a genus of games to which cricket either also belonged, or from which it subsequently crystallized, there is no record of a game *by that name* being played before the middle of the sixteenth century. The uncertainty which surrounds the precise origins of cricket has given rise to a prolonged debate, in the course of which many, highly imaginative arguments have been advanced. For example, there is in a Decretal of Pope Gregory IX (*c.* 1230) an illumination showing two figures – a young boy holding a straight club and a ball, and an older man, presumed to be his tutor, demonstrating a stroke played with a long stick. This has been claimed as evidence that cricket was played as early as the thirteenth century. Joseph Strutt's interpretation of a later illustration is remarkably similar:

In the Bodleian Library at Oxford, is a M.S. (No. 264) dated 1344, exhibiting a female figure in the act of throwing a ball to a man who elevates the bat to strike it. Behind them at a little distance appear, in the original delineation, several figures of both sexes, waiting attentively to catch or stop the ball, when returned by the batsmen. (p. 125)

In 1787, the London Society of Antiquaries published a series of manuscripts pertaining to the Wardrobe Account of the 28th year of the reign of Edward I, 1300, which contained the following entry:

> To Master John Leek, Chaplain of Prince Edward, the King's son, for monies which he has paid out, personally and by the hand of others, for the said Prince's playing at 'creag', and other games at Westminster, March 10th – 100s. And by the hand of Hugo, his Chamberlain, at Newenton in the month of March, 20s. Total.........£6. 0. 0.[3]

Interest in this entry centres on the identity of the game 'creag'. If it could be shown that this was an old English form of cricket, then the game could genuinely lay claim to a royal ancestry. H. S. Altham's argument is typical of the many attempts which have been made to prove this connection.

> In the mother tongue of the northern branch of the Aryan race there was a syllable beginning with 'cr', ending with the hard 'c', having for its letters every variety of the vowels according to the tribal predilection, and meaning staff or stick. . . . Furthermore, the termination 'et', though it sounds French, need not be anything of the sort; it may be really good Old English stock, a variant of the diminutive terminal 'el'. Hence, 'cricket' is simply a small 'crick' or staff, and cricket bat a redundancy exactly paralleled by golf-club, hockey-stick, or billiard-cue. . . . Reverting then, for a moment, to Prince Edward, let us now see what can be made of the puzzle. With the hard terminal 'c' or 'cric' a 'g' was virtually interchangeable; now suppose that Piers or one of the French play-fellows of Edward attempted to pronounce the word, he would sound the 'i' as 'ea' or 'ee', and straightaway we have 'creaget', which the clerk of accounts, following his consistent practice, shortened down to 'creag'. (p. 21)

Ingenious though this argument may be, it is also a little far-fetched. The original passage suggests only that a game involving Prince Edward took place at Newendon on the edge of the Weald of Kent in 1300. Apart from wishful thinking, there is very little evidence to support the claim that 'creag' was in fact an early form of cricket.

The etymological derivation of some of the basic terms in cricket's vocabulary, however, is a more promising line of enquiry. In the first place, it throws considerable light on the varying regional influences behind the crystallization of the earliest forms of the game. *The Oxford Dictionary of English Etymology* (1966) reveals that the words 'cricket', 'wicket', 'bat' and 'crease' first appeared in the English language in Anglo-Saxon times. The derivation of 'cricket' is uncertain, though it may have come from the Old French 'criquet' or alternatively the Old English 'cricc-crycc', meaning a crutch. 'Wicket' comes from the Old North French 'wiket', meaning a small gate, and 'bat' from either the Old French 'batte', a verb meaning to beat, or the Old English (Gaelic) 'batt' meaning staff. 'Bail' comes from the Old French 'beil', which was the name of a horizontal piece of wood fixed on two stakes. The word 'stump', however, derives from the Old Norse (Icelandic) 'stump-r' and does not appear in an Anglo-Saxon form. But it was closely related to the Old English 'stob' or 'stub', both of which referred to the stump of a tree. Various dictionaries of English regional dialects add a further dimension to this line of enquiry. For example, 'wicket' was part of Sussex dialect, and referred to the entrance to a downland sheep-pen. The latter consisted of a small hurdle, two uprights and a moveable cross-bar known as the 'beil'. This word was probably introduced into the language at the time of the Norman conquest and appeared primarily in dialects of Kent and Sussex. Similarly, the word 'stump' was part of Sussex and Hampshire dialect and meant the portion of a fallen tree left in the ground. The same meaning is attributed to the word 'stool', while 'stob' is included as another dialect variant. 'Stool-ball' was played in Sussex, Wiltshire and Somerset, while 'stob-ball' appears to have been confined to Gloucestershire.

By the middle of the sixteenth century, it seems that the name 'cricket' was becoming more closely associated with a particular species of folk-game, and that in this form, it had achieved a wider popularity. When, after the Reformation, Stoneyhurst School was forced to move to Rouen, it took with it the game of 'Stoneyhurst Cricket'. In the Malden Corporation Court Book of 1562, a presentment against John Porter alias Brown, and Robert, a servant, for 'playing an unlawful game called "clykett"' is recorded. The following reference, found among the records of the Borough of Guildford, mentions a game of cricket that was played by the boys of the Royal Grammar School in Guildford about 1550:

> Anno 40, Elizabeth. (1598) Memo, that atte this day came John Derrick of Guldeford aforesaid gent, one of the Queenes Majesties Coroners of the County of Surrey, being of age of fyftye and nine years or thereabouts and voluntarily sworn and examined saith upon his oath that he hath known the parcell of land lately used for a garden ... and did know the same lay waste and was used by the Inhabitants of Guldeford to lay timber and for sawpittes ... And also this deponent saith that he was a scholar at the Free Schoole of Guldeford and hee and divers others of his fellows did runne and play there at crickett and other plaies. And also that the same was used for the Baiting of Bears in the said Town untill the said John Parvishe did enclose the said parcelle of land.

Though these references tell us nothing about the way cricket was played, they contain at least two specific points of interest. It appears that cricket was a particularly popular game amongst schoolboys; but there is no evidence that cricket or any other game (save perhaps archery) was included in schools' *curricula*. It is equally clear that, under certain circumstances, the playing of cricket could be deemed an illegal activity.

The significance of these points only becomes apparent when they are seen against the backcloth of changes in sixteenth- and seventeenth-century society. Then we can begin to understand why cricket and other folk-games evolved as they did, and why they were frequently banned. For much of the previous two centuries, England had witnessed a succession of bloody feuds between members of an aristocracy who cared little for the claims of loyalty and obedience advanced by the Crown. Their defiance undermined the traditional stability of the feudal order to the point at which a state of near anarchy prevailed. Recalling these times, a contemporary observer remarked, 'Nothing hath plagueth England more than the many breaches and ever unsure, never faithful, friendshyppe of the Nobles.'[4]

Under the strain of repeated challenges from 'over-mighty' subjects, the capacity of the Crown, and the whole apparatus of government it controlled, to maintain law and order became seriously impaired. Evidence of this weakness is to be found in the proliferation of folk-games, some of which presented a serious threat not only to the law, but also to the physical safety of their players. Several attempts to suppress these games were made. For example, an order from Edward III to the Sheriffs of the City of London in 1365 forbade 'under the pain of imprisonment' participation 'in the hurling of stones, loggats, and quoits, hand-ball, foot-ball or other vain games of no value'. Another statute, passed in 1477, sought to prohibit 'playing at Cloish, ragle, half-bowle, quakeborde, handyn and handout'; in addition, it laid down that 'if any person permits even others to use these pastimes in his house or yard, he is to be imprisoned. Those who play at such games are to forfeit ten pounds and continue in gaol for two years.' Though these orders and statutes, and others like them, indicate an awareness of the dangers of folk-games, their continued popularity bears witness to the ineffectuality of the rule of law at this time.

That none of these bans specifically mentions cricket is not surprising. Since the variations and fluidity inherent in the nature of folk-games would have made precise legislation impractical, if not impossible, the decision as to whether or not playing cricket constituted a threat to law and order was probably left to the discretion of the local sheriff. Moreover, since it involved a minimal degree of physical contact as well as being a much less mobile game, folk-cricket presented less of a threat than football. As the following extract from the Middlesex County Records of 1581 shows, the latter was all too frequently the occasion of violence and death:

Coroner's inquisition – postmortem taken at Southemyms, Co., Midd., in view of the body of Roger Ludford, yeoman, there lying dead, with the verdict of the jurors that Nicholas Martyn and Richard Turvey both late of Southemyms, yeomen, were on the third instant between three and four pm playing with other persons at footeball in the field called Evanes Field at Southemyms, when the said Roger Ludford and a certain Simon Maltus, of the said parish, yeoman, came to the ground and that Roger Ludford cried out, cast him over the hedge, indiciating that he meant Nicholas Martyn, who replied, 'come thou and do yt'. That thereupon Roger Ludford ran towards the ball with the intention to kick, whereupon Nicholas Martyn with the forepart of his left arm and Richard Turvey with the forepart of his right arm struck Roger Ludford a blow on the forepart of the body under the breast, giving him a mortal blow and concussion of which he died within a quarter of an hour and that Nicholas and Richard in this manner feloniously slewe the said Roger.[5]

If the rivalry between the House of York and Lancaster – perhaps the original Roses match – contributed to a situation in which folk-games flourished, the arrival of the Tudor dynasty marked the beginning of a royal clamp-down on lawlessness and indiscriminate violence. While the monarchs themselves concentrated their efforts on barons, wives and Spaniards, the restoration of the sovereignty of the Crown over which they presided affected all sections of society. Aristocrats and artisans alike found that many of their favourite pastimes were now frowned upon, if not actually forbidden. Even such a seemingly harmless pursuit as cricket could end up in court, as the unfortunate John Porter and Robert of Malden found to their cost.

The Crown's attempts to prohibit many of the traditional pastimes of 'merrie England' were born of an ingrained fear of civil disorder. Many contemporaries believed that 'casual labour was the good basis of a mob, and a mob a valuable part of a well-organised riot'. The same sentiment was repeated in public pronouncements through the first half of the Tudor era. For example, among the reasons given for the abrogation of Holy Days in 1536 was the fact that they provided 'the occasion of much sloth and idleness, riot and superfluity'.

Besides the Crown, there were two other groups who were intent on imposing a greater degree of order on the everyday lives of the ordinary people. For the growing band of sixteenth-century capitalists, facing an increasingly competitive European market, the unpredictability of the agricultural labourer was a major handicap. 'Divers artificers and labourers', wrote Nicholas Bownde in 1608, 'waste too much part of their day in late coming unto their work, early departing therefrom, long sitting at their breakfast, at their dinner, and noon-meat, and long time sleeping in the afternoon.' He might also have referred to the number of saint's days and other religious festivals that were celebrated by the majority of the labour force. While few succeeded in emulating the Sheffield miners who, as late as 1579, still observed thirteen saint's days, in addition to having a week off at Christmas, four or five days at Easter, and another three at Whitsun, the number of working days devoted annually to 'piping, potting, feasting and factions' was enough to upset even the most phlegmatic of entrepreneurs. From the labourer's point of view, an additional attraction of saint's days was that they were the occasions on which many of the most popular folk-games were played. The Cotswold Games, for example, medieval in origin, but revived by Robert Dover in the early seventeenth century, took place at Campden in Gloucestershire over Whitsun: they involved 'leaping', 'dancing', 'leap-frog' and the ominous-sounding 'shin-kicking'. Events like these were obviously a major distraction, and it is therefore not surprising that during the sixteenth and early seventeenth centuries a series of attempts were made to impose a greater degree of discipline and order on the agricultural labour force, the most notable of which were the Statute of Artificers and Apprentices of 1563 and the Act of 1597–8 for the maintenance of husbandry and tillage.

The other major source of opposition to folk-games and other aspects of 'merrie England' were the Puritans. There was no more passionate advocate of the belief that work was a social duty than the Puritan preacher. During a sermon at St Pauls in 1581, James Bisse condemned all 'who live in no vocation, no craft, no trade, no profession', while William Perkins declared that 'such as live in no calling, but spend their time in eating, drinking, sleeping and sporting' were guilty of an offence against God. Many games were seen as a threat to the physical and the spiritual health of the populace, as the following dire prognosis indicates: 'If we should come into a house and see many Physic boxes and glasses, we should conclude that somebody is sick; so when we see Hounds and Hawks, and Cardes and Dice, we may fear that there is some sick soul in the family.'[6] Even the quietest pastimes could prove dangerous if taken to extremes. Congregations were exhorted to take the precautions: 'Watch against inordinate sensual Delight, even in the lawfullest sports. Excess of pleasure in any such vanity doth very much corrupt and befool the mind.'[7]

One of the first explicit denouncements of folk-games and other traditional pastimes by a Puritan is contained in a memorandum written in 1588. It singles out 'wakes, ales, greens, May-games, rush-bearings, bear-baits, dove-ales, bonfires, and all such manner of unlawful gaming, piping and dancing ... in all places freely exercised upon the Sabbath; by occasion whereof it cometh to pass that the youth will not by any means be brought to attend the exercises of catechizing in the afternoon; neither the people to be present at the evening service'. By the beginning of the seventeenth century, the die was cast. A Bill placed before Parliament in 1601 sought to prohibit the holding of fairs and markets on Sundays, and to make Justices of the Peace responsible for enforcing church attendance. This Bill failed to gain the Royal Assent, as did similar Bills introduced in 1606 and 1621. But in 1625, an Act was passed prohibiting the playing of unlawful sports, especially in towns.

The effectiveness of these restrictions is difficult to assess. That a large number of statutes and orders were aimed at preventing breaches of the Sunday observance code does not mean that they were necessarily successful in achieving that end. In fact, their profusion might well be taken as a sign of failure. However, there are indications that attempts to suppress folk-games were most numerous and, by and large, most successful in London and the larger towns, where Puritanism was strongest and law enforcement most rigorous. In London, for example, all play-houses and bear-pits were closed during the Interregnum. Nor did cricket escape the heavy hand of Puritan retribution. In 1654, the churchwardens and overseers of the parish of Eltham fined seven of their parishioners for playing the game on a Sunday. Similar prosecutions, though not necessarily involving cricket, were recorded in Ipswich, Rochester, Manchester, Rochdale, Liverpool, Lincoln, London, Southwark, Preston, Canterbury, Shrewsbury, Salisbury, Cambridge, Norwich, Maldon, Okehampton, Exeter and York.

Pitted against such powerful opposition, folk-games would seem to have had little chance of survival. Yet, as the records show, this reading of history takes too much for granted. In the first place, they were an integral part of a centuries-old tradition of rural entertainment and, as such, not easily destroyed. Secondly, while the forces ranged against folk-games – Puritanism, early capitalism and the law – were generally strongest in the larger towns, this was not universally true. Thus, it is not surprising to find a Puritan minister from Maidstone revealing with evident disgust how he had seen 'Morrice Dancing, Cudgels, Stool-ball, Cricketts, and many other sports [played] openly and publickly on the Lord's Day'. Again, though the likelihood of being arraigned for failing to keep the Sabbath was greater in towns than in the country, the following indictment, recorded in 1622, by a churchwarden from the Boxgrove Deanery in the diocese of Chichester, indicate that the intrepid village cricketer did not always go scot-free:

I present Ralph West, Edmund Hartley, Richard Slaughter, William Martin, Richard Martin Junior, together with others whose I have no notice of, for playing at Cricket in the Churchyard on Sunday, the fifthe of May, after sufficient warning had been given to the contrarie, for three special reasons: first, for it is contrarie to the 7th Article; second, for that they are used to break the Church windows with the balls; and thirdly, for that little children had like to have their braynes beaten out with the cricket batt.

And I also present Richard Martin Senior, and Thomas Ward, the old Churchwardens, for defending and mayntayning them in it, and Edward Hartley for playing at cricket in evening prayer time on Sunday XXVII of April.[8]

In general, opposition from the Crown, Puritans and the business community affected folk-games neither consistently nor conclusively. Some games, particularly those which involved large numbers of players, came under constant attack, while others were hardly mentioned. The most striking conclusion to emerge from a study of folk-games is that, more often than not, their decline owed less to direct prohibition than to the inexorable processes of economic and social change which culminated centuries later in the emergence of the first urban-industrial state.

At the same time as folk-games were coming under attack in Parliament, courts and churches, they were also being subjected to a more hostile evaluation by elements within the aristocracy and gentry. At Court, in particular, a growing preoccupation with exclusiveness manifested itself in a more selective attitude towards forms of entertainment. Archery, wrestling and bowls were favoured, while football and other folk-games were increasingly shunned. As early as 1541 an Act of Parliament had established bowls as the preserve of 'noblemen or others, and having manors, lands or tenements to the yearly value of £100 or above'. The logic behind such legislation is unmistakeable: if the capacity to enjoy a life of leisure was to be a mark of a gentlemen, it was vital that the games he played should not be sullied by the presence of lesser mortals.

This theme occupied a prominent place in contemporary writing on sport and leisure. In *The Governour* (1531), Sir Thomas Elyot praised the favourite sports of the nobleman – hawking, hunting, horse-riding and tennis – but scornfully dismissed the equally traditional skittles, quoits, ninepins and football, finding in the last of these 'nothing but beastly fury and extreme violence'. The same distinction was emphasized by Lawrence Humphrey in his *Of Nobilitye* (1563); for him, moderation in dress, diet and leisure was the essence of the courtly tradition: 'As in fare, apparayle, buyldings, they must observe dignitye, so in their playes and sportes, ought they keep the golden meane.'

By the early seventeenth century, the distinction between folk-games and the pastimes worthy of a courtier was firmly established. Robert Burton's *Anatomy of Melancholy* (1621) lists the pastimes of 'base, inferior persons', though no mention is made of cricket. In a defamatory reference to Oliver Cromwell, however, Sir William Dugdale claimed that, in his youth, he had been 'famous for foot-ball, cricket, cudgelling and wrestling', as well as having gained the undesirable reputation of being a 'royster'! Later in the century, John Stow left us in no doubt about cricket's reputation – or lack of it – when he wrote: 'The more common sort divert themselves at Football, Wrestling, Cudgels, Ninepins, Shovelboard, Cricket, Stowball, Ringing of Bells, Quoits, pitching the bar, Bull and Bear Baiting, throwing at Cocks, and lying at Alehouses.'

One factor which certainly counted against cricket was its association with violence. We have seen already how the Boxgrove churchwardens feared that 'little children had like to have their braynes beaten out with the cricket batt', and a similarly violent association is to be found in a work by Edward

Phillips (a nephew of Milton), entitled *The Mysteries of Love and Eloquence*, subtitled *The Arts of Wooing and Complementing: As they are practised in the Spring Garden, Hide Park and the New Exchange* (1658): 'Ay, but Richard, will you not think so hereafter? Will you not when you have me throw a stool at my head, and cry, "Would my eyes had been beaten out with a cricket ball, the day before I saw thee."'

All the evidence points to the fact that by the middle of the seventeenth century, cricket had reached a crucial watershed in its history. Being a folk-game at a time when folk-games in general were being viewed by 'respectable' people with the greatest suspicion, it could easily have faded into obscurity together with the traditional world into which it had been born. But cricket was destined for greater things. Barely a hundred years later, it numbered among its patrons no less an eminence than the Prince of Wales. How this transformation was accomplished will be considered in the next chapter.

3 The Adoption of Cricket

When, in 1677, the treasurer to the Earl of Sussex, a son-in-law of Charles II, made the following entrance in his ledger, 'Pd. to my lord when his lordship went to the cricket match at Dicker – 03.00.00', he could not have been aware of its historical importance. For, as the first recorded instance of a member of the aristocracy attending a game of cricket, the visit to Dicker testifies to the existence of an unbroken line in the development of cricket from folk-game to modern sport, and also suggests why this transformation occurred. As the Dicker match shows, the aristocracy did not find cricket a totally unorganized pastime. Early forms of competition, basically contests between neighbouring villages and parishes in Kent, Sussex and Surrey, existed around the turn of the century. In 1697 the *Foreign Post* announced a 'great cricket match in Sussex, eleven-a-side, for fifty guineas'. An entry in the diary of a Kentish farmer recalls a match played in 1708: 'Memorandum, June ye 23rd, 1708. Wee beat Ash Street at Creckitts.' In Sussex a match attended by the Earl of Sussex – at which his wife, it was also noted, 'tired of the prevailing amusements, hunting, hawking, nine-pins and cricket' – was only one of several recorded.

By 1700 the popularity of cricket had reached a point at which it earned a mention in the columns of the recently-founded local press. Most references took the form of an advertisement of a forthcoming match, and it is these advertisements that provide the clearest evidence of the direction in which cricket was evolving. In the first place, their very existence is an indication of the extent to which cricket had succeeded in overcoming the stigma of its folk origins amongst the literate sections of the population. An entry in the *Post Boy*, 30 March

24

1700, reveals that 'gentlemen' were playing the game even in London where, as John Stow has told us, its prestige had been lowest: 'These are to inform Gentlemen and others, who delight in Cricket-playing, that a match at Cricket, of ten gentlemen aside, will be played on Clapham Common near Fox-Hall, on Easter Monday next, for £10 per head each game.'

The second interesting feature of this notice is the reference to gambling. The size of the stakes – considerable by eighteenth-century standards – is in itself an indication of the presence of wealth. The same format involving gentlemen and gambling was used in another match advertised in the *Postman*, 24 July 1705: 'This is to give notice that a match of cricket is to be played between eleven gentlemen of a west part of the county of Kent, against as many of Chatham, for eleven guineas a man, at Moulden in Kent on August 7th next.'

While these press notices tell us little of the matches themselves, or of the players that took part, they do confirm the involvement of 'gentlemen' in what, only forty years earlier, had generally been thought of as a rural folk-game. Why these gentlemen should have looked to cricket to occupy their seemingly endless leisure hours, and why their involvement led eventually to cricket becoming a modern sport and the national game are questions that have baffled successive generations of cricket historians. However, an answer must be found if the subsequent history of the game is to be understood.

The association between cricket and the landed aristocracy and gentry was born in an era of rapid and fundamental social change. A great increase in the power of the state, together with the growth of bourgeois capitalism had resulted in the aristocracy surrendering much of its monolithic, warrior-like character. A new social order emerged, within which the aristocracy was often to command great authority, but never again as an entirely autonomous body. By and large, this change met with surprisingly little opposition: peers, it seems, were not attracted by the prospect of a fight to the death. There were a few, it is true, who bitterly resented any challenge to their traditional pre-eminence, particularly those old-established families whose estates were farthest from London – the Percys, the Cliffords, the Dacres, the Stanleys and the Talbots. Time and the executioner's axe were to show how misguided their obduracy was. By the end of Elizabeth's long reign, all resistance had been overcome either as a result of frontal assault or, more insidiously, by a combination of legal sanctions and natural biological decline.

There are a number of reasons for thinking that the English ruling class at the beginning of the seventeenth century was not the homogeneous entity that it had been during the Middle Ages. Changes in both personnel and values had occurred in the course of a rapid increase in size during the previous century. Between 1540 and 1640, the aristocracy and gentry approximately trebled in size while the rest of the population barely doubled. The numbers of peers rose from 60 to 160; of baronets and knights from 500 to 1,500; of squires from perhaps 800 to 3,000; and of armigerous gentry from around 3,000 to 15,000. This increase in numbers was only one of the changes that overtook the aristocracy and gentry during the Tudor and Stuart eras. Just as important from our point of view was the gradual loss of its traditional military strength. This loss, and the subsequent shift of interest to more peaceful forms of economic and political activity, hold the key to the aristocracy's associations with cricket.

While it is difficult to disentangle the precise cause of the aristocracy's decline as a military force, there is no doubt that the major beneficiaries were the Crown and the business community. Throughout the years of Tudor rule, the Crown and Parliament were, for the most part, united in their determination to be rid of the over-mighty subjects whose military strength had previously outweighed, and could still challenge, their own. To this end, Henry VII passed a number of acts which established beyond all doubt that the first loyalty of every subject was to the Crown, and only thereafter to his 'good lord'. Unfortunately for Henry, much of the sting was taken out of these measures by the fact that both he and his son, Henry VIII, depended on the aristocracy for an army in the event of an attack by a foreign power. Though, in theory, the monarch could raise a conscript army from a national levy of all able-bodied men between the ages of 16 and 60, in practice the administrative difficulties of mustering, training and arming such a force were immense. Without a standing army of its own, the Crown still had to rely on the armed retinues kept by the great magnates of the day. As late as 1523 the aristocracy was responsible for producing one third of the total army. From the 1540s, however, the importance of private armies declined. Henry VIII and Mary encouraged the development of conscript armies for foreign as well as domestic use; the office of the Lord-lieutenant came to include responsibility for supervising the musters. In 1573 Elizabeth decreed that out of the general body of the militia there should be groups of picked men who would be equipped at public expense and trained regularly in the use of weapons. Moreover, these 'trained bands' were to be controlled by the lord-lieutenants rather than the magnates.

In pursuing these measures, the Crown was undoubtedly helped by the absence of any substantial threat from overseas, save, of course, for the Spanish Armada. Prolonged periods of peace meant that by the beginning of the next century few members of the aristocracy had any experience or knowledge of war. In other words, their traditional qualities, bravery and strength in direct physical combat, were fast becoming anachronistic. Not only were there very few occasions when peers could employ these fighting talents, but even when the opportunity did arise, they found themselves involved in a type of warfare which was very different to anything they could have experienced. As the scions of countless families have since discovered, bravado, *élan* and *esprit de corps* provide little defence against a hail of bullets.

By 1650 many of the great feudal families were in the process of dispensing with the trappings of their military heritage. The most obvious sign of this adaptation was a reduction in the size of the retinues they maintained. Until the mid-sixteenth century these had frequently included as many as five hundred servants and retainers, but by the middle of the following century few numbered more than fifty. The Earl of Derby, for example, kept a staff of one hundred and eighteen as late as 1587, but his successor managed to live quite comfortably with only thirty-eight servants. Not only were these appendages too expensive, but against the growing ascendancy of the state they were becoming increasingly superfluous.

But a much reduced complement was not the only evidence of the extent to which aristocratic households were changing during the seventeenth century. Just as significant from the point of view of cricket was the more gradual change in the social origins of servants. During the Middle Ages it had been the custom for the younger sons of the gentry to enter upon a period of service in the household of one of the great magnates.

Young 'squires' were thus educated in aristocratic values, in correct ways of behaving and in the more physical and combative techniques of riding and swordsmanship. But from the seventeenth century onwards, this tradition gradually fell into neglect. The change was most noticeable amongst the lord's close personal attendants. At the beginning of Elizabeth's reign, the Duke of Northumberland had forty gentlemen and thirty yeoman ushers in his household. A century later, his successor was accompanied by only six footmen and two or three pages. No doubt this reduction was partly the result of a deliberate economy campaign. But it is also true that, about this time, the gentry began to view the prospect of committing their sons to a period of personal attendance upon one of the 'great lords' of the day with less enthusiasm than before. As Lord North observed, 'It is certain that families of noblemen are clean other than they were anciently, for within living memory of some yet alive, it was usual for persons of the inferior gentry to put their sons into such service for breeding.'

The growing ambitions of many members of the gentry, and of prosperous merchants and financiers from London, Bristol and other business centres, were fired by a realization that entry to the aristocracy no longer depended on being descended from one of the great feudal lineages, and that membership of the ruling class was no longer confined solely to aristocrats. Throughout the seventeenth century, it was common to find solid gentry stock and many of the great merchants of the day 'succeeding' to positions previously held by aristocratic families. But their presence did not challenge the time-honoured superiority of the aristocracy. These *arrivistes* were generally more intent on consolidating their new-found status than with destroying its foundations. Far from championing the end of privilege, the majority were desperately concerned to ensure its survival.

After the extraordinary influx of new blood into the ranks of the landed gentleman during the sixteenth and early seventeenth centuries – a consequence largely of the release on to the market of great acreages previously owned by the Crown or the Church – the rate of mobility into the aristocracy and gentry fell during the second half of the seventeenth century to its earlier levels. The result was the resurgence of a distinctive élite whom many admired, but to which few gained entry.

However, it was not only ambitious yeomen and merchants who profited from a gradual realization of the social and economic potential of land. From the sixteenth century onwards, examples of much-respected landed gentlemen participating in undisguisedly capitalistic activities became more and more common. As land was the basis of their wealth and authority, it was natural that the majority should devote their energies to finding ways of extracting greater revenue from their estates. But here an important distinction must be made. Much of the entrepreneurial activity which involved members of the landed aristocracy and gentry was decidedly speculative. It was, in effect, a further manifestation of that passionate love of gambling that was, and still is, part and parcel of life in high places. If such ventures were successful, the profits that accrued went towards financing an even more lavish presence at Court. If not, the losses were written off, and soon forgotten.

But not all the great landowners were equally enthralled by the prospect of life at Court. Indeed, this is one of the most important differences between political life in France and England during the seventeenth century. Unlike Louis xiii and xiv, the early Stuarts never managed to transform all the aristocracy into 'courtiers'. Many continued to prefer the life of a country gentleman to the expense and intrigue of London. Like their successors, the great Whig landowners of the eighteenth century, they looked upon the country house as the centre of their political world, and the surrounding estates as the source of the wealth needed to maintain it. Thus measures designed to improve the efficiency and profitability of the latter, like the introduction of more advanced systems of estate management, were as much a political as an economic investment. Away from the endless hubbub of Court, the country gentleman could settle down to enjoy a life of uninterrupted leisure, based on 'huntin', shootin' and fishin' '. And it was to this list that cricket was destined to be added.

The likelihood is that the transformation of cricket from a folk-game to a sport of princes (if not kings) was directly related to the changing patterns of seventeenth-century landowner-ship. The key to the game's 'adoption' lies in part in the unusual situation that confronted the new generation of landowners, most of whom, as we have seen, came from a farming or business background. Under normal circumstances, social climbers adapt very quickly to the perceived standards and values of the class into which they have moved. But in the seventeenth century, this process of assimilation was disrupted by the absence of a clear model of aristocratic standards and behaviour. Instead, the *arrivistes* found themselves faced by two conflicting models – the one based on the traditional virtues of rural life, and the other on the exotic, bohemian standards of Court.

The most widely accepted explanation of cricket's transformation into an élite pastime, put forward by H. S. Altham, is based on the assumption that folk-cricket was 'adopted' by members of the Court nobility who had been 'exiled' from London after the Civil War. In *A History of Cricket*, Altham advances the following argument:

> The truth seems to be that the last half of the seventeenth century was really the critical stage in the game's evolution, the era in which it developed from the pastime of boys, or, at best, of yeomen of the exclusive Weald into a game with a national appeal, enjoying in ever-increasing measure the patronage of leaders of Society. To this, it would seem that political history may have decisively contributed. With the temporary eclipse of the Royalist cause, it is probable that many of the nobility and gentry would retire to their country seats and here some of them . . . would find themselves watching the Wealden game as played by their gardeners, huntsmen, foresters and farm hands, and from sheer *ennui* would try their own hand at it and find that it was good. (p. 23)

The simplicity of this explanation makes it deceptively appealing, but on closer scrutiny a number of serious weaknesses appear. First, it fails to explain why an essentially Court-based nobility, accustomed to a sophisticated, urbane existence, should suddenly develop a liking for a simple folk-game. It also contains a fundamental misunderstanding of the activities of peers during the Interregnum. On this point, Professor Joan Thirsk has shown that between 1649 and 1660 the lands forfeited by the two greatest landowners in England, the Crown and the Church, were broken up for sale into hundreds of parcels. By 1660 some 200,000 acres in south-east England forfeited by fifty Royalists had been redistributed among 257 people.[1] It was not until after the Restoration that some of these

Royalists successfully reclaimed their lands.[2] Neither of these findings tie in with Mr Altham's idea that 'many of the nobility and gentry [retired] to their country seats'. Thus the notion of the existence of a temporarily domiciled group of nobles, possessing sufficient influence to change the life-style of the aristocracy, is open to doubt.

Nevertheless, the fact remains that the aristocracy's liking for cricket was a crucial factor in its subsequent evolution. Likewise, there is little doubt that this affinity was born about the middle of the seventeenth century. Altham's mistake lay in assuming that the landed aristocracy and gentry of Stuart times was the same as the 'warrior' élite of the Middle Ages. Nothing could have been further from the truth. Gone was the feudal order, and with it, many of the great aristocratic dynasties. The survivors populated a very different world, one in which they were obliged to associate with many whose origins lay in the gentry and commerce, but who had achieved respectability through the purchase of land.

It is against this background that cricket's adoption by sections of the landed aristocracy and gentry has to be considered. Two basic pre-conditions can be identified immediately. Efficient financial management by the more astute survivors of the old aristocracy, together with an injection of new blood and wealth from the farming and business communities, ensured that there was no shortage of money to stage matches and pay players. In addition to wealth, most landowners were well endowed with another vital resource – time. Except in the rare case of a life dedicated to the service of the Crown, or to political self-aggrandizement, the seventeenth-century gentleman had time on his hands.

The reconstitution of the aristocracy and gentry also provides several clues to the circumstances under which such an exalted collection of individuals first came into contact with a simple folk-game like cricket. For example, it is not difficult to imagine that many landowners first discovered the game in the course of supervising the management of their estates. Alternatively, the first acquaintance may have come about as a result of the gradual change in the social origins of domestic servants that occurred during the second half of the seventeenth century. By the turn of the century, 'the domestic retinue of the great house had been completely altered ... even the upper servants were in the majority of cases the sons of labourers, artisans or small farmers rather than recruits from the ranks of reduced gentlemen'.[3] 'The sons of labourers, artisans or small farmers' were exactly the type of people who would have played folk-cricket. Again, it is not necessary to delve too far into the realms of fantasy to imagine a situation in which the lord of the manor comes across some of his servants playing cricket and, being stirred by the prospect, decides to try it out for himself.

Both of these explanations assume that established members of the aristocracy and gentry actually 'adopted' cricket from the folk-culture in which it had previously existed. But this was not necessarily the case. It is just as likely that cricket was introduced into high society as one of the accoutrements of those yeomen and merchants who had purchased landed estates before the Civil War. As we have already seen, during the first half of the seventeenth century the aristocracy did not possess a single, distinctive life-style which all newcomers automatically copied. Thus the new landowners might not have felt quite so anxious to dispense with the trappings of their mundane past. Moreover, they may well have been encouraged to retain many facets of their previous way of life by the presence of a strong party within the established ranks of the aristocracy and gentry who were themselves staunch supporters of traditional rural life, the environment in which cricket existed at this time.

While the coincidence of these three factors helps to explain how cricket may have come to the notice of landed gentlemen, it does not tell us why they should have wanted to play such a game. However, a clear insight into the motivations involved can be gained by looking again at the changing structure and functions of the aristocracy and gentry during the previous century. When the descendants of the great feudal barons reluctantly began to disband their private, para-military retinues, it marked the end of an era during which they had frequently enjoyed total autonomy. While the most obvious indications of this military decline were to be found in the replacement of castles by country mansions and standing armies by domestic servants, it also involved an equally fundamental change of life-style.

During the Middle Ages, the power of the great barons had allowed them to behave more-or-less as they pleased, a licence that many had exploited to the full. But once the Crown had succeeded in imposing its authority over all its subjects, the peers of the realm, and even mere gentlemen, found themselves under growing pressure to accept the standards and conventions of court. As far as we can tell, it was about this time, the first half of the seventeenth century, that landed gentlemen began to take a greater interest in simple folk-games like cricket. The coincidence is too striking to ignore. What cricket and other folk-games offered was the chance to escape temporarily at least from the claustrophobic predictability of court life. Not only did these games provide gentlemen with an opportunity to act out their personal rivalries without resorting to duelling swords, but also with another gambling medium. More will be said of the aristocracy's legendary love of gambling in later chapters: here it is sufficient to note that the lure of betting and wagers easily outweighed any doubts concerning the respectability of the games in question. For example, in 1711, a visitor from France noted: 'Cock fighting is one of the great English Diversions; they build Amphitheatres for this purpose and Persons of Quality are seen at them. Great wagers are laid and I'm told that a man may be damnably bubbled if he is not very sharp.'[4]

Thus, it is not surprising that the first references to gentlemen watching or playing cricket also record that large sums of money were usually at stake. In short, cricket's adoption by members of the landed aristocracy and gentry in the seventeenth and early eighteenth centuries was born of a gradual realization that the game offered an opportunity to re-enact vestiges of an earlier life-style in a setting which combined the maximum of excitement with the minimum of danger.

4 'Gamesters, Jockeys and Cricket Players'

The first stage in cricket's evolution from medieval folk-game into modern sport took place under the patronage and direction of a collection of wealthy landowners within the boundaries of Kent, Sussex, Surrey and Hampshire. Though records show that cricket was played as far away as Gloucestershire as early as 1729, the major diffusion of a more advanced form of the game did not occur until the second half of the eighteenth century. Until that time, the organization and standard of performance in matches staged in the Midlands and the north of England did not compare with those found in the south-east.

Though competition in the form of local village contests already existed, it was not until members of the aristocracy and gentry began to patronize and play cricket that it acquired a degree of organization unknown in folk-games. The first record of a peer playing, as opposed to watching, cricket occurs in 1725, when the Duke of Richmond took part in a two-a-side match against Sir William Gage, from Firle near Eastbourne. The Duke was responsible for suggesting and organizing this contest, which was staged at his country seat at Goodwood. In a letter accepting the Duke's challenge, Sir William wrote,

My Lord Duke,

I received this moment your Grace's letter and am extremely happy your Grace intends us ye honour of making one a Tuesday, and will without fail bring a gentleman to play against you, One that has seldom played for several years.

I am in great affliction from being shamefully beaten Yesterday, the first match I played this year. However, I will muster all my courage against Tuesday's engagement ... I wish you success in everything but ye Crickett match.[1]

July ye 16th 1725

The reference to an earlier match illustrates one of the major difficulties of dating the early evolution of cricket. In the early eighteenth century, newspapers were comparatively rare, and their circulation was limited to the literate sections of the population.[2] Thus, as Sir William's letter suggests, several matches between wealthy landowners were almost certainly played before 1725 without being recorded for posterity in the pages of the local press.

Whether the Duke or Sir William won this contest we will probably never know, but it is clear that by the early decades of the eighteenth century matches of this type had become very popular. Announcements of matches involving members of the aristocracy and gentry began to appear in the press quite frequently. In 1726, two matches were reported, both involving teams led by Mr Edwin Stead, Esq. The first of these was played on Kennington Common for twenty-five guineas, the second on Dartford Heath. In the following year, the Duke of Richmond played a match against Mr Alan Broderick at Peperharrowe, near Godalming in Surrey. At least five matches were played in 1728: the Duke of Richmond and Sir William Gage met again, this time at Lewes, while the Duke 'and his Club' also played against Mr Edwin Stead 'and his company' for what was reported to be 'a great sum'; Sir William also played against Mr Stead 'at the Earl of Leicester's Park at Penshurst' and, not to be outdone, the Gentlemen of London took the field against the Gentlemen of Middlesex. In 1729, Kennington Common was the scene of a 'great match ... between the Londoners and the Dartford men for a considerable sum of money', while other matches were played at Penshurst and at an unknown venue in Sussex 'between Kent, headed by Mr Edwin Stead, Esq., and Sussex, Surrey and Hampshire, by Sir William Gage, for 100 guineas, eleven on a side'. In 1730, the Duke of Richmond played a match against Mr Andrews on Merrow Downs, near Guildford, at which 'were present the Rt. Hon. Lord Onslow and Lord Middleton, Sir Peter Soame, Mr Stead and a great many persons of distinction', and yet another game against Sir William Gage at Lewes. Of the twenty matches reported in 1731, six were contests between teams of Kentish men, led either by Edwin Stead or Lord John Sackville, and the Gentlemen of London, four involved teams of Gentlemen from various London boroughs such as Fulham, Chelsea and Brompton, and two were between the Gentlemen of Kent and Surrey. In 1733, the rapidly growing popularity of cricket was, in a sense, legitimized by the presence of HRH the Prince of Wales, who donated a silver cup to be competed for by a team selected by Mr Stead and one made up of 'the Prince's men'. That the Prince himself played in several matches is confirmed by the following report which appeared in July, 1735:

> The great cricket match was played at Moulsey Hurst, in Surrey, between H.R.H. the Prince of Wales and the Earl of Middlesex, son of the Duke of Dorset, for £1,000 a side: eight of the London Club and three out of Middlesex played for the Prince, and the Kentish men for the Earl. His Royal Highness came into the field between 12 and 1 o'clock, and the stumps were immediately pitched. Kent won with three men to come in. This day fortnight, the second match is to be played at Bromley Common.[3]

From 1735 until his death in 1746, the Prince was involved in several matches, played either in London or Surrey, between teams selected and sponsored by various members of the aristocracy. The Duke of Cumberland, the Earl of Middlesex, and the Lords Waldegrave, Baltimore, Montford and Sackville, to name but a few, were fervent supporters of the game. Few 'great matches' did not involve 'several persons of Distinction'.

These reports indicate that the aristocracy's involvement in cricket reflected the position it occupied in society at large. By the beginning of the eighteenth century, the aristocracy had clearly regained the political ascendancy it had temporarily lost during the previous century. In the process, it had also regained the essential qualities of an élite – exclusiveness and stability. Now, however, its authority was founded on land rather than military strength. 'Landed property', wrote William Marshall in 1804, 'is the basis on which every other species of material property rests: on it alone mankind can be said to live, to move, to have its being.'[4]

To most contemporaries, the aristocracy's pre-eminence was not only acceptable – it was seen as the foundation of a stable society and, as such, right and just. Thus Samuel Johnson, in a conversion recorded by the faithful Boswell, was heard to declare, 'Sir, I would no more deprive a nobleman of his respect than of his money. I consider myself as acting a part in a great system and do to others as I would have them do to me. Sir, I would behave to a nobleman as I would expect he should behave to me, were I a nobleman and he Samuel Johnson.'[5] The aristocracy's dominance was partly due to a swelling in its own ranks, for this meant that its collective influence over other sections of society was more direct and widespread than ever before. But the basis of this influence remains the ownership of land, and the wealth that accrued from it. The early eighteenth century was a period of great increase in the size of landed estates. Between 1640 and 1740, for example, they grew on average by around 15 per cent, most of which resulted from the enclosure of common lands. Gregory King's calculations suggest that the top 10 per cent of families measured by rank received over 20 per cent of all incomes received from land. Add to this the vast inherited wealth of the landed aristocracy and one sees very clearly how it was that eighteenth-century England could accurately be described as 'a federation of country-houses'.[6]

These estates lay at the heart of a web of authority in which the central figure was the landowning magnate. As Justice of the Peace, landlord and employer, his influence pervaded every aspect of the community's life. By subtle use of patronage, he created a complex network of dependencies and obligations among the local inhabitants. The efficiency of this network was improved by the highly personalized relationships which existed between the lord of the manor and his tenants and servants. It was upon these personal face-to-face relationships that the elaborate system of paternal dependence which legitimized the authority of the magnate rested.

The exercise of authority, however, was only one aspect of the magnate's role in society. As well as being the titular head of a local community, and often the holder of a governmental or Crown office, he was also part of a social circle, the very distinctiveness of which reinforced his superiority. The uniqueness of this cadre prompted G. M. Trevelyan to claim that,

Perhaps no set of men and women since the world began enjoyed so much zest as the English Upper Class at this period. The literary, the sporting, the fashionable and the political 'sets' were one and the same. When the most unsuccessful of all great politicians, Charles Fox, said on his death bed that he had lived happy, he spoke the truth. Oratory was at its highest, politics at its keenest, long days tramping after partridges, village cricket, endless talk as good as ever was talked, and a passion for Greek, Latin, Italian, and English poetry and history – all these and alas, the madness of the gambler.[7]

Within the values of this élite, leisure enjoyed a clear primacy over work. When the Earl of Sandwich, in answer to a summons to attend a governmental meeting, replied, 'I'll at your board [the Admiralty] when at leisure from cricket', far from being capricious, he was simply conforming to the dictates of a lifestyle which was as important to the aristocracy as the unearned income and wealth upon which its existence was based. Above all, it was this ability to live a life of uninterrupted leisure which set the true gentleman apart from the rest of society. For him, work was an anathema, something totally irreconcilable with his rank in society.

Descriptions of cricket matches played during the eighteenth century suggest that there were four main reasons why the aristocracy patronized and played the game. First, through playing cricket, the local magnate came into contact with a wide cross-section of those living on his estates and, by imposing his presence, increased his personal authority over them. In this respect, playing cricket may be seen as one of those unlikely activities which gave the eighteenth-century aristocracy its distinctive quality:

Instead of keeping themselves aloof from the other classes, and 'hedging their state' round with thorny but insubstantial barriers of heraldic distinction: instead of demanding half a hundred quarterings with their wives, and galling their inferiors by eternally dwelling on their inferiority, they may be said to have mixed more largely and with more seeming equality with all classes than with any other aristocracy in the savage or civilised world.... Their hospitality, their field sports, the agricultural meetings they attended in order 'to keep up the family interest', mix them with all classes. . . .[8]

Secondly, cricket matches between members of the aristocracy and gentry were an occasion for renewing old friendships and making new ones. They were a great way of keeping up-to-date with the latest gossip, scandal and intrigue. The early patrons of cricket had two things in common: they all owned country estates in Kent, Sussex, Surrey or Hampshire, and, with the exception of Edwin Stead who unhappily died a bankrupt in 1735, all were either Members of Parliament or Crown appointees. The Duke of Richmond was Lord High Constable of England, Lord of the King's Bedchamber, Master of the Horse – an appointment which by 1805 was worth over £27,000 a year – and member of the Privy Council. He also maintained a presence in local politics by being Mayor of Chichester, the constituency he represented in Parliament as the Earl of March, and which he secured for an uncle on his eventual departure to the House of Lords. Furthermore, he controlled the constituency of Seaford in Sussex, for which his cricketing friend, Sir William Gage, was the member. Alan Broderick, son of Viscount Middleton, whom he succeeded in 1728, was the Member for Midhurst, a Commissioner of the Customs, and subsequently Joint Controller of the Army accounts. Lord John Sackville, second son of the Duke of Dorset, was the Member for Tamworth. It is not difficult to visualize the matches patronized by these gentlemen, played either at one of their country estates or in the vicinity of London, as part of that annual round of events and visitations which satisfied both the governmental and social responsibilities of the ruling class.

The third attraction of cricket matches lay in the opportunities they provided for peers to act out their personal rivalries without risking the vicissitudes of duelling. The presence of these rivalries is reflected in many aspects of the matches that were staged. Though a team might play under a variety of titles, its members were essentially the personal representatives of their patron, brought together with the specific intent of defending or improving his immediate standing. The introduction of an element of serious rivalry prompted the development of a much higher level of skill amongst the players than had existed previously. Unlike the sides that had contested games of folk-cricket, those which represented the likes of the Duke of Richmond and Lord John Sackville included a number of 'professional' players, selected purely for their technical skills. In this respect, they were the forerunners of the modern 'team'.

Lastly, cricket provided a source of entertainment, exercise and excitement for a group of people who possessed almost infinite amounts of time and money to devote to the cause of leisure. The complete absence of self-consciousness, coupled with a sublime indifference to the presence of large, often unruly, crowds, testifies to the extent to which the eighteenth-century magnate had come to believe in the legitimacy and permanence of his exalted rank. An incident recorded in the *Morning Post* 16 July 1778), involving the Duke of Dorset, provides a superb illustration of the typical urbanity of the aristocrat. The Duke, who was playing for England against Hampshire, had 'run a considerable number of notches', when

> the Hampshire people very impolitely swarmed round his bat so close as to impede his making a full stroke; his Grace gently expostulated with them on this unfair mode and pointed out their dangers, which having no effect, he, with proper spirit, made full play at a ball and in so doing so brought one of the Gentlemen to the Ground.

Though cricket's ability to excite and entertain was due in part to its basic competitiveness, there is no doubt that it was the betting and wagering – by the middle of the eighteenth century an integral part of any match – which sparked off much of the aristocracy's interest in the game. In fact, cricket was only one of a number of activities which catered for this particular foible. Given sufficient imagination, almost any situation containing an element of competition could become the vehicle for a hefty wager. For example, in a letter to Sir Horatio Mann written in 1756, Horace Walpole described how, 'My Lord Rockingham and my nephew, Lord Oxford, have made a match of five hundred pounds between five turkeys and five geese to run from Norwich to London.'[9]

In *The Old Betting Book of All Soul's College*, a record of bets struck by fellows between 1795 and 1870, an entry for 1815 reads: 'Cartwright bets Birens £10 to £1 that some Jurist Fellow of the College will marry before D'Oyley does.' And so it went on. But it would be wrong to suppose that this penchant for gambling was confined to the aristocracy. At the end of the seventeenth century, the comment appeared in the *London Spy*: 'The gentry indeed might make it their diversion, but the common people make it a great part of their care and business, hoping thereby to relieve a necessitous life; instead of which they plunge themselves into an ocean of difficulties.'[10] As this observation suggests, while a love of gambling was common to all sections of eighteenth-century society, amongst the aristocracy it was motivated by entirely different expectations to those found amongst less privileged groups. For the landowning gentleman, the result of a bet was not as significant as the excitement it engendered. By stimulating suspense and uncertainty, betting satisfied important emotional needs for people who found their lives becoming more and more predictable. If the diaries and letters of the period are any guide, the everyday life of a typical gentleman, securely ensconced within a social circle which admitted changes only on the occasion of death or disgrace, was extremely tedious. Though initially considered improper, by the seventeenth century gambling had become a socially acceptable, even obligatory, form of behaviour. A willingness to stake large sums of money was seen by contemporaries as evidence not only of the possession of considerable wealth, but also of a suitable disregard for any thoughts of future well-being or planned investment. It was said of the court of Charles II, for example, that 'unless one gambles freely, it is quite impossible to be counted a gentleman, or, for that matter, a lady of fashion'.

By 1750, the attentions of the aristocracy had begun to have several noticeable effects on the game of cricket. It was no longer the folk-game of old. Not all the changes were the result of innovation: alterations in the laws of the game followed more from attempts to standardize the many local variations than to create an entirely new code. One way of illustrating how much had changed by the mid-eighteenth century is to compare the description of the game contained in a Latin poem, entitled 'In Certamen Pilae', composed by William Goldwin in 1706 with a later account found in the Articles of Agreement drawn up for two matches played in 1727 between the Duke of Richmond and Mr Alan Broderick. In the first, the teams, drawn it appears from the same village, converge upon the venue – 'a meadow yields with smooth expanse' – carrying curved bats, a style which was not superseded until the 1770s and 1780s – the Hambledon era. At this stage in the poem, an argument over the rules develops which is only resolved by the intervention of a 'Nestor' – 'a grey veteran',

> a Daniel come to judgement, he to all speaks equity.
> Though now his arms be laid aside
> and marred by years his early pride,
> yet rich is he in cricket lore,
> and proves that they need strive no more.[11]

Two sets of wickets – two stumps and a 'milk-white Bail' – are pitched, and two sides equal in number prepare to play. A coin is tossed to decide who has first innings, and when both sides are ready one of the umpires – 'the Moderates bini' – calls 'play', and the contest begins. The fielding side, using a leather ball – 'Coriaceus Orbis' – bowl four-ball overs, while the batsman can be dismissed by being 'caught', 'bowled', or 'run out'. To score, a batsman has to touch with his bat a piece of wood held by the umpire at the opposite end, and these 'runs' were recorded by cutting notches in a piece of wood. As late as 1823, runs were still described as 'notches'. Ways of gaining a runout varied: in Goldwin's poem the dismissal is not clearly recounted, but from other sources it appears that one method involved placing the ball in a 'popping hole' before the striker could place his bat therein. No doubt the mangled fingers that resulted were responsible for the 'popping hole' being superseded by the less dangerous 'popping crease'!

By the time the Articles of Agreement were drawn up, some features of the game remained unaltered, but the context in which it was played had changed dramatically. Because of the functions that cricket now served, and because of its almost permanent association with gambling, it was very much in the interests of the patrons and protagonists to minimize the chances of disagreement. Thus, in one sense, the 1727 Articles can be seen as an attempt to impose a standard code of rules upon the numerous local variations. For example, they defined the conditions under which a batsman could be 'caught out' and 'run out' – i.e. 'the wicket must be put down with ball in hand'. But in addition to this, they included specific clauses regulating the use of substitutes and the powers of the umpires, both of which could easily become highly controversial when large sums of money were at stake. As befitted men of their rank, the Duke of Richmond and Mr Alan Broderick were specifically excluded from the jurisdiction of the umpires. Finally, of course, the Articles stipulated the sum of money at stake – here, a relatively moderate 'twelve guineas of each side'. By 1727 then, though some of the eccentricities of the folk-game were preserved in, for example, the provision of a *twenty-three* yard pitch, the framework of the game had become relatively standardized.

On several subsequent occasions during the eighteenth century – in 1744, 1771, 1774 and 1788 – many of the sanctions and prohibitions included in the 1727 Articles were incorporated into specific codes of 'Laws'. One finds in these codes not only the first specification of the form that bat, ball, stumps and bails should take, but also a considerable elaboration of existing rules, with references to 'hit-wicket', 'no-ball', 'short-runs', and a type of obstruction closely akin to the modern LBW. The introduction of these new rules was related in several cases to advances in the techniques and tactics employed by the leading players of the day. In fact, on at least two occasions it is possible to trace a direct cause–effect sequence of events. In the first, a *cause célèbre* among cricket historians, the cause of the trouble was the size of the bat used by one 'Shock' White. The event was recalled many years later by John Nyren:

> Several years since (I do not recollect the precise date) a player named White, of Ryegate, brought a bat to a match, which being the width of the stumps effectually defended his wicket from the bowler: and in consequence, a law was passed limiting the future width of the bat.... I have a perfect recollection of this occurrence: also that subsequently an iron frame, of statute width, was constructed for and kept by the Hambledon Club; through which any bat of suspected dimensions was passed, and allowed or rejected accordingly.[12]

A similar series of events preceded the introduction of the third stump. In this case, as Nyren again recounts,

When Small went in, the last man, for fourteen runs, and fetched them, Lumpy was the bowler on the occasion; and it having been remarked that his balls had three times passed between Small's stumps, it was considered to be a hard thing upon the bowler that his straightest balls be thus sacrificed, the number of stumps was in consequence increased from two to three.[13]

While still not the responsibility of a central authority – the MCC did not produce its first code until 1788 – these modifications were incorporated into a set of rules which commanded a more widespread respect than any previous version. To explain this, it is necessary to look no further than the context in which they were formulated. Leaving aside the 'emergency' measures taken at Hambledon, the most comprehensive re-draftings (the 1744 and 1774 versions) were undertaken by the 'London Club' – whose president was none other than Frederick Lewis, Prince of Wales – and 'a committee of Noblemen and Gentlemen of Kent, Hampshire, Surrey, Sussex, Middlesex, and London'. It was from the prestige of these august bodies that the new laws derived their authority. The 1774 code contains an additional section which, as a final testimony to the strength of the aristocracy's influence on the development of eighteenth-century cricket, is particularly apt. Not content with deciding how it should be played, the noble lords were moved to insert the following clauses which regulate the very aspect of the game that they had done so much to encourage – gambling:

> If the notches of one Player are laid against another, the Bet depends on both Innings, unless otherwise specified.
> If one Party beats the other in one Innings, the Notches in the first Innings shall determine the Bet.
> But if the other Party goes in a Second Time, then the Bet must be determined by the numbers on the score.[14]

5 The Organization of Eighteenth-Century Cricket

The patronage lavished on cricket by the aristocracy was undoubtedly the most potent influence on the overall development of the game during the eighteenth century. The organization of matches became more elaborate; efforts were made to standardize the rules of the game; and the employment of the first 'professionals' encouraged a general improvement in playing skills. But it would be wrong to assume that the arrival of the cricket-loving peer signalled the demise of the earlier type of match. Until the death of the Hambledon club in the last years of the century, the organization of most matches depended on a combination of aristocratic enthusiasm and local village rivalry. Unlike most European élites, the English aristocracy did not try to detach all its leisure pursuits from the folk context in which many had been conceived. As a result, it is possible to identify two distinct patterns within the overall organization of the game. The first included all those matches played at the country seats of the great cricketing magnates, and those they organized in London. The second pattern was more complex since it superimposed the growing interest of the aristocracy, gentry, and, later, shopkeepers and craftsmen on to the established framework of local village contests.

Within the first general pattern, there were, in fact, two types of contest. The first consisted of matches between two great landowners, like the Duke of Richmond and Sir William Gage, which were played at one of the protagonist's estates or at a neutral venue roughly half-way between the two. Both in conception and in detail, these games bore the unmistakeable stamp of eighteenth-century aristocracy. They never became totally exclusive events, nor did their patrons seek to distance themselves from the other participants. Only in London did some measure of protection from the great crowds become necessary. The rise of this type of match marked an important step in the evolution of cricket. Based on the leisure habits of a ruling class rather than traditional rivalries between neighbouring villages it allowed the organization of matches to transcend local boundaries. So long as 'derbies' between neighbouring villages remained the basic axis of competition, local variations in the rules of the game were perpetuated, and playing skills rarely improved. By providing a basis on which the range of competition could be expanded, the involvement of members of the aristocracy and gentry paved the way for improvements in both the conduct and performance of the game.

Matches between patrons persisted for most of the eighteenth century. The central characters may have changed, but their approach to life was much the same. Most of the great patrons in the second half of the century mixed cricket and politics much as their predecessors had done. The Duke of Dorset was Ambassador to the Court of France as well as Steward of His Majesty's Household. Sir Horatio Mann represented Sandwich in five successive Parliaments between 1774 and 1807. Their counterpart in Surrey, the Earl of Tankerville, was Joint Post-Master General and a Privy Councillor. Between them, these three devotees were responsible for many of the 'great' matches played in south-east England. No description of their style of life betters that contained in the obituary of Sir Horatio Mann which appeared in *The Gentleman's Magazine* of 1814:

> His life was rather dedicated to pleasure than to business. Enjoying a good constitution, he was much attached to gymnastic exercise, specially cricket, which as he advanced in life, he relinquished for the more sedate amusement of whist. Of late years, he regularly passed his time between Bath and Margate, and was a warm promoter of every institution and improvement in these places. At Dandelion, near Margate, also several good matches came off under his patronage after he had left Bishopbourne.[1]

That a man like Sir Horatio should have played such an important part in the development of eighteenth-century cricket was largely the result of the amount of land he owned. Apart from Bourne House, Bishopbourne, where he played most of his cricket, Mann also owned estates at Linton, near Maidstone, and at Sissinghurst, together with half the parish of Frittenden. The Duke of Dorset and Sir Horatio Mann, while the most influential, were only two members of a larger set of cricket-loving, local landowners in Kent. Between 1751 and 1773, matches were played at Ashford, Bethersden, Bourne Paddock, New Romney, Wye, Canterbury, Egerton, and Swinfield. In some cases, the teams were named after the village in which the landowner lived, while others took the identity of the patron – for example, Mr Farrar's Club (Isle of Thanet), Mr Louch's Club (Chatham) and, predictably, Sir Horatio Mann's Club. In the case of Mr Stephen Amherst, not only did he form his own club, but he also employed the best players as his servants.

For most of the eighteenth century, the impetus behind these matches was supplied by the local landowners. It was not until 1787 that Stephen Amherst tried to place the organization of this, most exclusive, type of contest on a formal footing. In that year, the following notice appeared in the press:

> Cricket Meeting at Coxheath to begin in 1787. Subscription – Two Guineas a Year. To meet once a week except on those weeks when a great county match is to be played, of which Notice will be given at the Meeting nearest to it, for the encouragement of the Best Players to come, to chuse as equal a match as possible for one innings. To allow 5s for Winners, and Two Shillings and Sixpence to the losers, to pay all expenses of Horse Hire, etc. To allow One Shilling for each man for Eating and Sixpence for his drink. An ordinary to be provided at Two Shillings for Subscribers and Three Shillings for Non-Subscribers. The wines etc. to be paid for exclusively. No forfeit of any kind for Non-Attendance.[2]

The original notice of the meeting was accompanied by a list of the supporters of the venture which included the names of Sir Horatio Mann, two other baronets and three Members of Parliament. However, the provision of expenses suggests that it was also the intention to attract players regardless of rank and wealth. Amherst's initiative came at a time when, for different reasons, the major patrons of cricket in Kent were becoming less active. The Duke of Dorset's enthusiasm lapsed, never to be rekindled, on his appointment as Ambassador to France in 1784, and the last recorded match involving Sir Horatio took place two years earlier. Their disappearance no doubt partly explains the decline in the number of matches played in Kent towards the end of the eighteenth century. But there were other reasons too. The onset of industrialization, coinciding with the French Revolution, strained the traditional fabric of English society to the point at which growing distrust between classes manifested itself, at least in the case of the aristocracy, in a grow-ing concern with exclusiveness, even segregation. The other im-portant factor in a rapidly changing situation was the formation of the Marylebone Cricket Club in London. If the Coxheath Meeting was intended to restore flagging interest in the game, even the most passionate supporter of Kentish cricket could not pretend that it was anything but a failure. Lord Harris, who certainly falls into that category, reached the following con-clusion:

> From that date [1789], the horrors of the French revolution and the sanguinary career of Napoleon with his long-threat-ened, but never carried-out, intention of invading England, seemed to have almost put an end to cricket in this county ... So great was the falling-off of play that for the year 1801, Mr Haygarth was unable to record more than ten matches, for 1802 twelve, 1803 nine, 1804 seven, and like numbers up to 1811 and 1812, when the numbers dropped to only two for each year.[3]

The second type of contest within this first general pattern consisted of matches between rural- and urban-based teams, an example being the match between the 'Eleven Gentlemen of Sevenoaks' and the 'Eleven Gentlemen of London' played in 1731. Public parks and commons on the outskirts of London, like those in Kennington, Dulwich and Dartford, were popular venues for this type of contest. That the return leg of these contests was rarely played suggests that they were staged to coincide with visits to the capital of country-based peers in pursuance of their administrative or political careers. The 'London' teams included such notables as the Prince of Wales, Lord Strathavon, Lord Montford and Lord Waldegrave. Per-manently resident in London, they formed the nucleus of an influential coterie known as the 'London Club'. Between 1735 and 1751, this club served as the administrative centre of cricket in London and, in addition, was the source of one of the earliest sets of standardized rules (1744). Something of the atmosphere of those early days is re-captured in the following passage:

One can hardly suppose sides to have often taken the field without some sort of banding together for the purpose. But moneyed folk did the thing in full style. The local gentry, when at home, could play with the assistance of their neighbours: but when the Court or Parliament took them up to London, they had to seek out companions of their own class who were acquainted with the game, if they wished to indulge in it. To facilitate this, they formed associations of similarly inclined men: with exclusive membership, and big subscriptions, and with the primary object of assembling together for the game. These were incidental amenities particularly with regard to dissipating such stakes as they won. They whipped up the cricketers of their own set, rented grounds, hired players and ground men and before long, were charging admissions for the privilege of watching their agile exertions.[4]

As the venue for most of the matches organized by the London Club, the Artillery Ground acquired a reputation comparable to that of Lord's or the Oval today. While in 1731 only one match was played on the Ground, in 1748 it staged six matches involving Kentish teams alone. A remarkable feature of these matches was the number of spectators they attracted. If contemporary estimates are to be believed, a crowd of 'some thousands' saw Kent play a combined Sussex, Surrey and Hampshire team in 1731. By 1751, matches at the Artillery Ground were being watched by as many as 10,000 spectators – approximately one fiftieth of the total population of London at the time! So large and uncontrollable were the crowds that on one occasion, when the Prince of Wales was present, 'a poor woman, by the crowd bearing down on her, unfortunately had her leg broke, which being related to His Royal Highness, he was pleased to order her ten guineas'.

Why should so many people have wanted to watch these matches? In the first place, cricket matches were one of the few forms of organized entertainment open to the urban working classes. They also provided everybody with the chance to gamble. Finally, they were amongst the comparatively rare occasions on which many of the most powerful figures of the day were on display to the general public. Whilst playing, their whereabouts was spotlighted by the distinctive colour of the apparel they wore and, as spectators, they normally collected in special enclosures. In 1737, for example, a 'pavilion was erected for His Royal Highness, the Prince of Wales, who was accompanied by several persons of distinction'.

Many of the 'great matches' of the eighteenth century were played on grounds owned or leased by publicans. In 1668, the publican of The Ram in Smithfield was rated for a cricket field. Another ground was owned by a Mr Smith of The Pyed Horse in Chiswell Street, but whether this was the same Mr George Smith who managed the Artillery Ground is not known. From the way in which these grounds were managed, it is clear that they were business ventures. The first recorded admission fee was charged at the Artillery Ground on 18 June 1744, when Kent met an All-England side. Spectators were admitted to the ground on payment of two pence provided that they accepted the following conditions: 'Gentlemen are requested not to bring dogs to the ground. All persons that go out of the ground during the match and intend to return again, are desired to take a ticket, otherwise they will not be readmitted.'[5] This charge did little to deter spectators from watching that particular match. But when the charge was increased to sixpence, the effect was immediate. A notice appeared in the press in 1746: 'The small appearance of the company is a plain proof of the resentment of the public to any imposition, for the price of going in being raised from two pence to sixpence, it is not thought that there were 200 persons present when before there used to be 7000 to 8000.'[6] Smith eventually realized his mistake, and in 1749 announced his intention of reducing the cost of admission to its former level.

> Numbers of my friends have intimated that the taking of six-pence admission has been very prejudicial to me. This is to inform them that for the future, they shall be admitted for two pence, and the favour of their company gratefully acknowledged.
>
> Their Humble Servant,
> George Smith.[7]

The profitability of these early promotions is difficult to gauge. Though, by one estimate, each match cost eighty pounds to stage, the organization itself involved little more than the provision of refreshments and a rope. The latter served not to demarcate the boundary of the field of play – a nineteenth-century innovation – but to help control the movements of the crowd.

No historian of cricket has failed to appreciate the significance of the aristocracy's adoption of the game. But very few have realized that, at the same time as members of the aristocracy and gentry were besporting themselves at the wicket, another section of society was beginning to make its presence felt on the field of play. The urban middle classes were at this time a loose-knit collection of merchants, moneylenders, lawyers, entrepreneurs, tradesmen and independent craftsmen, all of whom had profited from the opportunities and incentives created by a burgeoning capitalist economy. Being by nature an ambitious set of individuals, it was not long before they perceived the social advantages that could accrue from playing, and being seen to play, the game that was all the rage amongst the aristocracy. Prompted by this consideration and, no doubt, by the pleasure they derived from playing cricket, merchants, tradesmen and the rest started to organize their own 'great' matches. The type of contest that resulted, a challenge match between middle-class 'gentlemen', was the first of two variations within the second major pattern of organization.

For centuries, merchants, tradesman and shopkeepers had always been looked down upon. No matter how honest or successful, they could never quite overcome the stigma of having worked for their living. 'Tradesmen in All Ages and Nations', wrote John Chamberlayne in 1669, 'have been reputed ignoble.' Yet even at this time, the validity of this judgement was being questioned. Contemporaries were divided over the question of whether the younger son of a 'gentleman' could enter the world of business without forfeiting his father's status. While this was going on, the group at the centre of the controversy, the urban middle classes, was growing almost daily in numbers and financial strength. In 1688 Gregory King estimated that the total income of the mercantile and profession sections of society was nearly as great as that of the landed aristocracy.[8] By 1725, Defoe could claim that,

> trade is so far from being inconsistent with a gentleman, that, in short, trade in England makes a gentleman ... for, after

a generation or two, the tradesmen's children, or at least their grandchildren come to be as good gentlemen, statesmen, parliamentarians, privy councillors, judges, bishops, and noblemen as those of highest birth and most ancient families.[9]

But wealth alone could not completely overcome the centuries-old prejudice against 'trade'. Old habits die hard, and those involved in trade were quick to realize that the key to being accepted as a 'gentleman' was to live like one. To this end, the most successful tradesmen set about converting profit into property, and in this way gradually became absorbed into the aristocracy and landed gentry. The scale on which this process of self-advancement took place was sufficient to bring it to the notice of contemporaries. Sir William Harrison, for example, commented that merchants 'often change estates with gentlemen as gentlemen do with them: by mutual conversion of one into the other', while William Lambarde, in his *Perambulations of Kent*, claimed, 'The gentlemen be not here (throughout) of so ancient stocks as elsewhere, especially in the parts nearest London, from which city (as it were from a certain rich and wealthy seed-plot) courtiers, lawyers, and merchants be continuously translated and do become new plants amongst them.'[10]

While the marriage of wealth and property helped to cement the social respectability of the *arrivistes*, the same concern persuaded them to take a much closer interest in the games and pastimes popular amongst the aristocracy. It is hardly a coincidence that at the same time as members of the aristocracy and gentry were experiencing the joys of cricket, so too were members of the urban middle classes. 'Quoits, Cricket, Ninepins and Trap-ball', wrote an anonymous observer, 'will be very much in fashion, and more tradesmen may be seen playing in the fields than working in their shops.' By the 1730s, when the heir apparent to the throne of England was to be seen on the cricket field, merchants, craftsmen and the like were playing cricket matches which bore the closest resemblance to those staged by their social superiors. Thus, in 1743 an advertisement was to be found in the press: 'September 21st, a cricket match will be played ... between some Gentlemen of London with Mr Littleboy, a book-binder in Creed Lane, at their head, and some Gentlemen of the Borough of Southwark, for 20 guineas a side.'[11] Without the calming influence of members of the aristocracy, these matches often degenerated into violent brawls. For example, after a game in 1731 between '11 of London' and '11 of Brompton',

> ...a quarrel happened between a Londoner and a Brompton Gentleman, occasioned by the latter's tearing the former's ruffles from off his shirt, swearing he had no property to them, when several engaged on both sides for nearly half an hour, and most of the Brompton Gents were forced to fly for quarter, and some retired home with broken heads and black-eyes, much to the satisfaction of the other side.[12]

The other variation in the second overall pattern differs from the type of match enjoyed by Mr Littleboy insofar as the competitive impetus came from entire communities rather than particular social groups like the aristocracy. Though many peers played in the matches which fall into this category, their distinctive feature was the bond of communal sympathy which motivated both players and spectators. The great patrons of cricket, men like the Duke of Dorset, took part not to settle personal scores but to enjoy the quality of the cricket and to bask in the reflected glory of the local heroes. As the general popularity of cricket grew, certain villages and small towns in southeast England became renowned for the strength of their teams. Reports suggest that these reputations were jealously defended in matches over the length and breadth of the counties. The Earl of Oxford, for example, came upon one such match during his travels in Kent: 'At Dartford, upon the Heath as we came out of the town, the men of Tonbridge and the Dartford men were warmly engaged at the sport of cricket, which of all the people in England, the Kentish folk are the most renowned, and of all the Kentish men, the men of Dartford lay claim to the greatest excellence.'[13]

It would be idle to pretend that the participation of members of the aristocracy left this type of match completely unchanged. The effect of their involvement was to add an elaborate superstructure to the original competitive format. While the central focus remained rivalries between local villages, increasingly the venue for these contests moved from the villages to the Artillery Ground. In July 1738 Chislehurst played three matches against Horsmonden, and two against a London XI. Similar matches were played in 1741 and 1742, and in the following year a combined Chislehurst–Bromley team played another London side. All these matches were played at the Artillery Ground. In 1747, the same ground staged matches between sides from as far afield as Dartford, Hadlow, Slindon and Horsmonden.

The best, and most famous, examples of this type of contest are those which involved the two small villages of Slindon and Hambledon. In both cases, members of the aristocracy took an active role in organizing the matches without diluting the original identity of the teams. Slindon's greatest successes were achieved during the 1740s. Since it was at this time that teams playing under the direct patronage of the Duke of Richmond disappeared from the fixture list, and as the village of Slindon is located only three miles from his estate at Goodwood, it has always been assumed that the Duke transferred his allegiance to the local team. That he derived great pleasure from the successes of the Slindon team is evident from his own comments: after one match, he recorded that 'poore Little Slyndon beat Surrey almost in one innings'. The Slindon XI's reputation spread far beyond the boundaries of the Sussex village. Amongst the London *cognoscenti*, it was hailed as the best team of its day, and many of its members – above all, Richard Newland – were rated amongst the leading players of their generation. Some idea of the excitement generated by their appearance in London can be gained from the following announcement:

On Monday 6th September, 1742, will be played at the Artillery Ground, the greatest match at cricket that has been played for many years between the famous parish of Slindon in Sussex and eleven picked gentlemen of London. And as 'tis expected that there will be the greatest crowd that was known on the like occasion 'tis to be hoped, nay desired, that gentlemen will not crowd in by reason of the very large sums of money which is laid if one of the Sussex gentlemen gets 40 notches himself. To begin exactly at 12 o'clock on the forfeit of 100 guineas. N.B. The above parish has played 43 matches and lost but one. The match between the county of Surrey and London that was fixed for the same day will by played next week.[14]

The matches played by Slindon, and later by Hambledon,

represented an important link between the more traditional local village cricket and the newer, relatively exclusive, inter-élite contest. The spectacle of these two sides, whose players hailed from obscure villages that no-one had heard of, pitting their skills against the strongest teams of the day, captured the imagination of all London. The crowds attending their matches were so large and volatile that a penalty clause was introduced to dissuade teams from arriving late, or not at all. Such delays or disappointments could prove dangerous for players and spectators alike. The importance of gambling at these matches is reflected in the provision for an extra day's play, should the first prove to be inconclusive.

The decline of Slindon from about 1750 coincides with the death of the Duke of Richmond, and the ageing of Richard Newland. Nothing is known of the composition of the team, nor of the relationships which existed between players and patrons. It is only with the rise of Hambledon that this type of detail becomes available. Hambledon retains a lasting importance as one of the few non-aristocratic institutions to influence the overall development of cricket. Memories of its greatest victories and leading players have been perpetuated as part of the game's folk-lore.

From contemporary accounts, it is clear that cricket was already quite popular in Hampshire at about the time the Hambledon club must have been formed. In 1750, a Hampshire team played a London XI at the Artillery Ground, whereas Hambledon itself is first mentioned in 1756 when a side under that name played against a Dartford XI, again at the Artillery Ground. In 1764, the 'gentlemen of Hambledon called Squire Lamb's Club' met a team from Chertsey with 'great sums of money depending upon the match'. The following twenty-five years were the golden era of Hambledon cricket, and during this period the club exerted an influence upon the development of the game which has been exceeded only by that of the MCC. Yet, even now, it is far from clear how this came to be. From an historical and geographical perspective, Hambledon's existence seems to be much more a freak than the predictable culmination of a long sequence of events.

The Hambledon club owed its formation very largely to the efforts of the Reverend Charles Powlett, a third son of the Duke of Bolton, who remained a steward of the club until its final collapse. The presence of men like Powlett, and also Squire Lamb, guaranteed the respectability of the club during its early days. Once established, the prestige of Hambledon was, for a long time, self-perpetuating. By numbering amongst its members the Dukes of Dorset, Lennox and Albemarle and the Earl of Tankerville, the club soon found that it attracted the support of many members of the local squirearchy who, unlike Powlett, had little or no direct interest in cricket. Though none of the original membership rolls have survived, a list of members prepared by F. S. Ashley-Cooper suggests that the majority were either local landowners or small businessmen.[15] Out of a total of 157, eighteen were titled, four were clergymen, twenty-seven held rank in either the army or the navy, six were MPs, two were county sheriffs, two were knights, two were wine-merchants, and there was one lawyer and a clerk assistant to the House of Commons. The importance of this list is not its comprehensiveness or numerical accuracy. What it suggests is that the crucial factor in the success of Hambledon was the delicate balance between aristocratic patronage and local enthusiasm. Once this balance was disturbed, the club's fortunes declined and the final break-up was not long delayed.

In its early days, Hambledon's survival depended almost entirely on the number of victories it gained. On at least one occasion, a long string of defeats nearly led to the affairs of the club being wound up. But this crisis was overcome, and between 1771 and 1781 'out of the fifty-one matches played by the same club against England etc., they [Hambledon] gained twenty-nine of that number'. During these years, attention focussed on the team itself. Of its members, John Nyren, whose father, Richard, was 'the chosen general of all matches', wrote, 'So renowned a set were the men of Hambledon that the whole county could flock to see one of their trial matches.'[16]

Unlike the teams assembled by the Duke of Dorset and Sir Horatio Mann, which contained a large number of 'imported' players, the members of the original Hambledon XI all lived within a twenty-mile radius of Broadhalfpenny Down. Between 1771 and 1781, the team's appearance was sufficient to attract crowds of more than 20,000. If John Nyren is to be believed, match days must have amounted to local holidays, such was the support the team commanded:

There was high-feasting held on Broad Halfpenny during the solemnity of one of our grand matches. Oh! it was a heart-stirring sight to witness the multitude forming a complete and dense circle round that noble green. Half the county would be present, and all their hearts with us. Little Hambledon pitted against All-England was a proud thought for the Hampshire men. Defeat was glory in such a struggle – Victory, indeed, made us only 'a little lower than angels'. How those fine brawn-faced fellows of farmers would drink to our success! And then what stuff they had to drink! – Punch! – and not your *Ponche à la Romaine*, or *Ponche à la Grosseille*, or your modern cat-lap milk punch – punch be-deviled: but good unsophisticated John Bull stuff – stark! – that would stand on end – punch that would make a cat speak! Sixpence a bottle! We had not sixty millions of interest to pay in those days. The ale too! – not the modern horror under the same name, that drives as many men melancholy mad as the hypocrites; not the beastliness of these days, that will make a fellow's inside like a shaking bog – and as rotten: but barleycorn such as would put the souls of three butchers into one weaver: Ale that would flare like turpentine – genuine Boniface! – This immortal viand (for it was more than liquor) was vended at two-pence per pint. The immeasurable villainy of our vintners would with their march of intellect (if ever they could get such a brewing), drive a pint of it out into a gallon. Then the quantity the fellows would eat! Two or three would strike dismay into a round of beef. They could have no more pecked in that style than they could have flown, had the infernal black stream (that type of Acheron) which soddens the carcass of a Londoner, been the fertiliser of their clay. There would have been this company, consisting most likely of some thousands, remain patiently and anxiously watching every turn of fate in the game, as if the event had been the meeting of two armies to decide their liberty. And whenever a Hambledon-man made a good hit, worth four or five runs, you would hear the deep mouths of the whole multitude baying away in pure Hampshire – 'Go hard! – go hard! Tich and turn!' To the honour of my countrymen, let me bear testimony upon this occasion also, as I have already done upon others. Although their provinciality in general, and personal partialities individually, were naturally interested on behalf of the Hambledon men, I cannot call to recollection an instance of their wilfully stopping a ball that had been let out amongst them by one of our opponents. Like true Englishmen, they would give the enemy fair play.[17]

How many of Nyren's complaints ring true today! High interest rates. Watered-down beer! But the main interest of the passage lies in the contrast Nyren draws between rural and urban life. Hambledon's success typifies the strength of rural traditions and values. Both players and spectators embodied those qualities of honesty and integrity which tended to be missing from the growing urban areas. In these latter, it was the rather effete, often bohemian, habits of peers at Westminster that held sway.

But Hambledon was more than just a collection of cricketers. From the beginning, it possessed a rudimentary club structure. The central administrative position was held by Richard Nyren, 'the head and right arm' of the club. He was for some time landlord of the Bat and Ball Inn at Broadhalfpenny Down, but later moved to the George Inn in Hambledon. He also owned a farm close to the village. Members of the club were elected, and were required to pay an annual subscription of three guineas. First Barber, a local tradesman and long-time stalwart of the club, and then Nyren, were deputed to collect arrears on which they received a commission. Like modern first-class cricketers, the Hambledon players were subject to a number of regulations, which were backed up by fines. In June 1773, playing members were instructed to appear on Broadhalfpenny Down at 12.00 am on 'Practice Days', when the team would be selected. However, the introduction of fixed monetary penalties one month later suggests that some players were not averse to 'forgetting' this rule. Those who arrived late were to 'forfeit three pence each, to be spent among those who came at the appointed time'. In June 1787, this penalty was doubled and it was stipulated that receipts were 'to be spent in punch for the benefit of the other players'.

The scale on which players were paid is not recorded, although a club minute of September 1782 noted that players should receive on 'Practice Days, four shillings if winners, and three shillings if losers', provided that they arrived by 'twelve of the clock'. The club also undertook to cover the travelling expenses of those players who lived beyond the immediate neighbourhood: a minute of the 17 August 1773 ordered 'That James Bayley be allowed the expense of his horse hire when he comes to the practice of a Tuesday meeting', whilst a similar minute of the 10 May 1774 allowed Purchase 'two shillings and sixpence whenever he attends the meeting'. Beldham and James Wells were allowed their expenses at the discretion of the stewards in 1785. The club also provided a caravan to transport the team to away matches, and paid the cost of hats for each player.

The Bat and Ball Inn was the centre of the social activities of members and spectators alike. The proprietors provided an 'excellent cold collation' at special booths during matches, and dinners for members in the evening. It was at the post-match gatherings that the *esprit de corps* which played such an important part in the team's continuing success was fostered. In *The Young Cricketer's Tutor*, Nyren recounts some of the musical evenings the players held: 'Leer was a short man of fair complexion, well-looking, and of pleasant aspect. He had a sweet counter-tenor voice. Many a treat have I had in hearing him and Sueter join in a glee at the Bat and Ball on Broad Halfpenny.' (p. 69)

Members who attended the club practice dined afterwards at the Bat and Ball. To improve gastronomic standards, they ordered a wine cistern and later built up a bin. On these occasions, six standing toasts were drunk, one of which 'was of the most undisguised impropriety'. Port was obtained at two shillings a bottle; dinner cost the same amount. Barber was responsible for collecting empty wine bottles, and returning to Smith, the wine merchant. The club also held an annual dinner at which the President traditionally provided venison.

From 1780 onwards, fundamental changes occurred within the structure of the Hambledon club which, in the long term, heralded its collapse. The disappearance of the local 'stars' signalled the beginning of the end, for with them went not only great skill and enthusiasm but also much of the local character of the team. Their replacements came not from the immediate vicinity of Hambledon, but from villages like Farnham in west Surrey. As a result, the great players who represented the club between 1780 and 1790, William Beldham, David Harris, Tom and Harry Walker, and John Wells, shared a more contractual and less emotional relationship with Hambledon and its supporters. They were no longer bound by the same bonds of birth and residence.

Once initiated, Hambledon's decline was encouraged by a number of other factors. The early 1780s saw a gradual withdrawal from the club of many of its most influential patrons, men like the Duke of Dorset, Sir Horatio Mann and the Earl of Tankerville, and once the early magnetism had been lost, Hambledon's remoteness counted strongly against its continuance. Apart from its obvious geographical advantages, London was the centre of the aristocracy's social world, and thus a ready source of employment for the best players. The formation of the MCC in 1787 sounded the final death-knell for the Hambledon club. But as F. S. Ashley-Cooper made clear in *The Hambledon Cricket Chronicle*,

> That the M.C.C. should at once have attracted the chief amateurs and patrons is not to be wondered at, seeing the Club had head-quarters in so convenient a centre as London: the surprising thing is that Hampshire organisation should have remained supreme for so many years in a part of the country so difficult of access. (p. 162)

In fact, Hambledon continued in existence until 1796 when an entry in the minutes sadly recorded that 'No gentlemen' were present. An attempt was made to collect outstanding subscriptions, but this served only to hasten the decline, since many members, following the example of William Powlett, the Earl of Darnley and the Hon. E. Bligh, paid their arrears and resigned.

Thus far, we have said little of the cricketers themselves. The reason is simple: before the aristocracy and landed gentry adopted it, the game could not have provided employment for even one full-time player. As a folk game, it lacked a precise form and a standard set of rules. Matches were usually spontaneous happenings; teams rarely possessed a distinct identity, except when they represented groups like 'the bachelors' or 'the husbands'. Normally, however, they were little more than quite arbitrary combinations of friends or neighbours. The major break-through came with the appearance of the patrons who had the time, ability and money to plan contests and to select teams. It was within the context of these matches, of personal rivalries, large audiences and never-ending gambling, that technical expertise was first recognized as an important criterion of selection. Though teams were still dominated by the presence of men like the Duke of Richmond and Lord John Sackville, batting, bowling and, to a lesser extent, fielding, were accepted as valuable skills. The time at which this occurred – around 1730 – marked the birth of cricket as an occupation.

From the beginning, an important distinction existed between 'retained' and 'independent' players. The difference lay in the allegiances of the two groups. 'Retained' players were employed by patrons in nominal positions as estate or household servants. The earliest recorded examples are Thomas Waymark, Stephen Dingate, Joseph Budd, Pye and Green, all of whom were in the service of the Duke of Richmond at Goodwood. Waymark worked as a groom and Dingate as a barber. The former, often described as the father of cricket professionals, was a decisive factor in the success of the Duke's teams between 1720 and 1740. After a match at Penshurst, one report noted that, 'a groom of the Duke of Richmond signalled himself by such extraordinary dexterity and agility ... and 'tis reckoned he turned the scale of victory which for some years past had generally been on the Kent side'.[18]

Later patrons followed a similar policy in selecting their teams. Sir Horatio Mann engaged Aylward, and George and John Ring, as his bailiff, huntsman and whipper-in; Boxall and Craute were attached to Mr Stephen Amhurst, while the third Duke of Dorset employed Miller and Brown as gamekeepers, and Minshull as a gardener. Even though these players are often referred to as professionals, their position differed significantly from that of the modern professional. Both were bound by a contractual relationship, but in the case of the eighteenth-century cricketer the scope of the contract was much wider. He was in every sense a 'lord's man'; it was not just his cricketing talents but his whole being which was owned by the patron. When not required on the cricket field, he reverted to the duties of an estate servant, though it is probable that he was afforded privileges not given to ordinary servants. In this minor role, his abilities were often limited; Aylward, for example, was described as 'the best batsman, but a poor bailiff'.

In contrast, the 'independent' player was not bound to any one team or patron. Because the demand for his skills was so great, he could 'free-lance' for any number of teams, regardless of who patronized them. Furthermore, the 'independent' player was usually in a better position, should his cricketing career end prematurely. While he would generally have come from the ranks of craftsmen or even 'reduced' gentlemen, the 'retained' player would otherwise have been an unskilled craftsman. This difference can be shown by a break-down of the Kent XI which played against an All-England XI at the Artillery in 1744. The players involved were, in batting order, Lord John Sackville, Long Robin, Mills, Hodswell, Cutbush, Bartrum, Danes, Sawyer, Kips, Mills and Romney. Lord John, the First Duke and Eighth Earl of Dorset, was naturally the patron of the side. Long Robin appears to have been a prototype of the modern drop-out. *The Connoisseur* of 1746 described him thus:

A young fellow of family and fortune, who was born and bred a gentleman, but has taken great pains to degrade himself, and is now as complete a blackguard as those he has chosen for his companions. He will drink purl in the morning, smoke his pipe in a night cellar, and eat black puddings at Bartholemew Fair, for the honour of the thing. All the while, he is reckoned by his friends to be a mighty good-natured gentleman and without the least bit of pride in him. In order to qualify himself for the society of the vulgar, Bob has studied and practised all the vulgar arts under the best masters ... his greatest excellence is cricket playing, in which he is as good a bat as either of the Bennets, and is at length arrived at the supreme dignity of being distinguished among his brethren of the wicket by the title of 'Long Robin'.

Of the others, Mills of Bromley was a bookmaker; Hodswell hailed from Dartford and was a tanner; and Cutbush was a clock maker from Maidstone. Nothing else is known of the rest of the side except that Kips came from Eltham, Sawyer from Richmond (in Surrey) and John Mills from Horsmonden. Nevertheless, these details do highlight two important features of teams raised by patrons like Sackville. In the first place, they would usually include at least three or four 'independent' players who were not totally dependent on cricket for their livelihood. Mills, Hodswell and Cutbush were skilled craftsmen and Long Robin was probably not entirely without means. In the second, the recruitment of players from as far afield as Richmond and Horsmonden indicates the lengths to which patrons were prepared to go in order to assemble a winning side. It also testifies to the excellence of their 'scouting' systems.

By 1750, a degree of specialization had become a common feature of the leading teams. Both 'retained' and 'independent' players were selected on the basis of their skill as batsmen (Romney and Waymark), or bowlers (Hodswell and Bartrum). From reference in the poem written by James Love on the occasion of Kent's heroic victory over England in 1744, it is clear that fast-bowling was Hodswell's forte:

'Observe', cries Hodswell, to the wondrous throng,
'Be judges now, whose arms are the better strong,'
He said, then pois'd and rising as he threw,
Swift from his Arm the fatal Missile flew,
Nor with more Force, the Death-conveying Ball,
Springs from the cannon to the Batter'd Wall
Nor swifter yet the pointed Arrows go
Launched from the Vigour of the Parthian Bow.
It whizzed along, with unimaginable Force,
And bore down all resistless in its Course
To such Impetuous Might compelled to yield
The Ball, the mangled Stumps bestrew the Field.[19]

The poem also contains a testament to Waymark's unrivalled fielding ability: he was, according to Love, 'as sure a Swain to catch as was ever known'. Lastly, the poem tells us that the side contained a wicketkeeper, in the person of Kips, who was responsible for the 'stumping of Bryan'.

If 'independent' players were outnumbered in the teams which were led by the great patrons, the reverse was true of the local village teams. At Hambledon, most of the original team were drawn from occupations which, in that milieu, would have been relatively prestigious. Peter Stewart was a publican; Edward Aburrow, William Barber and John Small were shoemakers, though Barber later became a publican; Thomas Sueter was an architect and surveyor, and in the church tower at Hambledon there is the following inscription: 'Tho. Sueter, and Rich. Flood : Builders AD 1788'; George Lee was a brewer in business at Petersfield, while Richard Nyren, Thomas Brett and Lambert were farmers. The same pattern is found among the later generation of players, even though they often lived some way from Hambledon. Noah Mann was a shoemaker and an innkeeper; Richard Purchase was a blacksmith; Tom and Harry Walker were described by John Nyren as farmers, but in the *Hambledon Cricket Chronicle* they were referred to as a shopkeeper and a maltster. John Wells was a baker; Andrew Freemantle was a carpenter and then an innkeeper, while his elder brother, John, was a master-builder. George and William Beldham were also farmers, and the great David Harris was a potter.

One reason for exploring the backgrounds of the Hambledon players in some detail is to illustrate a popular fallacy which is contained in innumerable histories of cricket. The writers in question try to explain the relationships between patron and player by employing a model of industrial society which stressed the social and political gulf separating the major classes. Seen against this background, the appearance of someone of the stature of the Duke of Dorset alongside innkeepers and farmers in a little village in Hampshire was indeed remarkable. Here was the irrefutable evidence of the uniquely egalitarian properties of cricket. But it is not difficult to see that this claim is based on a total misunderstanding of the structure of pre-industrial society. Within this framework, a person's status within the local community was as important a measure of respectability as his class. Because so many of the Hambledon players came from highly respectable occupations, they were able to develop relatively close, informal relationships with their aristocratic team-mates. However, there is no evidence that patrons were treated with anything other than the deference normally accorded to men of their rank. It was Richard Nyren who held the key to the situation. As a representative of the true yeoman stock, captain of the Hambledon team and an excellent player in his own right, Nyren commanded universal respect. John Nyren's description of his father may be a little biased, but it nevertheless gives some idea of the esteem in which the elder Nyren was held:

I never saw a finer specimen of the thorough-bred old English yeoman than Richard Nyren. He was a good, face-to-face, unflinching, uncompromising, independent man. He placed a full and just value upon the station he held in society, and this he maintained without insolence or assumption. He could differ with a superior, without trenching up his dignity or losing his own. I have known him maintain an opinion with great firmness against the Duke of Dorset and Sir Horatio Mann; and when, in consequence of his being proved right, the latter had afterwards crossed the ground and shaken him heartily by the hand.[20]

The strength of his own position allowed Nyren to act as an intermediary between players and patrons, a role in which he was conspicuously successful. Again, John Nyren is the narrator:

It may be worthwhile to mention a circumstance connected with poor Noah Mann ... as it will tend to show the amenity in which men of lower grade in society lived in those good old times with their superiors; it may prove no worthless example to the more aristocratic and certainly less beloved members of the same rank in society of the present day. Poor Noah was very ambitious that his new-born son should bear the Christian name, with the sanction, of his name-sake Sir Horatio Mann. Old Nyren, who, being the link between the patricians and plebians in our community – the 'juste milieu' – was always applied to in cases of similar emergency, undertook upon the present occasion to bear the petition of Noah to Sir Horatio Mann, who, with winning condescension, conceded to the worthy fellow's request.[21]

It is a comment on the supreme confidence of members of the aristocracy that occasional infractions of the accepted code of behaviour could be overlooked. It was always possible that, in moments of extreme tension and excitement, players might fail to observe the standard conventions of the day. In fact, one of the most memorable incidents in the history of Hambledon cricket occurred under precisely these circumstances:

He [Lambert] was once bowling against the Duke of Dorset, and delivering his ball straight to the wicket, it curled in and missed the Duke's leg stump by a hair's breadth. The plain spoken little bumpkin, in his eagerness and delight, and forgetting the style in which we were always accustomed to impress our aristocratical playmates with our acknowledgement of their rank and station, bawled out – 'Ah, it was tedious near you, Sir!' The familiarity of his tone, and the

65

genuine Hampshire dialect in which it was spoken set the whole ground laughing.[22]

Finally, a word about retirement. For eighteenth-century cricketers the prospect of giving up the game probably did not cause the anxiety and concern that it does today. The 'independent' player, of course, always had his craft skills to fall back on. Even the 'retained' player could view the future with cautious optimism. Patrons, it seemed, rarely neglected their former champions. Thomas Waymark, for example, received an income from the Duke of Richmond long after his playing days were over. While few were as fortunate as Waymark, many were 'found' a job so that they could support themselves. Boxall was a case in point: after fifteen years as a bowler, he was found a place 'as a tide-waiter at Purfleet' by his old employer, Mr Stephen Amhurst.

6 The Early Years of the Marylebone Cricket Club

During its heyday, Hambledon became the mecca of cricket. All other matches had to take second place behind the homeric clashes on Broadhalfpenny Down. But despite the obvious counter-attractions, matches played in London during the late eighteenth century still attracted the support of many members of the aristocracy. Games were arranged and teams assembled by many of the exclusive coteries which flourished at the time. The MCC's predecessor, the White Conduit Club, was formed in 1782 by a collection of gentlemen recruited from a still older institution, the *Je-ne-sais-quoi* Club, sometimes referred to as the Star and Garter Club, whose perpetual chairman was the Prince of Wales, later George IV. The existence of three apparently autonomous clubs does not mean that the aristocracy's influence over the game was in any way interrupted. To the outsider, it appeared, and indeed was often the case, that the same persons belonged to all three clubs. As late as 1786, the White Conduit Club was being mistaken for the Star and Garter Club. For in June of that year, it was announced in the press that a match was to be played between teams representing Kent and the Star and Garter Club, but when a report of this match appeared in the same periodical, the teams mentioned were Kent and the White Conduit Club.

These clubs ensured the continuation of a regular programme of matches in the capital. As an off-shoot of the White Conduit Club, it must be assumed that the MCC was a very similar institution – that is, a loosely structured association of gentlemen whose main purpose in gathering together was to organize cricket matches, either between themselves or against another club. The trouble with the White Conduit Club lay in the fact that its matches were played on common land far from the fashionable heart of London. In 1786, acting on the advice of the Earl of Winchilsea – once described as a 'man of enviable moral courage [who] withdrew from the 1789 England side because of cold weather' – and other members, Thomas Lord, an employee of the White Conduit Club, leased a piece of land from the Portman Estate in Dorset Fields (now Dorset Square), and in 1787 staged the first match – Middlesex *v.* Essex – at Lord's Cricket Ground. In 1808, under pressure from property developers, Lord was forced to move to another ground, this time at North Bank, Regent's Park. It was a short-lived move for, in 1812, plans for a Regent's Canal showed that the new waterway was destined to cross the main wicket at a point just short of a 'good length'. Taking, as before, a turf from the original pitch, Lord was obliged to move his ground to a third site – St John's Wood – where the MCC has resided ever since.

Unfortunately, very little is known of the early days of the club. Soon after William Ward had taken over the lease from Lord, a fire destroyed the pavilion, and with it, all of the early records. However, this loss has not prevented several of cricket's historians from concluding that at a very early stage in its life, the MCC assumed full responsibility for the organization and control of cricket and became in effect the supreme administrative and legislative body in the game. H. S. Altham, for example, argued that,

> By the year 1800, Lord's is an institution established high and dry beyond all rivalry. The Marylebone Club has twice again revised the laws of cricket, and is recognised to be the supreme authority on the game. All the leading amateur players are found on its members' list, and it is now strong enough to meet unaided such counties as Hampshire and Middlesex: its ground is the accepted venue for all the great matches of the year, the focus of ambition for every aspiring player. (p. 52)

R. S. Rait-Kerr puts forward a similar argument in his book, *The Laws of Cricket*: 'We see therefore that 1787 is an important constitutional milestone, since that year marks the passage from an epoch in which revisions were carried at irregular intervals by a committee appointed for the occasion, to one during which a single central authority has been in continuous session.' (p. 26)

The great advantage of this thesis is its convenience. If, as Altham and Rait-Kerr suggest, the MCC did assume the rôle of 'supreme authority' soon after its foundation, then it would follow that the authorities at Lord's instigated or at least actively encouraged all the important changes in the game thereafter. Beguiling though this idea may appear, the fact remains that it raises as many problems as it solves. There are many reasons for believing that the MCC, *as an autonomous institution* rather than an occasional collection of individuals, made little impact on the organization and control of cricket, or on its evolution, until the second quarter of the nineteenth century.

In the first place, if the MCC had been universally recognized from its foundation, or thereabouts, as cricket's governing body, it failed for a long time to stamp its constitutional or moral authority on the conduct of matches played outside of London. At the end of the eighteenth and beginning of the nineteenth centuries, local newspapers often carried reports of matches between neighbouring towns and villages which ended in violence. Games between Leicester and Coventry seemed fated in this respect. In 1788, a Leicester victory led to 'a scene of bloodshed ... scarcely to be credited in a country so entirely distinguished for acts of humanity'. In the following year, a return fixture 'could not be played out' owing to a dispute between the players:

> On Wed. morning, the bets were £10 to a crown, but to the surprise of all, Clarke, who was declared out by both umpires the preceding evening, made his appearance with his bat at the command of Mr Needham who exclaimed, 'Clarke, keep to your stumps: damm ye, Brown (the umpire), why do ye not call play?' ... Needham swore that if Mr Bunbury, the Coventry umpire, would not let him go in again, the match should not be played out. (*Coventry Mercury*, 13 October)

Secondly, it was not until some thirty years after its foundation that local clubs and teams began to refer disputes over rules to the MCC. The following report appeared in the *Leicester Journal*, July 1818:

> The rule of play in dispute between the Oakham and Melton Mowbray Cricket Clubs having been referred to the

Marylebone Club, a decision was last week communicated by Lord F. Beauclerk that the Umpire at the bowler's end should have decided whether the striker were out or not without reference to the other umpire, and consequently the Oakham striker was not out, and the Oakham Club won the game.

Even in this case, it is interesting that the judgement was provided not in the name of the MCC, but by an individual member, Lord Frederick Beauclerk. A report – in the *Norfolk Chronicle* – in the same year indicates that disputes were sometimes referred directly to Lord Frederick without mention of the MCC: 'Downing v Lynn – a batsman hitting at the ball lost his balance and fell on his wicket, and a dispute over this ended the match. A letter was sent to Lord Frederick Beauclerk requesting his opinion.'

Thirdly, any assessment of the MCC's influence before 1825 must take into account the fact that, at the time of its foundation, a competitive framework was already in existence, and that the staging of matches at Lord's depended largely on the efforts of Thomas Lord and, later, James Dark. There is little doubt that the early matches played by the MCC were based on a format established earlier in the eighteenth century. They were essentially contests between members of an increasingly exclusive circle of cricket-loving gentlemen, though within this broad framework, two distinctive variations developed.

In the first, a team composed of members of the MCC played a collection of gentlemen representing a club or a county. In 1787, for example, the MCC played the White Conduit Club, in 1804 Hertfordshire, and in 1820 Norfolk. The precise names given to the teams are irrelevant: they were simply a way of recognizing different combinations of gentlemen. Like the MCC, these clubs and counties did not possess the formal organization of a modern cricket club: they did not include formally defined positions whose incumbents were entrusted with specific administrative responsibilities. The MCC itself did not appoint its first secretary, Benjamin Aisalbie, until 1822, and then only in an honorary capacity.

The second type of match involved one or two players competing against a similar number over one or two innings. It was the quintessential expression of the personal rivalries which motivated the leading gentlemen cricketers of the day. Sometimes honour was not satisfied on the cricket field, and a more dangerous confrontation followed. In the following passage, Sir Pelham Warner recounts the events leading up to one of the most notorious duels of the early nineteenth century:

> The Squire [Osbaldeston] won a bet of 200 guineas from Lord George Bentinck, but Bentinck, on paying the bet, let slip from his lips, 'This is robbery'. 'This will not stop here', said Osbaldeston, and a challenge to a duel followed, which took place at Wormwood Scrubs. Two versions are given of the encounter – one that Osbaldeston fired in the air, the other that a ball went through Bentinck's hat, missing his brain by two inches.[1]

Osbaldeston, a great huntsman who, it has been said, 'batted as well on four legs as most men on two', resigned from the MCC in an impulsive gesture he was to regret. When he later applied to regain his membership, supported by two of the most respected 'gentlemen' cricketers of the day, E. H. Budd and William Ward, his application was permanently vetoed by Lord Frederick Beauclerk, another of his old adversaries.

The establishment of three annual fixtures which were destined to become highlights of the Lord's season, Eton v. Harrow, Oxford v. Cambridge and the Gentlemen v. the Players, is frequently cited as evidence of how the initiatives of the MCC added a new dimension to the programme of matches played in London. But the history of these matches hardly bears out this claim. Games of cricket were a familiar sight at schools and universities throughout the second half of the eighteenth century. The first recorded inter-school match, between Eton and Westminster, was played in 1792, but teams of Old Etonians had been playing fixtures against the Gentlemen of England and Cambridge University since 1751.

Like all élite matches, these appear to have been arranged on an impromptu basis by the players themselves, rather than any outside body. In fact, the informality of these arrangements testifies to the power and autonomy of pupils in the eighteenth- and early nineteenth-century public school. In their attempt to gain a greater measure of control, one of the activities that masters tried to prohibit was cricket. From bitter experience, they knew that matches were often the signal for uncontrollable outbursts of violence. In 1792, the boys of Westminster so provoked local residents by their habit of breaking windows on the way to their matches that one incensed householder tried firing shots over their heads. This incident ended in court. Though these matches were frequently forbidden, masters were in general unable to prevent them taking place. In 1796, the match between Eton and Westminster, banned by Dr Keate, headmaster of Eton, resulted in a victory for Westminster by 66 runs. In the face of this blatant disregard for his authority, the doctor resorted to repressive measures and flogged the entire team. Though the first match between Eton and Harrow at Lord's took place in 1805, it was not repeated until 1818 and did not become an annual event until 1822.

The first Varsity matches provide further evidence of the extent to which the organization of this type of contest depended on the enthusiasm of the players involved, rather than the efforts of the MCC. The initial match, played at Lord's in 1827, was very much the work of two players, Charles Wordsworth and Herbert Jenner, who had first met while playing in the Eton–Harrow match of 1822. A second match was played the following year, but from then until 1836 the universities met neither on the cricket field nor on the river.

But of the three 'new' contests, it is the Gentlemen v. Players match which, at first sight, seems to bear the clearest imprint of the MCC's influence. First played in 1806, it was apparently a different type of contest, based on conflict between classes rather than rivalries within them. Appropriately enough, it was always played at Lord's. But first impressions are often misleading, and in this case, they certainly were. Like so many of the 'great matches' of the eighteenth century, the Gentlemen v. Players match owed its existence more to the aristocracy's love of gambling than to underlying class conflict. The great danger was not the threat of riots, but the superiority of the Players' teams. Such was the difference in the standards of the two sides that, for odds to be quoted, the Gentlemen had to be assisted in a variety of ways. In 1806, they 'borrowed' two of the most successful professionals of the day, Beldham and Lambert, and no doubt the Gentlemen's triumphs in 1825 and 1827 were not unconnected with the fact that their teams included at least sixteen players. The victory in 1829 was due entirely to the efforts of the two Sussex professionals, Lillywhite and Broadridge, who took nineteen wickets between them and the twentieth was run out. In the notorious 'Barn Door' match of 1837, the Players were obliged to defend wickets twice the normal size, but still managed to win by an innings. By this time, far from expressing the realities of class conflict the match had become a completely contrived affair. Neither gamblers nor spectators showed much interest, and often members of the Gentlemen's XI failed to appear, their places being taken by anyone available on the ground at the time.

Previous assessments of the MCC's influence on the organization of early nineteenth-century cricket have consistently overlooked the efforts of the original proprietor of the Lord's Ground, Thomas Lord, and his successor, James Dark. It was clear from the start that the founder members did not wish to become involved in the day-to-day administration of the club's affairs. This gave Thomas Lord the opportunity to take over the organization of matches in London. He was in many respects a typical example of the late eighteenth-century entrepreneur. Born in Yorkshire in 1755, the son of a gentry farmer who was stripped of his possessions after supporting the Young Pretender in 1745, Lord first came into contact with the London aristocracy while employed as a bowler and general factotum by the White Conduit Club. From his earliest dealings, there is little doubt that Lord was motivated more by the chance to make a profit than by any love of the game. Before the purchase of the first Lord's, the rate books of St Marylebone indicate that he was the lessee of the Allsop Arms. As well as trying to find a permanent home for the MCC, he was involved in a series of transactions involving property in Gloucester St, Orchard St and Wardour St. The success of these transactions enabled Lord to become a respected citizen in the neighbourhood of St John's Wood, for in 1807 he was elected to the Marylebone Vestry. To these property dealings he later added a flourishing business in wines and spirits. On the sale of Lord's in 1825, he retired to West Meon where he died in 1829.

Founding the MCC was no easy task. In addition to their aversion for any kind of administrative responsibility, many of the members showed very little enthusiasm for cricket itself. In the three years that Lord leased the second of his grounds, the club only played three matches, all of which were lost. To overcome this lack of support and to guarantee a reasonable return on their investment, both the original proprietors were obliged to seek other profitable forms of popular entertainment. Lord organized military parades at the Dorset Fields, and it was from here that Monsieur Gamelin made his celebrated ascent in a hot-air balloon. Dark introduced canary shows, hopping races and pigeon flying, as well as displays of archery and dancing by a troupe of Ioway Indians, and a marathon by John Joseph Grandserre on his velocipede.

Outside of London, there are few signs that, during its early years, the MCC was a major factor behind the organization of matches. Most of the impetus, particularly in the case of the 'great matches', was still provided by local landowners, though there are indications that towards the end of the eighteenth century their enthusiasm was beginning to wane. But records suggest that, in the event, it was local enthusiasts drawn from amongst the increasingly respectable urban middle-class occupations who stepped in to ensure the continuation of matches. The *Leicester Journal* carried a report in 1790: 'At a meeting at the White Head's Inn, *Leicester*, on Thursday, 25th, it was ordered that public notice should be given of a meeting to be holden at the said Inn on Mon., May 29th at 7 p.m. to give gentlemen an opportunity of becoming members of a Cricket Club in Leicester, formed upon eligible principles.'

Contrary, then, to the views put forward by Altham and many others, there is little evidence to support the argument that, by the turn of the nineteenth century, the MCC had established itself as the 'supreme authority' in the world of cricket. At this time, and for many years after, the club had no administrative structure, nor a staff. Lord's was managed by a largely independent proprietor, and members were more than happy with this arrangement. Few seemed to be interested in playing more than one or two matches a season. Like the White Conduit and the *Je-ne-sais-quoi* Clubs, the early MCC existed as a select gathering of landed gentlemen, sharing in common a love of cricket. Had the most prestigious amongst this group, men like the Earl of Winchilsea, decided to meet under a different name, the MCC would have disappeared forthwith. The numerous revisions of the laws of cricket made between 1787 and 1830 are often cited as evidence of the authority of the MCC. But these were probably the work of small *ad hoc* committees, made up of the most influential members of the club. In fact, proposals for changes in the laws

74

were first referred to a General meeting of the club as late as 1828.

Though the formation of the MCC had little immediate impact on cricket, there were signs by the beginning of the nineteenth century that a fundamental change in the organization and outlook of the game was imminent. The key to the situation inevitably lay with the hitherto all-powerful landed aristocracy and gentry. As individual landowners gradually realized the extent to which the Industrial Revolution and the related growth in towns and cities threatened their traditional preeminence, they tended to withdraw from the popular spotlight, preferring instead the exclusiveness and seclusion of more élitist surroundings.

There had been criticism of the aristocracy's presence on the cricket field throughout the eighteenth century. In the early years, it was the Puritan lobby who were most offended by the cricketing lords. An anonymous pamphlet of 1712, entitled *The Devil and the Peers, or a Princely Way of Sabbath Breaking*, recounted 'a famous cricket match between the Duke of M........, another Lord and two boys, for twenty guineas', and denounced Sabbath-breaking, corruption of the electoral system, and the prevalence of gambling. None other than Alexander Pope was moved to comment on the irresponsibility of certain members of Parliament: 'Truants midst the Artillery Ground ... With Shoe-blacks, Barber's boys, at Cricket Playing.'[2] The poet believed that the appearance of great landowners in such undistinguished surroundings could only bring the entire aristocracy into disrepute. And, on the Day of Reckoning,

> When Death (for Lords must die) your doom shall seal,
> What sculptured Honors shall your tomb reveal?
> Instead of Glory, with a weeping eye,
> Instead of Virtue pointing to the sky,
> Let Bats and Balls th' affronting stone disgrace,
> While Farce stands leering by, with Satyr face,
> Holding, with forty notches marked, a board –
> A noble triumph of a noble Lord![3]

For the eighteenth-century capitalist, 'great matches' were the signal for large-scale absenteeism. Such dissipation of productive capacity could prove fatal to a nation as dependent on trade as Britain. As a contributor to *The Gentleman's Magazine*, September 1743, made clear, the aristocracy were free to indulge in whatever pastimes amused them, but the rest of society was not:

> In diversions as well as business, circumstances alter things mightily, and what in one may be decent, may in another be ridiculous ... neither is it at all impossible that exercise may be strained too far. A journeyman shoemaker may play from five o'clock on Saturday until it is dark at skittles, provided that he has worked all the rest of the week ... Noblemen, gentlemen and clergymen, have certainly a right to divert themselves in what manner they think fit: nor does it dispute their privilege of making butchers, cobblers and tinkers their companions provided they are gratified to keep their company. But I very much doubt whether they have the right to invite thousands of people to be spectators of their agility at the expense of their duty and honesty. The time of fashion may be indeed of very little value, but in a trading country, the time of the meanest man ought to be of some worth to himself and to the community. The diversion of cricket may be proper in holiday time and in the country: but, upon days when men ought to be busy, and in the neighbourhood of a great city, it is not only improper, but mischievous to a high degree ... It brings together crowds of apprentices and servants whose time is not their own. It propogates a spirit of idleness at a juncture when, with the utmost industry, our debts, taxes, and decay of trade, will scarce allow us to get bread.

Gambling, like idleness, involved a dissipation of scarce resources. This, combined with the enormous element of risk involved, meant that it too was anathema to the capitalist. Divested of its association with gambling, cricket was morally and physically beneficial; otherwise it represented a threat to players and spectators alike. In delivering judgement on a case arising out of a disputed wager on a cricket match, a London magistrate observed that, 'It [cricket] is a manly game, and not bad in itself, but it is the ill-use that is made of it by betting above £10 that is bad and against the law, which ought to be constructed largely to prevent the great mischief of excessive gambling.'[4] And a report in the *St James Chronicle*, May 1765, shows the judge's forebodings were not exaggerated: 'Monday last; a young fellow, a butcher being entrusted with about £40 by his mistress to buy cattle in Smithfield Market, instead went into the Artillery Ground and sported away the whole sum in betting upon the cricket players.'

However, it is not to these sporadic criticisms, but to more fundamental processes of economic and social change, that we must look to find the reasons behind the aristocracy's growing distaste for such popular spectacles as 'great matches'. These will be considered in the next chapters: here it is enough to identify some of the consequences of this change of habit. First, as we have already mentioned, it led to Thomas Lord being asked to provide a private, enclosed ground where members of the aristocracy could perform without having to subject themselves to scrutiny by the masses. It also led to a preference for the more exclusive single- or double-wicket type of context, in which a hired 'professional' would either represent or play alongside his illustrious employer. By the turn of the century, the rivalries between the leading patrons became so intense as to outweigh all considerations of honour. In 1810, for instance, Lord Frederick Beauclerk refused to consent to the cancellation of a double-wicket match against his old enemy, Squire Osbaldeston, although the latter was too ill to play. In the event, Beauclerk's lack of charity rebounded on him. Osbaldeston's partner, William Lambert, one of the best players of his time, took the field alone and inflicted an ignominious defeat on Lord Frederick and his partner, T. C. Howard.

The growing popularity of single- and double-wicket matches had far-reaching consequences for players too. It meant that the leading professionals had more opportunities to exploit the market value of their skills. On the other hand, the substitution of a short-term contract for the relative security of a retainer left the players far more exposed to the vagaries of their occupation. Of these, perhaps the most disruptive was the prevalence of gambling. Because the outcome of matches depended to a large extent on their performance, professionals were an obvious target for the unscrupulous gambler, bent on reducing to an absolute minimum the element of risk involved in his wagers. To achieve this end, he usually resorted to one of two subterfuges, bribery or a false report. William Ward recalled that 'one artifice was to keep a player out of the way by a false report that his wife was dead'. The susceptibility of professionals to the corrupting influence of the gamblers, or 'legs' as they were called, grew as their activities became increasingly predictable. Once it was known that most professionals spent the winter in Hampshire, it was a relatively easy task for the 'legs' to visit this area at the beginning of each season and, as Billy Beldham, the old Hambledon player, put it, 'buy them up'. In London, professionals were equally accessible. Again, it was Beldham who recalled the precise details: '... these men [the "legs"] would come down to the "Green Man and Still", and drink with us, and always said that those who backed us, or the "nobs" as they called them, sold the matches.'[5]

The 'Green Man and Still' to which Beldham refers was a public house in Oxford Street. During the season, it was the hub of the professional's life. Here he stayed whilst in London and here he could be contacted by potential employers – or the 'legs'. But the cost of staying at the Green Man was the undoing of many a young player, for it could not be met by match fees alone. As H. S. Altham wrote, 'The best of wine and beef was their normal fare, living such as five guineas for a win and three guineas for a loss could never pay for, and many a young countryman fresh to and dazzled by the glamour of London life, must have fallen easy victim to the free drinks and the wiles of the "legs".'[6]

The raw professional thus found himself in a very vulnerable situation. Nothing in his previous experiences equipped him to deal with the demands now placed upon him. He no longer had family or kin to fall back on: the relationships he formed in London involved fellow cricketers with whom he was competing, and employers with whom he was bargaining. On top of everything else, he was often poorly paid. Under these circumstances, the temptations offered by the web of corruption organized by the 'leg' were hard to resist.

The career of at least one famous professional was destroyed as a result of succumbing to these temptations. William Lambert was permanently barred from Lord's after it had been alleged that he had 'sold' the match between England and Nottingham in 1817. While less dramatic, the effects of such corruption on relationships between professionals was no less damaging. The frequency and ease with which players were known to accept bribes undermined the basis of trust both on and off the field. In a conversation with the Revd J. Mitford, another famous player, Fennex, described how at one stage mistrust reached such a pitch that even the most innocuous of actions seemed suspicious: 'You may hear that I sold matches. I will confess I was once sold myself by two men – one of whom would not bowl, and the other would not bat his best – and lost £10. The next match at Nottingham, I joined in the selling and got my money back. But for this once, I could say I was never bought in my life, and this was not for want of offers from C... and other turf men, though often I must have been accused. For where it was worthwhile to buy, no man could keep a character, because to be without runs or to miss a catch was, by the disappointed betting men, deemed proof as strong as the Holy Writ.'[7]

The gradual withdrawal of members of the aristocracy from the dominant position that they had occupied throughout the eighteenth century also had consequences for the professional at the end of his playing days. Retainers, and the close personal relationships associated with them, had provided an invaluable cushion against the privations of old age. Early in the nineteenth century, this advantage had largely disappeared. The prospects of the 'contract' player at the end of his career were scarcely encouraging, for there was no other market for his skills. Nor did the fact of having been a professional cricketer carry the kudos that it acquired later. The majority of players were faced with two choices. They might return to the neighbourhood, even the job, which they had left to become a cricketer. William Lambert, for instance, returned to Nutfield, his birthplace, where he worked as a miller, 'but he was also in the fuller's earth trade, having several men in his employ'. The alternative, for players who possessed no other skills, was to stay in cricket as long as was physically possible. Thus William Fennex was employed as a coach by the Ashford family of Eye in Suffolk, but this was only a temporary reprieve, for Fennex died a pauper in a London work-house. But it is Pycroft's description of the fate of the once renowned Thomas Beagley of Hampshire which best portrays the poverty and desolation which, all too frequently, was the lot of the old professional:

Yes, we have a painful recollection of poor Thomas Beagley

– one of the finest batsmen of Lord Frederick's day, and the very model of a long-stop – sitting neglected and alone under the lime trees at Lord's, while the ground was resounding with just such cheers for others in his day yet unborn, that had been raised for him. At length a benefit was attempted in acknowledgement of his former services; but the weather rendered it of little worth to him, and time after time we saw him looking more threadbare and more pitiful, till at last a notice in 'Bell' told us what Thomas Beagley had been, and what – alas! – he was.[8]

7 The Second Transformation

At first glance, it appears unlikely that the twenty years after Waterloo were a critical turning point in cricket's evolution. Obvious changes seemed few and far between. But these were the years when the game came face to face with the realities of the new industrial society, when it exchanged patronage, paternalism and the mingling of classes for entrepreneurial enterprise, the rigours of wage labour and the separate worlds of the amateur and the professional. The extent of these changes prompted contemporaries like Mary Mitford to look back nostalgically at the comfortable, unhurried world of the eighteenth century.

> I doubt if there is any scene in the world more animating or delightful than a cricket match. I don't mean a set match at Lord's for money, hard money, between a certain number of gentlemen and players as they are called – people who make a trade of the noble sport and degrade it into an affair of betting and hedgings and cheatings: nor do I mean a pretty fete in a gentlemen's park, where one club of cricketing dandies encounters another such club and where they show off to a gay marquee of admiring belles; No! the cricket I mean is the real solid, old-fashioned match between neighbouring parishes where each attacks the other for honour, glory and a supper for a half-crown.[1]

Cricket is seen here in the same light as 'Merrie England' – a remnant of the goodness of a society as yet unafflicted by the evils of industrialization. The Industrial Revolution loosened the bonds of paternalism and deference which had cemented the fabric of eighteenth-century society. In Victorian

81

England, the traditional dominance of the aristocracy, based on land and a particular life-style, was challenged by industrialists, manufacturers, financiers and members of the professions – a collection usually known as the middle classes. Another important change involved the freeing of labour from the personal obligations and ties traditionally associated with a master-servant relationship, and the rise of a wage economy. As contractual employment became the norm, conditions of work became more rigorous and demanding. Rather than relying on the beneficence and protection of the aristocracy, the working population was expected to look after itself; hard work was the first step on the road to self-improvement. The importance of leisure was similarly reassessed. In the face of the increasing demands from capitalists intent on maximizing profits, the complementarity of work and play characteristic of pre-industrial society was shattered. Henceforth, there was to be no doubt that work was the real business of life. Ironically perhaps, no summary of the relationship between work and play in the early nineteenth century can better that offered by Karl Marx:

> The industrialist has to be hard-working, sober, economical, prosaic; his enjoyment is only a secondary matter; it is recreation subordinated to production, and thus a calculated, economic enjoyment for he charges his pleasure as an expense of capital and what he squanders must not be more than can be replaced with profit by the reduction of capital. Thus enjoyment is subordinated to capital and the pleasure-loving individual is subordinated to the capital-accumulating individual whereas formerly (in feudal society) the contrary was the case.[2]

In the calculations of the Victorian entrepreneur, leisure had three main virtues. It stimulated the appetite for work amongst both privates and captains of industry. In many cases, especially cricket, it provided an opportunity to mingle with the aristocracy. Lastly, it provided one means by which future generations might be imbued with that quality of moral integrity which, for many, was to be the hall-mark of the upper classes.

At the same time as radical changes were affecting the structure of society at large, cricket began to develop a more complex organization as well as a wider popularity. Nor were the players left unaffected. The status of the professional, and the requirements and responsibilities of his role in the game, were gradually clarified. From being a little more than an aristocratic diversion, by 1850 cricket was well on the way to becoming a sport, an occupation and a career. But it is not enough to suggest that there might have been a link between the history of cricket and industrialization. The critical question concerns the working-out of this relationship. Why did cricket develop a new structure between 1830 and 1870, one which was to survive virtually unchanged for another seventy years?

If the stability of eighteenth-century England was largely a reflection of the power of the landed interests, the fluidity of the nineteenth century can be linked just as certainly to what Thomas Carlyle described as the 'abdication on the part of the governors'[3], and the events which, later that century, were to culminate in the 'triumph of the plutocracy'.[4] Carlyle's phrase refers to the gradual abandonment by the aristocracy about the turn of the nineteenth century of that obligation to protect their tenants and servants in return for which they had demanded, and received, obedience and loyalty. While isolated examples of *noblesse oblige* appear later in the century – notably in the person of Lord Shaftesbury – the essentially personal relationships which had been the basis of the local magnate's authority fifty years before were irretrievably lost. Without them, the aristocracy became increasingly distanced from the rest of society. Even the conservative *Blackwood's Edinburgh Magazine* concluded in 1820 that,

> Everywhere, in every walk of life, it is too evident that the upper orders of society have been tending, more and more, to a separation of themselves from those who nature placed beneath them ... The rich and the high have been indolently and slothfully allowing the barriers that separate them from their inferiors to increase and accumulate ... Men have come to deride and despise a thousand of those means of communicating that in former days knit all orders of men together.[5]

To many members of the aristocracy, the break-down of paternalism was a blessing in disguise since they had become just as committed to capitalism as the middle-class entrepreneur. Yet despite the inexorable progress of the Industrial

Revolution, in the course of which many vestiges of the eighteenth century soon became anachronistic,

> The aristocratic element continued to rule the roost right to the end of intact and vital capitalism. No doubt that element – though nowhere so effectively as in England – currently absorbed the brains from other strata that drifted into politics; it made itself the representative of bourgeois interests and fought the battles of the bourgeoisie; it had to surrender its last legal privileges – but with these qualifications, and for ends no longer its own, it continued to man the political engine, to manage the state, to govern.[6]

The middle classes themselves remained as convinced as ever of the social value of land. They went to great lengths to ensure that, as far as was possible, the distinctive life-style which had grown up around the country estate was not disturbed by the change of ownership. It was this element of continuity, as Samuel Coleridge realized, that prevented the complete disruption of the English ruling class:

> It will not be necessary to enumerate the several causes that combine to connect the performance of a state with the land and the landed property. To found a family, and to convert his wealth into land, are twin thoughts, births of the same moment, in the mind of the opulent merchant, when he thinks of reposing from his labours. From the class of *novi homines* he redeems himself by becoming the staple ring of the chain, by which the present will become connected with the past, and the text and evidence of permanency be afforded.[7]

Why did the relationship between Coleridge's 'opulent merchant' and the great aristocratic lineages become one of interdependence and not mortal rivalry? The simple answer – and in this case, probably the right one – lies with the gentry. By the middle of the nineteenth century, it had become '... a more fluid class than the aristocracy, permitting easier exit and entry, and as a result of the provincial limits prescribed by their resources and way of life, fundamentally a more conservative class ... Taken together, these two factors played a substantial part in the prolongation of the aristocratic control of society.'[8]

Purchase of land and inclusion in the social world of the

county gentry were standard steps in the 'opulent merchant's' pursuit of respectability. If successfully negotiated, they led the wealthy entrepreneur to the desirable bosom of provincial gentility. However, the parvenu origins of many of the aspirants did require some changes in the traditional concept of gentility. Since it had always been an attribute of birth, a strict interpretation would have permanently excluded most members of the middle classes. Resolution came in the form of a compromise by which the meaning of gentility was widened to take account of the ownership of property, wealth and such personal qualities as loyalty and self-discipline. By 1860, one of the most important attributes of the county gentleman was his utility: far more readily than anyone else, he would serve the state through performing the everyday duties of local government. Ideally, *le gentilhomme anglais* was expected to possess, 'a sense of honour [which] would generally make expensive supervision unnecessary: his personal status would supply him with the power he might officially lack: his standards would be those of the manor house, the rectory, the club, so that he would never push professional zeal to inconvenient or dangerous lengths.'[9]

As the nineteenth century continued, the county gentleman moved into many other spheres, including cricket. But if the intention was to emulate the style of the eighteenth-century noble, the result was a very different form of involvement. Far from assuming an inherent superiority, the nineteenth-century gentleman went to great lengths to emphasize his authority. Some games and pastimes were ignored completely; in others, two separate roles were created, one of which was to be occupied by the gentleman, and the other by his 'inferiors'. In cricket, as in other games, these came to be known as the 'amateur' and the 'professional'. While, in cricket, these terms had originally only indicated whether a player accepted payment for his services, they soon came to denote a much more comprehensive distinction, covering not just remuneration but the whole gamut of relationships on and off the field. It is not a coincidence that many of the games that first achieved widespread popularity during the nineteenth century – cricket, rugby and tennis – were administered on a county basis and had the amateur–professional distinction at the heart of their organization and identity.

Moreover, these games, and cricket in particular, were more

than just desirable sources of exercise and entertainment. As the *curriculum* of the nineteenth-century public school indicates, cricket played an important part in perpetuating ruling-class values. Sporting prowess and intellectual development were believed to be mutually compatible. When a member of the 1864 Royal Commission on the Public Schools asked an assistant master at Eton 'whether or not boys who excel at games are pretty good at work?' he received the following reply:

I think you could not say that there was a regular tendency for intellectually distinguished boys to come to the top in other things; I do not think you will find that; but at the same time, I do not think you will find that the eight and the eleven were particularly stupid fellows, or that they did not care about intellectual distinction.

The questioner then asked:

Is there any difference between games in that respect? Do you think that cricketers are less well up in their school-work than others?

And to this the master replied:

No, I do not think so: I think that they are on a par with the others.[10]

Through playing games like cricket, the sons of the upper classes acquired those qualities of self-discipline and loyalty which were fundamental to Victorian gentility. Perhaps the best description of these values, and of cricket's role in their inculcation, is to be found in a famous extract from *Tom Brown's Schooldays*:

'What a noble game it is too.'
'Isn't it? But it is more than a game. It's an institution,' said Tom.
'Yes,' said Arthur, 'the birthright of British boys old and young, as *habeas corpus* and trial by jury are of British men.'
'The discipline and reliance upon one another which it teaches is so valuable, I think,' went on the master, 'it ought to be such an unselfish game. It merges the individual in the eleven: he doesn't play that he might win, but that his side may.'[11]

A similar theme is propounded in the following passage taken from an article published in *Belgravia* in 1871, only here the professional element is specifically excluded:

Cricket is the purest of all games, for the simple reasons that it is followed up for itself alone,and no material reward is held out as an inducement to play ... It is free from the evils of betting. It encourages obedience, discipline, tact: it engenders health and strength, and it leads to no possible ill results except the spending of a summer's day in the summer air rather than crouched over an inky desk.[12]

The significance of the character-building properties attributed to 'amateur' cricket cannot be overstated. Throughout the Victorian era, they had an influence on the game and its players which can only be compared with that of the landed aristocracy in the eighteenth century, or the mass audience and demands of economic viability in the second half of the twentieth.

'Amateur' cricket had its origins way back in the early nineteenth century. The rise of the MCC reflected a desire on the part of many members of the aristocracy for a different role in the organization of the game. Several were attracted only by the chance to gamble, and almost all preferred to play or watch in enclosed, private grounds, rather than on common land as before. From this point of view, the opening of the Lord's Ground was a logical development, though it robbed matches of much of their old-fashioned charm and vitality. The intrusion of the middle classes probably reinforced the trend toward exclusiveness. By 1833, the MCC could scarcely be described as an aristocratic institution since only twenty-five, out of a total membership of 202, possessed titles. At about the same time, non-aristocrats began to fill key positions in the administration of the club. It was William Ward, a prosperous City banker, who purchased the leasehold of the ground from Thomas Lord in 1825, thereby preventing its sale to property developers. In 1822, Benjamin Aisalbie, a wine merchant by trade, became the club's first secretary, albeit in an honorary capacity. Mr G. T. Knight's move to alter the 'no-ball' rule in 1828 was the first occasion on which a proposed change in the laws of cricket was submitted to a general meeting of the MCC. In 1835, it was decided that, thereafter, suggested changes should be published in *The Sporting Magazine* at least seven months before the meeting at which they were to be presented.

The lack of interest shown by members of the MCC in the day-to-day administration of the club, and in many of the matches played at Lord's, removed one potential obstacle to these changes. In 1835, James Dark purchased the leasehold of Lord's from William Ward, who had 'experienced a reverse of fortune'. He remained the 'Proprietor of the Ground' for almost thirty years, and more than once during this period 'Dark's' threatened to replace 'Lord's'. In the 1830s, 'Lord's was more like a field pure and simple': there was a 'cottage-like pavilion with a few shrubs in front of it . . . a miniature hill and a valley between the farthest corner of the pavilion and the lower wicket', two ponds and, penned in one corner, a flock of sheep which were allowed onto the ground the day before a match was due to be played to prepare a wicket. Dark was responsible for several improvements in the ground's facilities, and in the fixture list. The MCC committee minutes of 1850 recorded that 'Lord's was drained by Mr Dark at his sole expense'. He took charge of organizing the Players' team, and in 1835 actually played in the side himself. In 1853, the minutes recorded that 'Mr Dark receives all subscriptions and Entrances and undertakes the expense of all matches made by the Committee'. This is confirmed four years later in a minute which reported that, 'owing to the proposal made four years ago by Mr Dark, and accepted by us, viz., that he should receive the whole amount of the subscriptions and provide for every expense, matches have been paid for by him at an annual cost of £507. Those of last year cost £583. 15., the largest sum ever expended in one year'. The ownership of Lord's did not pass into the hands of the MCC until 1866. For eighty years, members were content to leave the administration of their club to a man who was ostensibly their servant, but who really dictated the type and number of matches played at Lord's.

Before 1830 the best games of cricket and the most skilled players were to be found almost without exception within a thirty-mile radius of London. The major barrier to the diffusion of skills had always been the difficulty and cost of long-distance travel. For this reason, the arrival in the provinces of teams from London created immense excitement. When the MCC, responding to an invitation from Col. the Hon. Charles Churchill, first ventured as far as Nottingham, it was reported that 'booths were erected and the days of play being, with one exception, remarkably fine, the attraction drew to the scene more than ten thousand spectators'. In a similar match in 1817, the crowd, estimated to be between 12,000 and 14,000, was a cause of great concern to the local dignitaries. As a member of the MCC team, E. H. Budd, recalled,

> The concourse of people was very great: these were the days of the Luddites, and the magistrates warned us that unless we would stop our game at seven o'clock, they would not answer for keeping the peace. At seven we stopped, and simultaneously the thousands who lined the ground began to close in on us. Lord Frederick lost his nerve and was very much alarmed, but I said they didn't want to hurt us. No: they simply care to have a look at the eleven men who ventured to play two against one![13]

The fact that the MCC XI could play and beat a Nottingham XXII is an indication of the superiority of London cricket. If these odds seem unfair, they should be weighed against the technical limitations of the Nottingham players described in the following recollection.

> Woodward, who is a hale and hearty old man, describes graphically the professional tutorage he received from Gilbert, the captain of the 22. He was instructed to take his station at the wicket, with his feet firmly fixed on the ground, a foot or 18 inches asunder, and to strike resolutely at any ball that came within his reach. Consequently, he had no freedom of action, and could not, unless by accident, return the ball in any other than one direction. 'Leg hits', 'forward cuts', and similar modes of dealing with the ball were not even thought of. No wonder that under the influence of such instruction, and with reliance on nothing but strength of arm and quickness of eye, our townsmen should have proved unequal to the task assigned to them.[14]

The visits of the MCC were a great stimulus to local cricket. As the following report in the *Nottingham Journal*, (19 July 1817) indicates, the example set by the leading players of the day

triggered off a great surge of interest among the local enthusiasts:

> Such is the rage for cricketing amongst all classes of the com-
> munity of Nottingham, since the successful issue of the late
> grand contest between the Nottingham and London clubs,
> that men and boys, young and old alike, are emulous of
> becoming proficient at the game: hence bats and balls are
> held in perpetual requisition and strangers, in traversing the
> outskirts and avenues of the town, can scarcely avoid being
> complimented with some notable proof of superior dexterity
> in the noble science.

From the 1840s, however, far-reaching innovations in transport greatly extended the distance that teams could travel,
and as a result the number of matches played in a season increased dramatically. Gradually, more elaborate matches and
superior techniques emerged in the north and west of England
and in the Midlands. More often than not, these involved
players not recruited from, or supported by, the aristocracy and
gentry.

It was in this rapidly changing situation that the MCC first
acquired a reputation for being conservative, parochial and exclusive. The trend was most evident in the club's attitudes towards the organization of matches, and in its relationships with
'professional' cricketers. In 1863 the MCC was playing the
same number and the same type of match as it had been in
1836. Yet during the same period, the total number of matches
played in England each season approximately trebled. By 1850
the three most popular fixtures at Lord's – the Gentlemen
versus the Players, Eton versus Harrow, and Oxford versus
Cambridge – mirrored divisions in the wider society. The first
was based on the rivalries between upper-class 'amateurs' and
working-class 'professionals', while the other two were, in
spirit and in practice, the apotheosis of the amateur ideal.
Though probably unintentionally, Dark's devotion to profit confirmed this élitist trend. By raising entrance fees, he made it
more difficult for ordinary people to watch the matches at
Lord's. Thirty years later, this 'accident' had been adopted as
club policy. A report of the annual general meeting of the MCC
held on 8 May 1875, clearly suggests that the raising of admission fees was seen as a way of producing a predominantly upper-

class audience – which, of course, would add to the dignity of the event:

> The increase in the price of admission at the Public Schools match tended to lessen the number of visitors, but the good order which to some extent is due to this measure, coupled to the fact that no objection was raised by the regular audience to Lord's Ground, encouraged the Committee to maintain the minimum price this season [2/6d per person].[15]

By the 1860s the popularity of the public schools and Varsity matches led to their being added to the annual calendar of events which made up the London 'season'. For the privileged few, the season involved a number of more-or-less obligatory appearances at events like Royal Ascot and Henley. For the social climbers, it represented the summit of their ambition. 'Many go to Lord's as they go to Ascot simply for the pleasure of enjoying a picnic, and as at Ascot those who are utterly ignorant of racing, and never even bet to the extent of a pair of gloves, are numerous, so at Lord's there are hundreds who come to see or be seen, without any ulterior object of watching the play.'[16]

In engaging its first professionals in 1825, 'four practice bowlers and two boys', the MCC established conditions of employment which were to be perpetuated in clubs, schools and universities throughout the first half of the nineteenth century. Earlier the development of an occupation had been restricted by the relative lack of opportunities open to cricketers. At any one time the number of players who could find employment in teams supported by members of the aristocracy and gentry was very small. The gradual decline of patronage in the nineteenth century, however, was more than offset by the creation of permanent coaching positions in clubs, schools and universities. By 1835 the MCC had increased its permanent complement of professionals to ten – five bowlers and five boys. Little is known of these earliest appointments other than the match fees that were paid. An extract from the committee minutes of 1827 records that 'Players at Lord's on the winning side [would receive] £6 per head; on the losing side, £4. It was settled that after this year, players on the winning side would receive £5 and on the losing side, £3 per head, except in the case of a match lasting over two days, when the old pay would be given.' These became the standard rates of pay for professionals in England, and remained substantially unaltered until the County Championship was founded in 1873, when match fees gave way to a weekly wage throughout the playing season. Piece-rates such as these were in one respect well suited to exigencies of Victorian capitalism. They allowed employers, in this case the MCC, to exercise a largely arbitrary control over players, while apparently giving them the opportunity to realize the full market value of their skills. In several cases incentive payments were added to the basic rates. For example, players representing Surrey received £1 talent money for scoring over fifty runs, and in 1846 the MCC decided that 'all players on the winning side [were to be] paid £1 in addition to the foregoing scale, except in a one-day match at Lord's in which the remuneration shall never exceed £1.' The principle on which the payment of professionals was based was self-dependence. High wages could be earned by the skilled player who was willing to go in search of work. All other considerations, notably his home and family, had to take second place. In this respect, his situation was identical to that of most skilled workers of the period.

Apart from playing in matches, a professional at Lord's was required to spend most of his time bowling to the members, while 'the boys' acted as fielders. By 1862, the MCC had 620 members, and Lord's was said to be 'devoted exclusively during the months of May and June to the matches and practices of the Club'.[17] This meant that the professional had few chances to improve as a batsman. Soon the roles of batsman and bowler came to reflect class divisions in society at large. By 1850 the pattern of amateur batsmen and professional bowlers was well established. Though great professional batsmen were not unknown, they were a comparative rarity. Thus William Denison concluded, 'The batting of professionals was not like to be strong because, as Corbett said to me, "We have no practice but in bowling; our batting must come of itself, except with Pilch and one or two of the others." '[18]

Faced with working conditions over which they had less and less control it is perhaps a little surprising that the professionals did not take collective action to improve their lot. But this was not the twentieth century, and in fact they did the reverse. Professionals looked upon cricket first and foremost as a source of income, and this inevitably led them to compete against each other for the privilege of being included in essentially amateur teams. Less easy to explain are the protracted, and often embittered, arguments which divided the amateur camp during the 1830s and 1840s.

Though the views of the MCC were not totally representative of the upper classes, they were becoming increasingly influential. The only serious opposition at this time came from a more progressive group, made up of county gentlemen and city businessmen. The way in which they neither abhorred the idea of cricket as a source of income nor merely suffered the presence of professionals stamped them as the earliest proponents of an ideal which was to be realized with the launching of the County Championship in 1873. It was not the MCC's power, but its opposition to the more popular types of match, which led this group to support leading professionals like William Lillywhite and James Broadridge. How much of the rivalry between the professionals and the MCC was a reflection of the worsening climate of industrial relations in society at large is difficult to say. No doubt it helped to fan the flames, but the main source of trouble was the MCC's determination not to give way in the face of the professionals' efforts to establish a new style of bowling. The longer the controversy raged, the more the MCC became cast in the role of defenders of an outdated technique, and the more intransigent became its opposition to the idea of change. Members of the club saw the issue as a trial of strength. Could they prevent a style of bowling, practised mainly by professionals, from becoming generally accepted? The origins of the dispute were outlined in a series of letters from Mr G. T. Knight of Godmersham Park in Kent which were published in *The Sporting Magazine* in 1827 and 1828. The gist of his arguments have been conveniently summarized by H. S. Altham.

(i) It is universally admitted that batting dominates bowling to an extent detrimental to the best interests of the game.

(ii) The new style is not really new at all: the Kent bowlers (i.e. John Willes and Ashby) practised it twenty years earlier, and it was only because they raised their arm too high that the MCC went too far in the opposite direction and condemned all scientific progress by demanding that the hand be kept below the elbow.

(iii) There has been no attempt to regulate the new style reasonably by law.

(iv) The proposal to redress the balance of the game by increasing the size of the wicket is retrograde: it would reduce not stimulate the science of the game.

(v) To describe the new style as 'throwing' is nonsense: the straight arm is the very antithesis of a throw: moreover, it makes it quite impossible to bowl fast and dangerously.

(vi) Let us keep a middle course, avoiding the tameness of the old chuck-halfpenny school and the extravagancies of the new alike.

The MCC's answer to these suggestions came from Mr W. Denison.

(i) The new style is fatal to all scientific play, putting a premium on chance hits, and placing a scientific defence at a discount.

(ii) It is throwing, pure and simple.

(iii) It must lead to a dangerous pace, such as cannot be faced on hard grounds, save at the most imminent peril. (p. 62)

In an attempt to resolve the problem once and for all, Knight organized three 'experimental' matches between teams representing England and Sussex. After the Sussex XI, which included Lillywhite and Broadridge, the foremost exponents of 'throwing', had won the first two matches, nine members of the England team, including all the professionals, signed a declaration of their intention to withdraw from the third match 'unless the Sussex bowlers bowl fair – that is, abstain from throwing'. Though this was little more than a gesture, it does show how much professionals resented the advantage that Lillywhite and Broadridge had gained through their mastery of the new style. It was not just that they were unplayable, but that, as a result, their services were constantly in demand.

On this occasion the MCC succeeded in maintaining the *status quo* by passing an amendment to Rule 10 which reaffirmed the illegality of any bowling action in which the arm was above the elbow at the point of delivery. But the reprieve was short lived. By continuing to bowl round-arm, Lillywhite and Broadridge spotlighted the MCC's basic weakness – an inability to impose its authority on the leading professionals of the day. In part, this weakness was a reflection of the impotence of the umpires. It was common knowledge that many were unfamiliar with the laws of the game, and partial in their implementation. Even at Lord's, umpires found it impossible to apply Rule 10 as a general principle, because of the difficulty of defining a round-arm action. In a match there in 1829, Lillywhite and Broadridge were no-balled during the first innings, but allowed to bowl uninterrupted in the second. This was to prove to be the thin edge of the wedge. Once admitted at Lord's, umpires found it impossible to prohibit the round-arm action elsewhere. In the *Bury and Norwich Post* of July 1831, it was noted that, 'as throwing was tolerated at Lord's, the umpires (Bentley and Matthews) did not dare call "no-ball" in the country'.

By 1835 the MCC were obliged to accept round-arm bowling and to alter Rule 10 accordingly. The action was deemed legitimate so long as the ball was not 'thrown or jerked' and the hand did not rise above shoulder level. To add to its difficulties, the club had to contend with the rapid spread of cricket's popularity. Matches in the provinces were, to all intents and purposes, beyond the jurisdiction of the MCC. So it is not surprising to find amongst the rules of the St Austell Club, the following concession: '[Games should] be played according to the rules of the Marylebone Club, but if the majority of the members wish to play the rough game, they may do so.'[19]

Furthermore, secure in the knowledge that he was 'a law unto himself', Lillywhite extended his repertoire to include over-arm bowling, which enabled him to bowl straighter without sacrificing any pace. So great was his reputation that few umpires were willing to question the legality of his action. As William Caldecourt, one of the foremost umpires of the day, pointed out, 'if Lillywhite was not watched as by country umpires who thought that what Lillywhite did must be right, he bowled one hundred times better than any man did bowl: it was cruel to see how he would rattle about either the knuckles or the stumps'.[20]

As before, the MCC tried to outlaw this advanced technique. In 1845 Rule 10 was reformulated and umpires were henceforth required to call 'no-ball whenever the bowler shall so closely infringe this rule as to make it difficult for the umpire at the bowler's wicket to judge whether the ball has been delivered within the true intent and meaning of the rule or not'.[21] A month later the MCC tried to isolate the main transgressors by prohibiting them from any match in which the 'Laws of Cricket' were in dispute. For the next eighteen years the issue was held in abeyance, waiting for the time when the Victorian establishment could overcome its differences and finally agree upon the role professionals were to play in the evolution of first-class cricket. That the eventual reconciliation was so long delayed is an indication of the gulf that divided the MCC, with its élitist preferences for amateur teams playing in private grounds, and the 'progressives', led by men like G. T. Knight, who favoured allowing professionals to play alongside amateurs in a regular series of 'county' matches. In the meantime, the professionals took the opportunity to go their own way and it was not long before the first of the great touring elevens appeared.

The strength of the opposition to the MCC, and its consequences, can best be illustrated by looking at the circumstances surround the formation of 'county cricket' in Kent. With Gloucestershire and Derbyshire, also established in 1870, Kent was the last of the nine original participants in the County Championship to be founded, the others being Sussex (1839), Surrey (1845), Nottinghamshire (1859), Yorkshire (1863), Lancashire (1864) and Middlesex (1864). From the start of the nineteenth century, matches and clubs in Kent combined elements of two traditions. Alongside the spontaneity and individuality of the eighteenth-century match, one can detect signs of formality and exclusiveness. In the West Kent Club, founded in 1812, with the exception of two professionals or 'scouts' all the members were or believed themselves to be gentlemen. Here, as at Lord's, members practised regularly and, if enough were present, a double-wicket match was played after which all adjourned to dinner. The organization of matches was left to individual members. As a result, the teams rarely reflected the strength of the club, and on many occasions they were made up largely of outsiders. Both this and the happy-go-lucky spirit in which most matches were played were recalled by Herbert Jenner-Fust, later President of the MCC:

I once arranged (in 1834) to take a team representing the West Kent Club to play Norfolk ... I got promises of a full team, but when the day came close those who had promised all cried off except for a man who was subject to fits and not good enough for a run ... I set off to play the county match determined to make a team on the way as best I could. At one place ... I came across three young men who seemed nice fellows, and as they said they could play cricket I pressed them into service for my match. Then we went on to Cambridge and I ransacked King's College and found four more men to join me. Two others were met on the ground in Norfolk, and with this strange combination, we won the match.[22]

Formed fifteen years later, the Town Malling Club was to become the focus of cricket in Kent for players and spectators alike between 1836 and 1845. It owed its existence to the efforts of Thomas Selby. Like William Ward, he was a successful businessman, and had subsequently purchased an estate outside Town Malling. Selby led sides as far afield as Hyde Park, Sheffield, where he played against a team captained by a Mr Barker. Through cricket, Selby met the second Lord Harris, a relationship which resulted in the foundation of a small syndicate who were responsible for inducing Fuller Pilch, one of the greatest players of his time, to move to Town Malling. The conditions of Pilch's employment were particularly interesting. Unlike the 'retained' players of the previous century, he was not supported by a wealthy patron. Instead, he received £100 a year as a ground attendant, which supplemented his earnings as landlord of a nearby pub. To assist him, Pilch 'brought in Martingell', a Surrey-born professional, for a salary of £60 a year. Though the pub gave Pilch a measure of independence from the Town Malling Club, he was still expected to treat members of the club with the deference that characterized the eighteenth-century master-servant relationship – a fact that Pilch himself recalled: 'Gentlemen were gentlemen, and players much in the same position as a nobleman and his headkeeper maybe.'

As early as 1835, the matches played at Town Malling were described as 'county' matches, though they bore little resemblance to the modern equivalent. Because travel was both difficult and costly, these early matches were arranged on a regional basis. Kent, Surrey and Sussex, and occasionally Middlesex and Hampshire, played each other, while other clusters included Norfolk, Suffolk and Cambridgeshire, and finally

Yorkshire, Nottinghamshire and Leicestershire. Between 1835 and 1842 Kent played eleven matches at Town Malling, three of which were against 'England' XIs selected by the MCC. The appearance of many of the most famous players of the day made these games immensely popular. To control the crowds, one Thomas Bennet – like Smith in James Love's description of the 1744 encounter – 'proudly acted as a ringkeeper using his long lash with energy and some noise'. Frederick Gale's account recaptures some of the excitement that surrounded these matches:

> It is five o'clock in the morning and after a restless night, from anxiety and excitement, we are off in a trap of some kind for a twenty mile drive to the match, and as we leave Rochester and get to the Malling Road, we find no dearth of company, and the road is much like Derby Day at an early hour as the old hands know very well that if they are to get any stabling they must be early. Nor are the pedestrians less numerous than the riders. We pass many a poor fellow on the tramp, who has started over night, perhaps, to be on the ground in time to see the first over, and witness with his own eyes the feats of the mighty men of whom he has heard so much.[23]

The rapid decline of the Town Malling Club after 1842 was almost entirely due to rising costs and the resulting loss of profitability. Between its demise and the formation of the County Club in 1858, the organization of matches depended on the efforts of a number of closely related, cricket-loving families – the Nortons, Normans, Jenners, Deedes, Knatchbulls and the Knights. Their enthusiasm led to the emergence of a number of local centres which were to be the venues for future 'county' matches. At Gravesend, Mr Harman Brenchley and his brother, Captain Henry Brenchley, promoted matches between 1849 and 1859, while the Beverley Club played on the estate of the Baker family at Canterbury. John Baker and his brother, William de Chair Baker, were the prime movers behind the annual Cricket Week held at Canterbury. The first Canterbury Week match, Kent versus England in 1842, was played on the Bakers' private ground, but from 1847 the venue moved to the Saint Laurence Ground – now the headquarters of the Kent County Cricket Club.

It was to the service of the Baker family that Fuller Pilch moved in 1842. The Beverley Club, which became his responsibility, remained separate from the Kent County Club until 1870. The latter was founded in 1859 at a meeting held in the Mitre Hotel, Maidstone, and presided over by the 6th Earl of Darnley. Two particular points of interest emerged from this meeting. The first was a resolution, accepted by a committee composed of members of the leading county families – Captain Brenchley, Edward Leigh-Pemberton, W. W. Knatchbull-Hugessen – which laid down that 'matches to be played shall not be confined to any particular locality, and they shall be matches in which Kent as a County, without the assistance of "given" men, shall always be concerned on one side'. The second was that the original committee of the Kent County Club include two of the county's greatest players, Alfred Mynn and Edward Wenman. The presence of Wenman, a professional, on this committee suggests that success in cricket could overcome the stigma of humble origins. But, after only eighteen days, Wenman decided that he 'preferred not to act' and was duly replaced by the Hon. G. W. Milles. This resignation can be interpreted in at least two ways: it may have been that Wenman soon realized that his inclusion was only a token gesture, and that his continued presence on the committee was pointless; or he may have been unable to cope with such a dramatic change in his personal status.

Though nominally a 'county' association, the club's activities were confined to east Kent. It lacked the finances to promote more than a few matches, and apparently no attempts were made to recruit any professionals. The responsibility for arranging the majority of matches still lay with the individual members. In 1863, for example, Mr J. Walker assembled a Middlesex XI at his own expense to play the Kent Club on his private ground at Southgate. When the Beverley Club amalgamated with the Kent Club in 1870 to form the Kent County Cricket Club, it was more in the hope of reviving the declining fortunes of Kent cricket than anything else; since the retirement of Mynn and Pilch, victories had been few and far between. The centre-piece of the Canterbury Week was a game between Kent and England, but between 1860 and 1864, Kent were so weak that they had to increase their numbers to sixteen to put up any sort of resistance. This lent an element of artificiality to the fixture, which was soon reflected in declining attendances and financial loss. On six occasions between 1864 and 1873 gate money failed to cover expenses.

The foundation of Kent's supremacy between 1830 and 1850 was the exceptional skills of players like Mynn, Pilch, Wenman, Willsher, and Hillyer. In those days, it was rare for the XI to include more than one amateur – Mynn. Only Pilch continued the practice of 'keeping a couple of places in the Kent Eleven for the young amateurs from the public schools and the universities'. Under normal circumstances, it would have been difficult to replace players like Mynn and Pilch, but in the face of a growing preference amongst amateurs for 'country-house' cricket and the wandering XIs, it was virtually impossible. As the name suggests, 'country-house' matches were played between teams of amateurs at the private residence of one of their number. The élitist image of the wandering XIs was maintained by a rigorous selection process, and then by the cost of taking part. I Zingari, founded in 1845, was the first and probably the most elaborate of all the wandering clubs, but there were many others including Quidnunc (1851) and Incogniti (1862). There can be little doubt that the popularity of these two new types of cricket was detrimental to the progress of 'county cricket'. Contact between amateurs and professionals was drastically reduced, and thus an important means of recruiting young professionals to the 'county' game was effectively blocked. This is precisely the point made by Lord Harris in an article that he wrote for the *National Review* (September 1883):

> In the coaching days, young Hopeful, the squire's son, was at home for most of the summers of his cricketing career after he had left college, and having seen good cricket there and at school and perhaps taken a glance at the headquarters on his way down for vacation, his style was probably one in which it did the villagers good to emulate. So would it be now, but the village cricketers ... never see the young master play, unless it be for three or four days after the London season is over, when the great house is filled with his friends ... He is always playing with one or the other of the dozen wandering clubs, whose gorgeous colours he has permission to wear. (p. 164)

8 William Clarke
and the Professional XIs
1846–70

> Good Match old Fellow?
> Oh yes! Awfully jolly.
> What did you do?
> I 'ad a hover of Jackson.
> The first ball 'it me on the hand:
> the second 'ad me on the knee:
> the third was in my eye:
> and the fourth bowled me out!
> (*Punch*, 29 August 1863)

When William Clarke selected the first All-England XI in August 1846, his idea was to make money. The XI was a revolutionary concept: it was the first example of a wandering team of professional sportsmen in England, and possibly anywhere, and it represented a totally new type of cricket. Previously the game had been dominated to a great extent by its aristocratic heritage. After 1846, it began to develop an entirely new image. Whilst retaining upper-class associations, it became a national sport as well as big business.

In assembling a side composed of the best players in England, Clarke's idea was to tour the country playing a series of matches against local teams. To offset the obvious difference in standards, the 'home' team was allowed to field as many as twenty-two players. Clarke did not believe that its awesome strength would deter clubs from wanting to play the All-England XI. On the contrary, such was the honour of being matched against the most famous players of the day that local elevens would forget that they had little or no chance of winning. Not only would cricket gain in popularity, but Clarke and his aides would show a handsome profit on a minimal outlay of capital. During a conversation with another great entrepreneur, James Dark, the manager of Lord's, Clarke was overheard to claim that, 'It is a-going to be, Sir, from one end of the land to the other, you may depend on that; and what is more, it will make good for cricket – it will make good for you as well as for me: mark my words, you'll sell cartloads of your balls where you used to sell dozens.'[1]

During its heyday, the All-England XI played matches as far afield as Truro, Oldham, St Helens, Hull, Leicester, Macclesfield, Bristol, Melton Mowbray, Canterbury, Dublin, Maidstone and Sheffield. The popularity of the XI confirmed Clarke's judgement. Far from being overawed by its reputation, clubs queued up for the honour of entertaining the XI – a factor which guaranteed its financial success. As the Revd Pycroft recalled, 'So proud [are] provincial clubs of this honour, that, besides a subscription of some £70 and money at the field gate, much hospitality is exercised wherever they go.'[2] One member of the XI, Richard Daft, provided a vivid description of the excitement caused by the arrival of Clarke's team: 'Certainly one never sees such holiday-making and high jinks as we used to see in the All-England days. The match was the topic of conversation months before the event took place. Special committees were formed to get up entertainments in the evenings, and when the day arrived the excitement was often intense.'[3]

In many of the more rural venues, the conditions under which matches were played were, to say the least, rudimentary. Pitches, as we know them today, did not exist. The game usually took place on what one could be forgiven for mistaking for a field. This meant that 'before we could begin, old Pilch had to borrow a scythe and mow the wicket ... Even then, once at Truro one of our men, in fielding the ball, ran into a covey of partridges.'[4]

Of the circumstances leading up to the formation of the All-England XI, mention has already been made of the MCC's growing preference for predominantly amateur forms of cricket, of its hostility towards attempts to change some of the techniques and rules of the game, and of the great advances in transport and communications which extended the distance teams could travel to matches – though some journeys, particularly in the more remote northern and western counties, still proved troublesome. George Anderson, one of the original members of the All-England XI, long remembered:

> One difficulty we got into, going from Wisbech to Sleaford. We had to do it in one night by coach. Our driver got lost and we all wandered about the Lincolnshire roads in the darkness until we struck a guide-post. Old Martingell clambered up this post, struck a light and found the way we had to go. We landed at our destination at 6 am, and play began at noon.[5]

To these factors must be added another, perhaps decisive, consideration – the lack of opportunities for cricketers to exploit their talents. Before 1846 professionals did not think in terms of regular, secure employment. The best they could hope for was to gain work either with one of the growing number of amateur clubs or by a patron, though the latter became increasingly rare as the century progressed. Otherwise the number of matches played in any one area did not warrant the employment of full-time professionals. In the face of this uncertainty, it is not surprising that most professionals did not start playing cricket until they had mastered another craft or trade. In his *Sketches of the Players*, William Denison provides potted biographies of cricketers active between 1820 and 1850. These show that few were completely unskilled. A regional breakdown of Denison's players reveals that eighteen were born and worked in south-east England, eight came from Nottinghamshire and Leicestershire and eight from Cambridge. Only in the case of the Midlanders, five of whom had previously worked in textile industry, did there appear to be a clear recruitment pattern. Otherwise, the professionals were drawn from a wide range of occupations. Of those born in Cambridge, two were college servants, two had no recorded occupations besides cricket, and the rest included a cook, tobacconist, licensed victualler and a brazier. Amongst the southern-based players there was a butcher, a breeches maker, a licensed victualler, a sawyer, a tailor, plumber, a painter, a bricklayer, a carpenter a confectioner and a calico printer.

For the unskilled worker, the attractions of a cricket career were obvious. After all, he had nothing to lose and everything to gain. The chance to play cricket for a living must have seemed a heaven-sent opportunity to escape for a few months at least the misery of the factory or the field. And there was always the added incentive that a grateful benefactor might subsidize a comfortable retirement. Because craftsmen were less vulnerable to the vicissitudes of fortune, it is more difficult to explain their willingness to exchange a secure, respectable life for the imponderability of cricket. But this perhaps overstates the problem. In the early nineteenth century, a professional's responsibilities were not as demanding as they have become since. During the winter, and even in the summer, he could probably have found time to ply his trade between matches. Even when cricket did entail some financial sacrifice, professionals found compensation in other aspects of the game. Nineteenth-century society did not encourage mingling between the 'have's' and the 'have not's'. It was rare for an artisan, let alone a common labourer, to rub shoulders with the wealthy, yet cricket provided just such an opportunity. A few professionals were lucky enough to make business contacts which stood them in good stead after their careers were ended. Others were happy simply to bask in the reflected glory of their superiors. And for everyone, there was the glamour and the excitement of the match. From contemporary reports, it is clear that spectators were willing to travel long distances to see the great players in action. To watch the match between the North and the South played at Leicester in 1836, 'hundreds of Nottingham enthusiasts, unable to procure conveyances (all of which had been bespoken a week ahead) walked the whole way to view the game, and finding all the inns full on arrival, tramped back to Loughborough at the end of each day for sleeping accomodation.'[6]

If the money, the glamour and the chance to make potentially useful business contacts were the major attractions of a cricket career at this time, only a few of the most celebrated professionals appear to have been able to translate them into solid, lasting prosperity. For the majority, a career in cricket lasted on average for twenty years, during which time it was usual to play about twenty matches a season. The dearth of opportunities meant that professionals, particularly those from the North and Midlands, were normally forced to migrate south in order to find work. Samuel Dakin, for example, was born at Sileby in Leicestershire in 1808 and made his debut for that county in 1829. He was subsequently employed by the South Derbyshire Club, the Kingscote Club in Gloucestershire and, from 1847 to 1855, the MCC. Then he became an 'extra bowler' at Lord's until being engaged as a coach at Charterhouse School. He died at Cambridge in 1876. Fuller Pilch's career follows a similar pattern. Born in Horningtoft in Norfolk in 1803, he 'migrated into the north for bread and water at an early age, and learnt how to handle bats and balls at Sheffield where he became distinguished, and where he was found by a Suffolk spirit'. Between 1825 and 1829 he played for the Bury St Edmunds Club, before moving to Norwich where he became the proprietor of a public house and lessee of the Norwich Cricket Ground. In 1835 he was persuaded to move to Town Malling, from where, in 1842, he went to the Beverley Club in Canterbury. Here, apart from a few months spent at Oxford, he remained until his death.

Pilch's career illustrates another of the perils of the professional cricketer's life. Even if a player was able to save some of his earnings, there was no guarantee that he would invest them profitably. Pilch set himself up as a tailor, but went bankrupt. Two of his colleagues in the great Kent team of the 1840s, Alfred Mynn and Edward Wenman, were also reported to have run into financial difficulties during their retirement. Many players chose to put their savings into a public house. But, as Samuel Dakin pointed out, even this was not without its dangers: '... not a few find that the usual recourse of keeping a "Bat and Ball" public house brings more temptations to drink the return for their little investment.'[7]

Another popular form of investment was to buy or lease a cricket ground. Thomas Box, born in Ardingley in 1809, took over the Royal Gardens and the Cricket Ground at Brighton during the 1850s. The most ambitious professionals tried to combine the two operations, William Lillywhite being a prime example. Born in 1792, a bricklayer by trade, he was thirty-five before his reputation spread beyond his native Sussex. At that point, as Denison records, things began to go wrong: '... after he had taken his position as the first bowler of the day, somewhat unwisely because he could not attend to it, he became the landlord of a public house in Brighton, in addition to his proprietorship of the cricket ground. Both were financial failures and Lillywhite became one of the ground at Lord's.'[8]

Lillywhite remained at Lord's until his death in 1854, though for a while he was also the first professional coach at Winchester College. There is a striking similarity between the careers of Lillywhite and his contemporary, William Clarke. Coming from a similar background, and originally following the same trade, Clarke was a bowler who, at different times, owned a public house and a cricket ground. But there is one respect in which the lives of the two men differed fundamentally. Though for much of his career Lillywhite was a thorn in the side of the MCC, he never attempted to replace the club as the central authority in the game. Clarke, on the other hand, sought to establish a type of cricket which was largely independent of the authorities at Lord's.

He was born in Nottingham in 1798, the son of a bricklayer, the trade which he himself followed for many years before becoming landlord of the Bell Inn – headquarters of the Nottingham cricketers. In 1838 he moved from the Bell to the Trent Bridge Inn where, on an adjacent site, he laid down and opened the Trent Bridge Ground. Initially this was not a success, largely because, unlike the Forest Ground which it replaced, an entrance fee had to be paid. Clarke stayed at Trent Bridge until 1847, after which he devoted his energies to organizing the All-England XI. Earlier he had laid down several other grounds, most notably at Bedale where he also coached. Though Clarke's playing career extended over forty years, it was not until he had represented Nottingham for twenty years that he made his debut at Lord's. He did not play for England until 1844, and for the Players until 1846. He lost the sight of one eye before he was thirty and broke an arm in 1852. Amazingly he recovered to play for another three years, only to die a year after finally retiring.

There is little doubt that in planning the All-England XI, Clarke had in mind the need to improve the opportunities open to northern professionals. In 1842, for example, the Nottinghamshire team played only one match, and in 1845 only five. Under these circumstances, 'It was, of course, impossible for a professional to make a livelihood out of county cricket in the sixties – at least not out of Nottinghamshire cricket – so few in number were the matches played.'[9] To add to his difficulties, the professional also had to contend with a regular complement of amateurs:

Several of the Nottingham Elevens were weakened by an infusion of gentlemen who, though they acquitted themselves well in some departments of the game, were inadequate in other respects to the task they undertook.[10]

The All-England XI played between twenty and twenty-five matches a season, and 'could have had three times as many if we could have found the dates'. The addition of these fixtures greatly improved the professional's earning capacity. Full-time employment during the playing season at last became a real possibility. Richard Daft estimated that when he 'began to play for All-England, we used to play six days a week for five months, and never had a days rest except on Sundays and when it was wet ... If we had not the All-England matches, there were matches at Lord's or elsewhere.'[11]

Throughout its existence, one of the major drawbacks of the All-England XI was the frequent, long and arduous journeys which its members were required to undertake. This was the reason why the life of an All-England professional appeared to be so much more demanding than that of later generations of professionals. 'Cricketers who now go about the country in saloons and express trains have a much easier life than we were accustomed to. Dublin to London, London to Glasgow and Edinburgh and so on – these were the journeys we often had to do, often in one night, to be ready for the next day's match.'[12]

As well as being permanently on the move, the members of the Eleven had to contend with various threats to their well-being. There were the rough, unprepared pitches, the crude techniques employed by many of their opponents, and, perhaps worst of all, the completely unpredictable hazard. One of the stars of the Eleven, Job Greenwood, recounted how once at Hull, he was lucky to escape with his life: 'They used to let the "lunies" from the local asylum roll the ground. On the occasion I speak of one of the imbeciles was seized with a sudden frenzy, and taking an iron cross-handle out of the roller, he hit me a terrific blow on the head with it. I believe that lunatics have not been allowed to roll wickets at Hull since.'[13]

Though the All-England XI's fixtures increased the number of matches in which a professional could play during a season, he was still paid on the same basis, and at the same rate – £5 per match – as earlier professionals. Moreover, he was responsible for all the expenses incurred in travelling. Occasionally on particularly long journeys, the match fee was increased to £6, but all-in-all George Anderson was probably not exaggerating when he concluded that 'after paying expenses there was not much left to get fat on'.

In fact, it was Clarke's miserliness which eventually led to the break-up of the original All-England XI. In 1852, angered by his habit of pocketing most of the match receipts, several members of the XI (including most of the southern players) resolved, 'not to play in any match, for or against, wherein William Clarke may have the management or control (county matches excepted) in consequence of the treatment they have received from Clarke at Newmarket and elsewhere'. Led by John Wisden and James Dean, they set up a rival team, the United XI of England, and for more than ten years these two sides dominated English cricket. To the casual observer it must have seemed as though the professionals were destined to reign supreme for a long time to come. Above all, they were united by a fierce determination not to succumb to the repeated efforts of the MCC to undermine their position. These attacks took two forms. First, the club introduced a series of measures designed to restrict the independence of individual players. In 1840 the committee adopted the following motion: 'That any paid player, umpire or scorer, failing to appear at his post one moment after play shall have been called, do forfeit two shillings and six pence for such an offence. The Committee are earnestly desired to enforce the payment of the penalty.' Eight years later, an even heavier penalty was imposed on latecomers. Not only did they lose their match fees, but thereafter they were also liable to pay the cost of a substitute. The clause in question stated.

> That in future, all matches shall commence punctually at 11 o'clock. That all players engaged in every match at Lord's ground shall be in readiness to take their place at that hour, or to be excluded from playing in that match: (or if belonging to the Lord's Ground, pay for a substitute, if a substitute be allowed by the manager of the side.)

Until 1848, in addition to receiving a basic match fee, professionals playing at Lord's could also qualify to be paid a bonus. This was provided for by a fund which had been set up specifically to reward outstanding performances. But in that year the MCC adopted a motion which significantly altered the conditions under which this bonus would be paid. It read,

> That in order to encourage good conduct on the part of professional players, both of the ground, and who have been engaged in matches by the MCC, a fund be raised, to be called 'The Cricketers Fund' (in lieu of the present reward fund, which shall be abolished) for the purpose of giving donations in cases of illness or accident: the fund was to be under the sole control of the Committee of the MCC, and that the sum of £10 be annually taken from the funds of the Club, in the hope that members might be induced to add their contributions.

The intention of this resolution was to replace the reward system by an arrangement which, in effect, made the professional's future conditional on his continued 'good conduct' – a term which the MCC reserved the right to define.

The second line of attack pursued by the MCC involved attempting to outlaw the technical advances made by professional bowlers. The sequence of events which had preceded the acceptance of round-arm bowling was repeated twenty years later when the over-arm style became popular. After the club had made several abortive attempts to prohibit the new style, matters came to a head in a famous match at the Oval in 1862. Late in the afternoon on the second day, Edgar Willsher was no-balled six times in succession by John Lillywhite, son of the great round-arm bowler. Willsher stalked off the field followed by the rest of his team – except, that is, for the two amateurs, V. E. Walker and C. G. Lyttleton. Play was not resumed until the following morning, by which time Lillywhite had been replaced. It was rumoured at the time that he had been prompted to no-ball Willsher by pressure from Lord's, but this was never substantiated. Others, including Altham, attributed to Lillywhite far more altruistic motives: '[He] conceived it to be his duty to force an issue on the question [of over-arm bowling], and saw no better means than to no-ball the first bowler in England in almost the greatest match of the year.'[14] Whatever his intentions, Lillywhite's action forced the MCC's hand and in 1864 Law 10 was eventually amended to permit over-arm bowling.

This concession probably represented a high-water mark in the professionals' attempts to establish their own brand of cricket. It was not long before internal dissension, which in fact had never been far below the surface, broke through the brittle facade of unity. Torn between an obligation to close ranks in the face of opposition from supporters of amateurism and an equally pressing desire to cash in on their talents while the opportunities still existed, the professionals succeeded only in cutting their own throats. As early as 1860 there were indications that the northern and southern players were beginning to split once again into rival factions, each united by a profound distrust of the other. As before, the basic cause of the trouble lay in the difficulties professionals experienced in getting enough work to sustain a reasonable standard of living. In 1852 it was the southern professionals who felt that they were not receiving their just dues from William Clarke – a northerner. On that occasion, however, the promise of riches to come persuaded the players to bury their differences for the time being. It was a shrewd decision, for after Clarke's death the two XIs they had created – the All-England and the United England – met at Lord's over Whitsun in what was the most popular match of the year, and a great money spinner! But in the early 1860s a new crisis arose and the old divisions were once again laid bare, only this time it was the turn of the northern professionals to feel aggrieved. The origins of this crisis lay in what the northerners believed to be a pro-southern bias in the selection of teams for the great matches. Their protest was more than a display of idle peevishness. At a time when cricket's popularity was increasing almost daily, the players in question were genuinely concerned that they might be prevented from earning a fair share of the bigger cake.

One factor which probably encouraged professionals to take an optimistic view of their future was the appearance of the County Cricket Clubs. The point has already been made that the MCC did not represent all shades of upper class opinion. Many openly expressed their disapproval of the way the club had handled the over-arm bowling issue. In the middle of the final confrontation in 1864, there was an attempt to replace the MCC as the sovereign authority in the game. W. G. Grace described its failure with scarce-concealed pleasure:

An agitation was set going in one of the leading sporting newspapers which had for its aim, the formation of a 'cricket Parliament' to depose the Marylebone Club from its position as authority on the game: but it met with little countenance, and the old club, which had now played on its present ground for fifty years, was allowed to carry on the work which it and it alone seemed to be able to do with firmness and impartiality.[15]

That Grace, a legend in his lifetime and since, should not have approved of the ill-fated 'Parliament' is perhaps not surprising. The significance of the affair rests in the fact that it showed that opposition to the MCC's handling of cricket was not confined to a group of discontented professionals. Though Grace does not mention any names, it is likely that much of the support for the idea of a 'Parliament' came from persons connected with the new county clubs. For instance, in 1863 W. South Norton, the first secretary of the Kent Cricket Club, wrote in a letter, 'I understand the MCC have left Law 10 exactly as it was, which means, I am afraid, 'vengeance on Willsher' – I begin to be jealous of the MCC as lawgivers and am inclined to favour the suggestion of a congress of representatives for the cricketing counties with a view to superceding its authority.'[16]

But it was not Kent but Surrey that presented the greatest challenge to the traditional supremacy of the MCC. Profiting from the latter's inactivity, by 1860 the Surrey County Cricket Club had become a serious rival to the supremacy of Lord's. Between 1851 and 1861 its membership rose from about 230 to nearly 1,000, at which point it became larger than the MCC. The facilities offered at Surrey's headquarters, the Kennington Oval, and the quality of its teams were superior to anything that could be found at Lord's – with the possible exception of the professional XIs. In 1858 the Surrey Eleven was unbeaten, a record which even included an innings defeat of an All-England team led by George Parr.

Victories apart, the other important feature of the Surrey team was the number of professionals it contained. Seldom fewer than eight, the total often rose to eleven – the whole side! Being in the majority placed the professionals in a strong bargaining position in negotiations over wages and conditions of work. On one celebrated occasion before a match against

Sussex in 1859, two leading players, Julius Caesar and H. H. Stephenson, went so far as to refuse to play 'without a further increase in pay'. But numerical supremacy and bargaining power were not the only reasons for the prosperity enjoyed by the Surrey professionals. The most spectacular advances came about as a result of the organization of overseas tours. The first such tour, to Canada and the USA, took place in 1859. The party was made up of six members from the All-England XI and six from the United XI of England. As Altham has pointed out,

> ... its territorial composition is not a bad index of the relative strengths of that period. From Notts came Parr, Grundy and Jackson; from Sussex, Wisden and John Lillywhite; from Cambridge, their two famous 'cracks', Hayward and Carpenter, with Ducky Diver, while Surrey contributed no less than four – Stephenson, Julius Caesar, Lockyer, and Caffyn.[17]

If the composition of this party was acceptable to all the professionals, that of its successor, the first to visit Australia, most certainly was not. Like the North American expedition, the 1861 tour was planned with professionals in mind. It was underwritten and managed by a firm of tea importers, Messrs Spiers and Pond, who were said to have made a profit of £11,000. Each of the tourists was guaranteed £150 and expenses, a considerable sum in those days. In selecting the party, the promoters were persuaded by the secretary of the Surrey CCC, W. Birrup, to include seven members of the Surrey team, and to place the whole party under the captaincy of H. H. Stephenson. The choice of Stephenson in preference to George Parr was the last straw as far as many of the northern professionals were concerned. From that moment, relationships between the two groups grew steadily worse until, in 1865, open conflict broke out. The Surrey CCC was singled out as the target for major recriminations. Nottinghamshire players refused to play at the Oval with the result that there were no matches between the two counties until 1868. Five Yorkshire professionals, Anderson, Atkinson, Iddison, Rowbotham and Stephenson, similarly refused to play in a number of matches. The next act in the drama took place at the end of the 1865 season when the southern professionals withdrew from both the All-England XI and the United XI of England and formed the United South of England XI.

The consequences of this rupture were far-reaching. What began as a minor dispute between a number of professionals rapidly assumed the proportions of a major confrontation involving all sections of cricket's 'establishment'. Some saw the northern professionals' stand as a deliberate challenge to the *status quo*; the MCC certainly believed this to be true. When in 1866 the northerners dissociated themselves from all cricket played in the south, the worst suspicions were confirmed. From an entry in the club's minutes of 21 May 1866, it is clear that many members saw this withdrawal as an event comparable in its implications to the secession of the Confederate States of the USA in 1862 : 'Northern players secede from Lord's on the day of the Two Elevens match, played for the benefit of professionals, the ground being given to them for that purpose – Gratitude!'

By spurning the beneficence of the MCC, the northern rebels jeopardized all the improvements in pay and conditions of employment that professionals had won during the previous fifty years. The following article, published in *The Times* in August 1866, shows how quickly many sections of public opinion were antagonized:

The evidences are many that cricket is making rapid progress both in London and in the country. Matches, players, and spectators, grow more numerous every year: prince and pauper alike are proud of being one in an eleven; and the good cricketer is almost as famous as an eminent politician. But with this prosperity, a power has sprung up to which we wish to call attention. Two years ago, it was written that Lord's had plenty of players, but no ground to play on whilst the Oval had a good ground, but no players to play on it. Now, however, Lord's has its ground, but the players have left. The evil has arisen in this wise. Some years ago, a quarrel sprung up between the representatives of Surrey and Nottingham: it arose, we believe, in relation to the visit of Stephenson's Eleven to Australia, George Parr feeling himself aggrieved at the selection that was made of captain. The merits of this original dispute have become immaterial ... the northern men were irritated: they refused to play at the Oval. The southern men separated from the All-England and United Elevens, and so open war was proclaimed. Thus matters stood at the commencement of the season. The usual matches between the two Elevens were played at Lord's on Whit-Monday, for the benefit of the Cricketers' Fund. The Marylebone Club gave the ground gratuitously, the Players Association received the whole of the gate money. During the course of that match, Mr Fitzgerald applied to Carpenter to play in the coming match of North against South ... the request was refused and all the Northern players, except the ground men, supported him in his refusal ... The men were on strike, and the Committee had to decide what should be done. Wisely they determined not to be beaten, and with the aid of Grundy and Wootton, they chose the best northern Eleven they could ... it was determined that the players who refused to play should not appear at Lord's only when they chose, and that for the future they should play in the old-established matches or none ... the northern players refused to let a southern player bowl for a Twenty-Two against them, banished Wootton and Grundy from the ranks of the All-England Eleven, and although invited, absented themselves from Canterbury ... The cause of this unfortunate position of things is to be found in the too prosperous conditions of the players. So long as they can earn more money by playing matches against Twenty-Two's than by appearing at Lord's – so long as they can be 'mistered' in public houses, and stared at at railway stations, they will care very little for being absent from the Metropolitan Ground. But they are wrong. They may be certain that the 'Gentlemen' will not give way in this struggle.

And so the lines of battle were drawn. As the tone of the article suggests, the MCC and many members of the general public interpreted the secession as nothing less than a strike. In the mid-nineteenth century, the merest mention of this word was sufficient to invoke the spectre of massive working-class insurrection and, worse still, revolution. Immediately the professional cricketer was thrown into an ever-hardening stereotype of the 'working-classes', and as a result his relationship with the gentleman amateur was redefined in terms of class difference rather than a genuine, if sometimes grudging, respect for outstanding sporting ability. Henceforth, disagreement between amateurs and professionals could only be understood as examples of class conflict.

John Frederick Sackville, 3rd Duke and 10th Earl of Dorset (1745–99). One of the great eighteenth-century patrons of the game, he owned the famous Vine Ground at Sevenoaks and employed several of the leading players of the day. Once described as one of 'the two idlest lords in His Majesty's three kingdoms', a hotly contested title then and now.

Sir Horatio Mann, Bart. (died 1814). A contemporary of the Duke, Sir Horatio was responsible for organising many 'great' matches on his estates at Bishopsbourne, Linton and Sissinghurst. 'Agreeable, gay and affable', he once staged a match in which both teams played on horseback.

A scene during an early match (circa 1743) at the Artillery Ground. Either the batsman was a tail-ender or the scorer was extraordinarily courageous.

A typical late-eighteenth-century cricketing scene.

The LAWS of the NOBLE GAME of CRICKET,

as Established at the Star and Garter Pall-Mall by a Committee of Noblemen & Gentlemen.

THE BALL.

THE BAT.

THE STUMPS.

THE BOWLING CREASE.

THE POPPING CREASE.

THE PARTY.
which goes from home.

THE BOWLER.

THE STRIKER.
is out.

THE WICKET KEEPER.

THE UMPIRES.

BETS.

THE END

lence of the aristocracy's influence
he evolution of eighteenth-century
ket. The Star and Garter tavern in
Mall was a haunt of many
usive coteries from 1750 onwards.

THE BATSMAN.

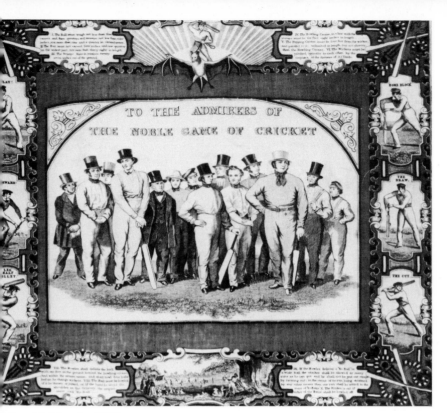

ndkerchief showing William
ke's All-England XI (1847), the
eam of touring professional
smen, and the forerunner of
y Packer's circus. Clarke himself
he sight of his right eye before he
hirty, but continued to play for
er twenty-five years. The first
er to dispense with a long-stop,
ok a wicket with the last ball he
bowled.

er Pilch (1803–70), beyond all
t the finest batsman in England
ng the 1830s. 'He seemed to crush
est bowling by his long forward
ge before it had time to shoot, or
or do mischief by catches.'

County Cricket 1873-1973

3ᴾ

The massive presence of W. G. Grace about to launch into a square-cut.

A century later, he remains an instantly recognizable figure.

The 'demon bowler', F.
R. Spofforth, in action
for the Australians
against C. I. Thornton's
XI in 1878. The
proximity of the wicket-
keeper, and the disdain
on the face of the non-
striking batsman make
one wonder if this is an
accurate representation.

C. B. Fry batting for
Sussex.

Australian TV tycoon, Kerry Packer, jokes with former England captain, Tony Greig, after announcing his intention of commencing court proceedings against the International Cricket Conference and the Test and County Cricket Board (3 August 1977).

The MCC's reaction to the northern professionals' secession was predictable. At a special general meeting, reported in *The Times* on 2 May 1867,

> The Earl of Sandwich, in an eloquent speech, brought forward the motion relating to the establishment of a Marylebone Club Cricketers' Fund ... It was finally proposed and carried 'That a fund be established called the Marylebone Cricket Club Fund; that the fund be in the first instance available for professionals on the Lord's Ground: secondly for the relief of all cricketers who, during their career shall have conducted themselves to the entire satisfaction of the Committee of the MCC.
>
> The Secretary then read: 'The Committee whilst deploring the existence of any misunderstanding among players, have adhered to the course adopted by them last season on the secession of certain of the northern players:– i.e. that of asking only those players who are willing to play together in a friendly manner. In reference to the match (England versus Middlesex) to be played on Whit-Monday, the proceeds of which will be devoted to the MCC Cricketers Fund, the Committee remember with great regret that a secession of the northern players last season occurred on the day which, for several years, has been given by the MCC for the benefit of the Cricketers' Fund.

Banished from Lord's, excommunicated by the MCC and strongly attacked by their own county clubs, the northern rebels became pariahs. Contact with the rest of the cricketing world was reduced to a minimum. After 1865, since both the All-England and United XIs were made up entirely of northern professionals, their annual match, the receipts from which went into the Cricketers' Fund, was played at Manchester.

Fortunately, the schism did not last for long. When matches between Surrey and Nottinghamshire were resumed in 1868, the implications were unmistakable. The professional XIs were rapidly losing ground in the face of growing public support for county cricket, and without a widespread popular following the XIs could not survive for long. Realizing the weakness of their position, professionals soon came to terms with the fact that in future the biggest employers of cricketers would be the county clubs.

With the benefit of hindsight, it is not difficult to spot the fatal flaws in Clarke's original conception of a team of touring professionals. In the first place, the XIs lacked all but the vaguest geographical identity about which supporters could rally. Secondly, the overpowering strength of such a team meant that the result of its matches was rarely in doubt. Thus, these occasions were drained of much of their intrinsic excitement. No amount of artificial manipulation of the conditions of the contest could totally overcome this problem. County clubs, however, did not have to face these difficulties. Their geographical links were obvious, and once the County Championship had overcome its teething troubles, there was no shortage of real competition.

The great rise in popularity of county cricket during the 1860s and 1870s was in part a reaction to the limitations of the professional XIs. It also owed much to the ingenuity of the administrators of the county clubs. For the framework of inter-county matches which they built up was essentially a compromise between the populism of professional cricket and the élitism of country-house contests. The success of this formula was reflected in the enduring popularity of the County Championship. Another important factor was the secession of the northerners in 1865 which probably poisoned many people's attitudes to the idea of professional cricket, but it is more likely that this event only confirmed what the majority had already begun to suspect. The great objection to professionals was that they were believed to be a threat to the sanctity of sport. For the Victorian gentleman, the most important attribute of sport lay in the mental and physical relaxation it provided from the pressures of work. The fear was that, if professionals were allowed to dominate games like cricket, they would soon lose their stimulating and restorative properties. Some believed that this was already happening:

Play is now-a-days becoming a mere matter of hard work, and what should be an amusement is very often the reverse of it. A match is really quite a serious and solemn piece of business, and grave faces are seen in it more frequently than grinning ones ... Play is too cut-and-dried a piece of work to please. A ball is bowled and hit and fielded as if by steam; and if the players fail to do precisely that they do not get jeered as much as sneered at. To my mind, this is not a whole-some alteration. When I am at play, I like to laugh and enjoy myself and half the pleasure of sport is gone if you abstract the fun from it.[18]

To make matters worse, the professional was also associated with a win-at-all costs approach to cricket. For him, the 'self' was more important than the team. 'Average hunting' and 'record breaking', examples *par excellence* of unbridled profes-sionalism, were anathema to the amateur. He saw the pro-fessional's pre-occupation with success as a serious threat to the *esprit de corps* and discipline which were integral features of the English public-school tradition, and which were believed to have played such an important role in the foundation of the Empire. In short, an extension of professionalism was a recipe for disaster.

They [the professionals] do not look upon themselves as part of a little army, who are fighting on equal terms against another army, and they are apt to go away before the match is over, and get a man to field for them if they have had the great *desideratum* – their innings. 'Self' has taken a great hold on cricket, and public cricket too often looks as if it was con-tracted for at so much per day ... The average mania is as fatal to cricket as trade unions are to commerce, and Jones, Robinson and Brown go about playing in scratch teams, in matches in which they have little interest beyond their innings.[19]

The analogy between professionals in cricket and trade unions in commerce is revealing. Both sport and commerce were symbols of Victorian excellence; both were activities which the Victorian gentleman was supposed to dominate – an assumption which professionalism and the growth of trade unionism now questioned. As far as cricket was con-cerned, the impact of the professional's challenge was intensi-fied by coinciding with the game's rise to the status of a 'national' sport; if there was to be something peculiarly English about cricket, it could hardly be the product of a largely work-ing-class body. The symbolic importance of the game was too great to allow that.

Cricket! There is a wholesome English smack about the word

which no-one but an Englishman can relish. To my notion, a cricketer *nascitur, non fit*. Men must be British to play it and like it. Your Frenchman is too volatile, your German too phlegmatic for it, and as for the other nations, they are mostly too lazy, or else too luxurious. Cricket requires steadiness as well as strength and quickness, and the union of these qualities distinguishes the English. I repeat then, none but the English know how to play cricket and only in their ears will the reaction to it waken any pleasurable response.[20]

These then were some of the reasons why the great era of professional cricket came to an end in the early 1870s. County cricket may not have been the ideal replacement, but it did allow the amateur to re-establish his traditional authority over the professional. Thus the 'natural order' of society, valued so highly by many Victorians, was restored. For the professional though, there were some compensations. His role in the game was now accepted, if not exactly welcomed, by most cricket lovers. This meant that the viability of a cricket career was finally established, and by this time jobs were more numerous and easier to discover. Previously players had started their careers as a result of being 'spotted', or personally recommended, but gradually advertisements for professionals began to appear in the sporting press. Luke Greenwood, brother of Job, described how, at the start of his career, he 'saw an advertisement in the papers that a young man was wanted as a bowler by the Duke of Sutherland in Staffordshire ... and stayed there for four years'.[21]

Unlike their predecessors, however, few mid-Victorian professionals had any other skills to offer a prospective employer. Retirement, either through old age or injury, thus presented an even greater threat than before. If a professional had neither savings nor the chance to stay in the game as an umpire or coach, he would be lucky to avoid succumbing to the miseries normally reserved for the labourer. The case of John Jackson, in his prime one of the most feared bowlers in England, illustrates how easily this fate could befall even the greatest players. Jackson was born in Suffolk in 1833, but moved to Nottingham before he was fifteen. He held five professional engagements, two at Southwell and one each at Ipswich, Newark and Edinburgh, as well as playing for Nottinghamshire and the All-England XI between 1855 and 1870. Then a ruptured blood vessel prematurely terminated his career. Though he subsequently managed to find several coaching jobs, none lasted for long, and by 1900, he had become 'a bent and grisly man of 67, with the remnants of a fine presence, subsisting for a pittance on five shillings and six pence a week, willing to work, but elbowed out by younger and more vigorous competitors in the battle of life, having no permanent address and always hovering on the thresh-hold of the work-house.'[22]

9 The County Championship 1873–94

Writing in 1902, Viscount Alverstone and Mr C. W. Alcock came somewhat begrudgingly to the conclusion that: 'Modern first-class cricket has become for good or evil almost exclusively county cricket: what the novel is now to literature, county cricket is to the game.'[1]

But thirty years earlier only the eternal optimist could have predicted that the County Championship was to become the centre-piece of first-class cricket. Though ideas for an inter-county tournament had appeared in the sporting press from time to time during the previous decade, it was not until 1873 that the nine county clubs then in existence – Derbyshire, Gloucestershire, Kent, Lancashire, Middlesex, Nottinghamshire, Surrey, Sussex and Yorkshire – first competed for the title of 'champion county'. Even then, the tournament was not an overnight success. The basic design left a lot to be desired, and day-to-day administration was almost non-existent. Not even when the last match of the season had been played were the difficulties over, for the early systems of awarding points for victories gave rise to interminable bickering. In the end it was usually left to the sporting press to decide who had won the competition.

What the Championship lacked above all during these early years was a strong central authority. The MCC was the obvious choice, but for twenty years the club eschewed this responsibility. Upset by the ignominious failure of their own knock-out competition, the Silver Cup, in 1873, the authorities at Lord's preferred to sit back and let the counties try to resolve the problem of the Championship. If they could come up with a viable blue-print, then, and only then, would the club agree to reconsider its position. So, from 1873 until 1894 crisis followed crisis as the county clubs tried to agree upon the best way to run the Championship. Yet the lessons of these early traumas were evidently well learned. After agreement had finally been reached in 1894, the Championship went from strength to strength until by 1902 one could say without fear of contradiction that it was the foundation of first-class cricket in England.

The story begins early in 1873 when, against a background of growing public interest in county matches and a corresponding decline in the popularity of the professional XIs, the Surrey County Cricket Club arranged a series of meetings to which were invited representatives of Middlesex, Kent, Sussex, Derbyshire, Gloucestershire, Lancashire and Yorkshire – Nottinghamshire was not represented, though they did take part in the inaugural Championship season. The purpose of these meetings was to establish the conditions under which the competition was to take place. Immediately, it became clear that this was not going to prove as easy as it sounded. The most intractable problem was to frame the residential qualifications each player, amateur and professional, would be required to satisfy. Failure to enforce these conditions in the past had created a situation in which certain players represented more than one county in a season.

The secretary of the Surrey club, Frederick Burbage, first consulted the MCC who, in turn, indicated that it would consider any proposals providing that they had the support of all the counties. Between February and June of 1873, meetings were held at the Hanover Square residence of Dr Evan B. Jones, a member of the Surrey committee. Agreement proved very elusive and finally it was only on the casting vote of the chairman, Frederick Burbage, that a set of proposals were adopted. The final recommendations, ratified at the Oval on 9 June 1873, were,

(a) That no cricketer, whether amateur or professional, shall play for more than one county during the same season:
(b) That every cricketer born in one county and residing in another shall be free to choose at the commencement of each season for which of these counties he will play, and shall during the season play for that county only:

(c) That a cricketer shall be qualified to play for any county in which he is residing and has resided for the previous years; or that a cricketer may elect to play for the county in which his family home is, so long as it remains open to him as an occupational residence:

(d) That should any question arise as to the residential qualification, that should be left to the decision of the Marylebone Club:

(e) That a copy of these rules be sent to the Marylebone Club, with the request that they be adopted by the Club.[2]

When the 'Qualifications for the County Cricketer' were submitted to the MCC later that year, the club proposed a modification: 'An amateur could play for any county in which he or his parents had property, or in which his parents, if dead, had property at the time of their decease.'[3] If this clause had been accepted, it would have allowed the amateur an additional method of qualifying. But in the event, the counties rejected it, and with it the prospect of an early *rapprochement* with the MCC. While negotiations proceeded, the club had attempted to steal a march on the counties by organizing its own form of county competition. The following statement was issued in January 1873:

With a view to promoting county cricket, and to bringing counties into contact which otherwise might not have had the opportunity of competing with each other, and to establish an interesting series of county matches on a neutral ground, the Committee of the MCC propose to offer a silver cup for competition. The matches will be arranged by lot, and the ties drawn by the Committee as soon as possible after acceptances are received ... The winner of the final tie will hold the cup for one year. The winner of the cup three times successively shall hold the cup in perpetuity. The name of the winning county, with the date, shall be engraved on the cup at the cost to the MCC.[4]

Six counties were invited to take part, but only Kent and Sussex accepted. Only one match was played, on what was described as a 'very dangerous pitch' at Lord's, after which the competition was abandoned.

The comings and goings that preceded that first Championship match have led many to believe that 1873 was a major watershed in cricket's history – the year that saw the birth of modern first-class cricket. In fact, this is far from the truth, as Major Rowland Bowen has made clear.

> There has been an uncritical acceptance and repetition of statements concerning earlier periods, or statements about earlier cricket, which would horrify the professional historian ... The only significant thing about 1873 was that for that season, rules governing qualifications for counties were agreed – nothing else was decided – certainly not how the championship should be run.[5]

The first important step towards setting up a central authority with responsibility for the overall organization of the championship was taken in 1882 when the county secretaries began to meet annually. This was followed in 1887 by the formation of the County Cricket Council. In the interim, it was left to individual counties to organize their own matches. The only difficulty was that no-one seemed to know which were first-class counties and which were not.

> There was no general agreement whether Hampshire and Somerset were to be considered amongst the 'celebrated' counties; averages often included all county matches even against such teams as Buckinghamshire. For example, W. G. Grace's published records for the first-class matches includes such matches as the MCC *v.* Hertfordshire. Moreover, there seems to be a distinction between county champions and the county championship. In other words, the county champions were the best county against all-comers; the idea of restricting the choice of champions by reference only to games against the other counties did not appear to exist, certainly in the minds of the editors of the *Companion* or *Annual* until some time in the late 70's or early 80's.[6]

One of the foremost problems facing members of the County Cricket Council when they started work in 1887 was thus to decide who should be eligible to compete in the Championship. A formula was soon drawn up which classified all counties into one of three divisions, with provision for automatic promotion and regulation. But it was to prove a wasted effort. Shortly after a final draft had been prepared, the bitter rivalries between the counties which had always threatened to undermine any attempt at collaboration brought about the collapse of the council. In 1890, with all prospects of reconciliation exhausted, it suffered the improbable fate of being dissolved *sine die* by the casting vote of its own chairman. When, in 1894, the MCC were invited to draw up principles for classifying counties, it was a final recognition by the counties of their inability to reach any form of lasting agreement.

In that year, a committee of the club produced a 'Classification of Counties' which laid down that,

> Cricketing counties shall be considered as belonging to the first-class or not. There is no need for a further sub-division. First-class Counties are those whose matches with one another, with the MCC and Ground, with the Universities, with the Australians, and other such elevens as shall be adjudged first-class by the MCC Committee, are used in the compilation of first-class batting and bowling averages.
>
> There shall be no limit to the number of first-class Counties. The MCC Committee may bring new Counties into the list, may remove existing ones from it, or may do both.[7]

The outcome of the Championship was henceforth to be determined upon the principles of 'one point ... for each game won, one point deducted for each loss, and the county which should have obtained the greatest proportion of points to the total of finished matches shall be reckoned the champion county'.[8]

Though other counties were admitted later – Worcestershire in 1899, Northamptonshire in 1905 and finally Glamorgan in 1921 – and many changes made to the original framework of the competition, there can be little doubt that the County Championship, as we knew it until very recently, dates from 1894. But if 1873 was not the year in which county cricket really came of age, did it mark the beginning of what might be called the modern era of cricket? Here again, the answer must be 'no'. The final stage in cricket's transformation from a crude, spontaneous, folk-game to a sophisticated, highly-organized sport occurred over a period of some fifty years between 1860 and 1910. Besides the rise of county cricket, these years saw the first international 'tests', notably those between England and Australia; after much protracted debate, the formation in 1909 of the Imperial Cricket Conference; the establishment in 1898 of a Board of Control to administer test matches played in England; in 1895 the formation of the Minor Counties Cricket Association and the Minor Counties Championship and in 1904 the setting up of the Advisory County Cricket Committee. In 1884 the MCC adopted a completely revised code of laws which brought many outdated rules into line with modern standards of performance. Boundaries were introduced and six-ball overs legalized. The 'follow-on' was made optional after 150 runs in a three-day match, 100 in a two-day and 75 runs in a one-day match. The old custom of allowing the same player to bowl two overs in succession was abolished and the conditions under which a new ball could be requested were clarified. In 1892 the MCC issued its first instructions to umpires. The purchase of a heavy roller at Lord's signalled a general improvement in the standard of pitches. From about 1880 coloured shirts were replaced by the standard white apparel. White buckskin shoes were worn for the first time in 1882.

1864 was notable for the debut of a player whose achievements and personality made him a legend in his own lifetime, and an immeasurable influence on the subsequent development of the game. W. G. Grace's record speaks for itself: he scored 54,896 runs and took 2,876 wickets. In 1895, at the age of forty-seven, he amassed 1,000 runs in twenty-two days in May. It is true that these figures have since been surpassed on several occasions but, by the standards of the time and under the prevailing conditions, they were little short of miraculous. Grace perfected techniques, particularly in batting, which changed the entire conception of the game. As the *Jubilee Book of Cricket* proclaimed, 'He revolutionised cricket. He turned it from an accomplishment into a science; he united in his mighty self all the good points of all the good players and made utility the criterion of style ... he turned the old one-stringed instrument into a many chorded lyre. But in addition, his execution equalled his invention.'[9]

But there was more to Grace than technical brilliance. An exceptional athletic talent joined with an unmistakable presence to make him the first great sporting hero. He did more than any other single figure to make cricket a national game. For H. S. Altham,

He was incomparably the greatest 'draw' of all sportsmen in history; he was the nearest approach to a living embodiment of John Bull that England has seen, and however much H. G. Wells might sneer at the 'tribal gods for whom people would die', I can believe the Bishop of Hertford read deeper into the heart of the man when he spoke of W. G. the words with which his memorial biography so fitly closes: Had Grace been born in ancient Greece, the Iliad would have been a different book. Had he lived in the Middle Ages he would have been a crusader and would now have been lying with his legs crossed in some ancient abbey, having founded a family. As he was born when the world was older, he was the best known of all Englishmen and the king of that English game least spoilt by any form of vice![10]

When Monsignor Ronald Knox suggested in jest that W. G. Grace and W. Gladstone might be the same person, he expressed a view with which very few contemporaries would have argued. Part of Grace's charisma sprang from the fact that he was worshipped by all sections of society. For those who revelled in the glories of imperial aggrandizement, he epitomized Britain's global supremacy. For the industrial worker, he presented an identity – an *alter ego* – which, by the very span of its achievements, had overcome the rigidities of a class-bound society. And in his freedom lay the hope of things to come.

While all these changes were taking place, cricket managed to maintain a coherent, upper-class image to a degree that was quite unique in the English sporting world. Though by the end of the nineteenth century professionals outnumbered amateurs in first-class cricket, it still remained a patrician pastime at heart. Other games, like football and rugby, which shared some of cricket's aristocratic heritage, did not adapt so readily to their new-found popularity. Neither could withstand the social strains created by a sudden influx of people from all walks of life, and eventually both suffered irrevocable, internal ruptures which gave rise to amateur football and rugby union on the one hand, and football league and rugby league on the other. While the former were genteel and discreet, the latter were professional and popular. Cricket's success in avoiding a similar break-up appears even more remarkable when one remembers that only a few years earlier the MCC and the great professional

XIs seemed to be heading for a violent confrontation. Of course, there were the northern leagues, but these never became as ostracized as did rugby league, and their players were never formally barred from first-class cricket.

The secret of success, however, was not to be found in the resilience of the game, nor in the diplomatic skills of its administrators. Benjamin Disraeli provided a clue when he observed that 'the aristocracy of England absorbs all other aristocracies'. This flexibility allowed the aristocracy to tap a rich vein of middle-class energy and talent, and to forestall much of the envy and hostility that otherwise might have brought about its downfall. Cricket is an excellent example of how this subtle 'divide and rule' strategy enabled a deeply conservative institution to withstand the challenge of new people and new ideas. Faced with the choice of removing the MCC or of becoming a member of it, the majority of self-proclaimed reformers were so hopelessly confused that they did nothing, while the astute few were content to hedge their bets. Either way, the impact of progressive opinion was decisively cushioned.

Though it was destined never to replace the MCC at the centre of the cricketing world, during its early days county cricket was an attractive alternative to the traditional fare served up by the *maître chef* at Lord's. It offered the best of both worlds – a regular programme of first-class matches with more than a modicum of privilege. In fact, the options open to the devotee from the 1870s onwards were not quite so obvious. It was not simply a question of the old-fashioned, aristocratic MCC versus the energetic, apparently more liberal, county clubs. Times were changing, and members of the aristocracy were soon to be found among the list of patrons of county cricket clubs just as often as members of the middle-classes were elected to the MCC. Yet for a period during the 1860s, the ideals represented by the MCC on the one hand and the county clubs on the other were in direct opposition. It seemed only a matter of days or months before cricket would be torn apart by the conflicting forces of tradition and progress.

But the great bust-up never happened. From being mortal enemies, the MCC and the county clubs in the space of thirty years settled their differences to the point at which they became inseparable partners in the great venture of first-class cricket. Quite how this unexpected reconciliation came about is, at first sight, something of a mystery. If it had been simply a contest between the aristocratic MCC and middle-class counties, then the fact that it was the latter who in 1894 solicited the advice and support of the MCC would suggest that tradition had triumphed. The only trouble with this argument is that it runs contrary to all analyses of the direction of social change in Victorian England. Walter Bagehot was only one of many to point out that by the end of the nineteenth century, 'The middle classes – the ordinary majority of educated men – are in the present day the despotic power in England.'[11] Bagehot's judgement was correct in all respects bar one. Uppermost in the minds of the late-Victorian middle classes was not the destruction of the aristocracy, but its reconstitution. Ambitious and energetic, their aim was to fuse business and social worlds in such a way as to allow a new ruling coalition to emerge, but before this could happen, centuries of tradition enshrined in the style and habits of a landed aristocracy had to be reconciled with the idea and practice of capitalism. In 1870 the differences between the two life-styles were unmistakable. Within the narrow world of cricket, the county clubs and the MCC had about as much in common as Hunslet and the Harlequins.

Twenty-five years later the situation had been completely transformed. The MCC had recognized (some would say rescued) the County Championship, and for their part the county clubs had accepted the ultimate authority of the MCC. Two series of events combined to bring about this *rapprochement*. The first was the economic and agricultural depression of the 1870s and 1880s, which disturbed the stability and eventually the structure of the aristocracy. The second were the violent criticisms to which the MCC was subjected during the 1870s, and which finally shook the club out of its languorous stupor.

As far as the landed aristocracy was concerned, the last twenty-five years of the nineteenth century saw the final whittling away of that unchallenged political supremacy which it had enjoyed for 200 years or more. Very few of the traditional lineages came through the Great Depression completely unscathed, and many disappeared without trace. The few who prospered did so through investing in industry or commerce. For example,

The Earl of Verulam, for instance, in the 1870s had an income of about £17,000 (which he usually overspent), of which £14,500 came from rents and timber sales. His son, the third earl, extended his small share portfolio to some fifteen companies, mainly in the colonies and other overseas parts, and became a multiple director of companies, again mainly of African and American mines. By 1897 almost a third of his income came from such unbucolic sources.[12]

Within the middle classes, a similar shake-up was taking place. The majority were, of course, no strangers to business; they had been brought up on a diet of profit and loss. But towards the end of the century, a rather superior genus emerged. By 1890 this 'business aristocracy' was both larger and richer than the landed aristocracy.

Compared with the 2,500 great landowners in 1873 with rentals of over £3,000 (excluding London property and other income) there were in 1850 under 2,000 businessmen with profits under Schedule D of £3,000. By 1880, there were over 5,000. And if 866 of the landlords had over £10,000 and 70 over £50,000, the corresponding figure for businessmen had risen from 338 to 987 and from 26 to 77 respectively.[13]

It was really a case of 'the aristocracy is dead: long live the aristocracy'. For apart from lineages, this new breed possessed all the trappings of an aristocracy – all, that is, save one. Like the seventeenth and eighteenth-century magnate, 'business aristocrats' owned land – often great estates. Unlike their predecessors, however, they still travelled daily to work. The company head-office in London, Birmingham, Manchester, Leeds or Glasgow was still the centre of their lives and the source of their wealth.

Business aristocrats and aristocratic businessmen united in the late nineteenth century to form a new ruling coalition, a plutocracy which flowered with unparalleled splendour in the Edwardian era – or, as some would have it, indulged in 'an orgy of conspicuous waste'.

Biarritz, Cannes, Monte Carlo, and Marienbad – the international luxury hotel was very much the product of this age and found in the 'Edwardian' style its best architectural form – steam yachts and larger racing stables, private trains, massacres of game birds and opulent country house weekends stretching into weeks: these consoled the increasingly lengthy leisure hours of the rich.[14]

Cricket was certainly one of the leisure pastimes which bene-fited from the attentions of the new coalition. The two decades prior to the outbreak of war in 1914 witnessed a succession of brilliant performances from some of the most memorable figures ever to play the game. Sandwiched between the ageing glory of Grace and the precocious excellence of Hobbs, were a collection of players whose talents may have been equalled but never surpassed. Fry, Ranjitsinhji, Jessop, MacLaren, Jackson, Hirst, Hayward, Palairet, Spooner and Rhodes – an incomparable synthesis of cricketing genius. It was, truly, a 'Golden Age'.

Volumes have been devoted to recounting its glories, but few have bothered to try to explain this extraordinary profusion of ability. A fortuitous coincidence? Perhaps. Yet just as great theatrical performances emerge out of a scaffolding of script and stage, so the stars of the 'Golden Age' needed a platform from which to launch their talents. The platform was county cricket. Here, as never before, cricketers had the opportunity to compete regularly against each other on equal terms, to learn at first hand, to practice all aspects of the game under the watchful eye of the acknowledged masters, in an atmosphere charged by genuine rivalry and thousands of (generally) appre-ciative spectators.

Before this could take place, however, a way had to be found of overcoming the MCC's indifference to the idea of a county championship. Without the club's blessing and active support, the Championship probably would never have survived the traumas of maladministration and jealousy that marked its early days. The solution, as it transpired, involved not so much a change of heart as a change of face. By 1870 the MCC had become a die-hard stronghold. Professionals and advocates of county cricket were looked upon with the utmost suspicion. At first, resentment at the club's attitudes was confined to out-siders – the professionals themselves and a few outspoken moderates. But the crunch came when a vociferous body of opinion *within* the MCC began to lobby for a radical re-appraisal of the club's position. In 1874, in the wake of the failure of its 'knock-out' competition, the secretary of the MCC made the following announcement at the club's Annual General Meeting.

> The match list will be found to differ from those of previous years. The counties having generally disapproved of the scheme entertained last year, the Committee have instituted a series of divisional matches. The North, South-East, and West will be represented at Lord's. The Elevens will be selected by the Committee, and they hope to bring out many players who, from various circumstances, may have been debarred from playing for their respective counties. Secretaries of clubs in all parts of England have been requested to forward the names of players, little known to the general public, but of local celebrity, who may, by this means, be enabled to advance themselves in their profession.

Reading between the lines, the issues are clear. In a final effort to outflank its new rivals, the MCC's 'old guard' tried to set up an alternative fixture list which owed nothing to the counties or to established players; the club would arrange the matches and pick the teams. It was a disastrous mistake. The standard of cricket at Lord's dropped alarmingly, with the result that both the better players and spectators began to drift away. Soon the club began to find it difficult to raise teams. But the secretary did not give in easily. In a speech late in 1874, he claimed that the poor quality of much of the cricket at Lord's was the result of factors over which he had no control: first, such was the superiority of W. G. Grace that in his absence, standards automatically seemed to have fallen; secondly, because of the surfeit of cricket, it had become very difficult to distinguish between the 'Gentlemen' and the 'Players' – the implication being that only the former were capable of attracting large crowds. Not everyone was convinced by these arguments. In a letter to the editor of *Bell's Life* (1875), Mr R. A. H. Mitchell wrote,

> I cannot think that Mr Grace's advent to the field of cricket can have in any way contributed to the decline of cricket ... It is professionals whose names we miss. Why is this? Those who say there is too much cricket appear to me to be stating only half the truth. There is too much cricket under the imperfect management of the MCC. The MCC, occupying

as it does the first position of any club in England, holds in its hands the remedy for the present state of affairs. What is wanted is a policy of conciliation with due regard to the interests of other clubs. Hitherto, the MCC has arranged their matches independently, and the argument advanced has been, 'We arrange our matches and others must make their own arrangements accordingly'. I hope the hard logic of facts may break down so infatuated a theory. Let the MCC invite representations from the County Clubs and the All-England Elevens to meet together in the autumn and arrange their matches for the next year, in such a way as may be most convenient to all ... In such matches as the Gentlemen versus the Players, I should like to see permission given to the Players to select their own side.

In another letter to *Bell's Life* (1875), an anonymous contributor expressed a similar opinion.

Let the Marylebone Secretary, if he has the time, pay a visit to the Kennington Oval, or to Prince's, whilst a good county match is proceeding without Mr Grace, and he will at either place receive a direct denial to his preposterous statement. The real fact of the case is that the public are more fond of cricket than ever, but they will not visit any ground that does not lay an attractive programme before them.

Neither was criticism of the club's approach to first-class cricket confined to newspaper articles.

At the Annual General Meeting of the Club on May 5th, 1875, a fierce attack was made not for the first time, by Mr Willoughby who criticized the expenditure on the Tavern, derived the match-list as rubbishy, and asserted that professionals were reluctant to play at Lord's being better treated elsewhere. He objected strongly to the introduction of lawn-tennis courts, and criticised the attitude of the Secretary to members.[15]

Though Willoughby, Mitchell and others had a powerful case, it is doubtful if they could have overcome the MCC's well-known antipathy to change had it not been for the illness which compelled the secretary, R. A. Fitzgerald, to resign on 2 October 1876. During the thirteen years that he had held the office, the 'number of members increased from 650 to 2,080'.

The arrival of his successor, Mr H. A. Perkins, was the signal for a dramatic expression in the MCC's membership. Between 1876 and 1898 more than 3,000 members were elected. By 1910, the total had risen to 5,219, an increase of more than 400 per cent in forty years. Moreover, the majority were elected under new conditions which were designed to improve the standard of the teams that represented the club. The question of 'playing members' had been raised for the first time at the Annual General Meeting in 1875.

> The Committee now approach a less satisfactory aspect and one scarcely befitting the reputation of the Marylebone Club. It is much to be lamented that the playing staff of the club does not appear to have advanced in due proportion to the increased roll of members. The members are earnestly reminded that something more is required of them than cursory support in order to maintain the Marylebone Club at the head of the cricketing world. It will scarcely be credited that on several occasions last season matches were either abandoned or otherwise injured, both by the non-appearance of members who agreed to play, and by the reluctance of others to take part at all.[16]

Next year, the committee took action to counter this threat

> A revised scheme of election was submitted to a special meeting of members on March 2nd, 1876 ... the new rules affecting election to the MCC have been substituted for those which have stood the test of many years, but which are found inadequate to the rapid expansion of the Club ... The object which the committee had in view ... is to secure a proper discretion in the election of new members. Cricketers possess the first claim on the Club, and it is not thought conducive to the best interests to suffer the welfare of the Club to depend upon so uncertain a basis as the popularity of certain great matches.

The second major improvement in cricket at Lord's was just as much a break with tradition. In 1877 the MCC concluded an agreement with the Middlesex County Cricket Club under the terms of which the county was allowed to play some of its home matches at Lord's. No charge was made for this concession, though Middlesex did generally make an annual donation to the MCC, 'larger or smaller according to the state of its finances'. Many, including James Lillywhite, felt this to be a major turning point in the affairs of the MCC.

Cricket at Lord's benefited greatly by the appearance there of the Middlesex Club, which has migrated from its former headquarters at Prince's and the addition of a few county matches to the Marylebone programme will certainly strengthen it at a point where it has been undeniably weak of late years. For some time there has been a complaint that there was not so much first-class cricket at Lord's as the revenue and the position of the Club warranted, and beyond all doubt, with the exception of the two fashionable meetings of the season, there has been for some time to the outside world an air of monotony and apathy about the cricket at Lord's. The addition of the Middlesex fixtures filled a decided blank in the Marylebone programme, and there was certainly more life in the appearance of matters at headquarters than in previous years.'[17]

The admission of county cricket to Lord's, though it preceded the MCC's official recognition of the County Championship by seventeen years, was nevertheless a sign of the times. No longer was county cricket an activity beyond countenance, nor the cricket field an arena fit to be graced only by patricians. Nor was the arrival of county cricket the only indication that a new broom was at work at Lord's. An enlarged ground staff, a new members' pavilion, a new stand (the Mound), and a press box had been added to the facilities available at the ground by the turn of the century.

The final pieces in the puzzle do not fall into place so conveniently. We know that great economic and social pressures were gradually shifting the foundation of the aristocracy from land to urban-based industry and finance. We know too that the MCC was undergoing a far-reaching re-examination of its role in the game. But we can only suggest how the two processes might have been linked. The most important clue is to be found in the changing face of the membership at Lord's. In 1877, out of a total membership of 2,291, 337 were titled members of the aristocracy. By 1886 the total membership had grown to 5,091, but the number who held titles had fallen to 327. By 1915 the position had been partially restored: of the 5,135 members, some 452 were now titled. In other words, not only did the MCC grow exceptionally fast during the last quarter of the nineteenth century, it also changed character. Whatever else the new members might have been, they were not landed aristocrats.

At the same time, a number of changes were taking place in the method of selecting new members. Traditionally, prospective members had to go through an elaborate process of recommendation and election before they were finally admitted to the MCC. But in 1888, against a background of increasing expenditure, the club publicly advertised 100 life memberships at a cost of £100 each. We do not know precisely who took advantage of this offer, but it is not difficult to guess the type of person that it would have appealed to. Most enthusiasts among the ranks of the landed gentlemen would have been members already. Among the middle classes, it was not a time of great prosperity – or, at least, so the majority believed. Belts were being tightened to preserve existing standards of living. It was hardly the moment to splash out on something as immaterial as the MCC; after all, there were other places where cricket could be watched! Perhaps the only group who possessed both the money and the motivation to become life members were the leaders of the business community. There was no doubting their reverence for aristocratic tradition, nor their determination to preserve the panoply of pomp and ceremony which surrounded it. The majority were content with the trappings of privilege, but for the lucky few a life peerage turned an ideal into reality. The fact of becoming a lord did nothing to reduce the attractiveness of belonging to the MCC. If anything, the reverse seems to have been the case, for of the 47 who were thus elevated before 1900, 17 went on to join the Club.[18]

These business aristocrats and their less exalted colleagues were a decisive influence on the affairs of the MCC. They brought a fresh vision and a new sense of purpose to its activities. Rather than closing their eyes to the County Championship and hoping it would disappear, the newcomers accepted the existence of the competition and sought instead to bring it within the club's jurisdiction. The events of 1894 were the natural consequence of their new approach.

The rejuvenation of the MCC, however, was only one half

of the story. During the same period county cricket was also having its problems. In the 1860s the county clubs were questioning the MCC's claims to sovereignty; yet by the early 1890s many were wishing that the club would use its powers even more extensively. Behind this *volte-face* lay a combination of disorganization and disillusionment. For many, the Championship just wasn't living up to expectations. As the foundation of first-class cricket, county matches were expected to provide entertainment and, above all, an example to everyone of how the game should be played, but by the 1880s many devoted supporters of the game were asking themselves, 'How can we expect our children to learn from playing cricket when the very matches they can watch during their school holidays – supposedly the zenith of cricketing achievements – carry the taint of jealousy, dishonesty, and selfishness.'[19]

In part, the fault lay with the organization (or lack of it) of the Championship. That the outcome of the most English of sporting competitions should be decided by the sporting press was to say the least an unsatisfactory state of affairs. No doubt the counties could have solved this problem themselves had it not been for one other factor. For, ironically enough, the greatest obstacle to reorganizing the Championship was its popularity. Between 1860 and 1900 county clubs sprang up all over England, Wales, Scotland – and even Ireland. Many people would be surprised to discover that clubs were formed in Denbighshire in 1864, in Clackmannanshire in 1868 and in County Donegal in 1871. Though many were little stronger than the average town XI, none were prepared to admit that they were not 'first-class' and thus unworthy of a place in the Championship. At this time the MCC had its head firmly embedded in the sand: to the authorities at Lord's 'all counties [were] equal'. After the only other body capable of restoring some order to the Championship, the County Cricket Council, had voted itself out of existence in 1890, the competition was in danger of becoming a joke. Yet against this background of confusion and chaos, county matches retained their enormous popularity. As the Revd Holmes noted in 1894,

Twenty-five years ago, the great matches of the season were North *v.* South and Gentlemen *v.* Players. The former have to all intents and purposes disappeared, whilst the latter no longer possess the charm they once did. County cricketers prefer fighting under the colours of their County. It is by no means certain that in twenty years time the annual matches between Amateurs and Professionals will be played. The fact is, all our interest is absorbed in the doings of the Counties. The crowds flock to County Matches.[20]

Faced with mounting evidence of their own impotence, the representatives of the county clubs had to act. Further procrastination would have damaged their credibility and, more importantly, might have endangered the future of inter-county competition. The Championship was undoubtedly the vital consideration because, apart from test matches, it attracted the largest crowds and was thus the biggest money-spinner. This was a fact that the counties could not afford to overlook. Their administrators appreciated better than anyone else the scale of rising costs. Facilities for spectators, the upkeep of grounds and the payment of professionals were the major items in an annual expenditure which could not be covered by donations and subscriptions alone. Even the richest counties relied on gate-money to balance their budgets. Against this background, it is clear that by 1894 the county clubs had little choice but to call in the MCC. The Championship was their bread and butter; if it failed, they might too.

The reconciliation of 1894 was a lasting success because it proved its worth. The counties needed to find a way of rationalizing the Championship. The MCC had finally come to terms with the idea of cricket as a 'national' game, and was seeking a way of unifying the administration of all facets of the game. The new partnership put county cricket on a sound organizational footing and secured its economic viability for years to come. Lastly, it paved the way for the consummation of one of the greatest double acts in the sporting history – the amateurs and the professionals.

10 Amateurs and Professionals
1873–1962

'Is it wrong to pray to beat the Australians?'
'My dear Warner, anything which tends to increase the prestige of England is worth praying, for.'

At first sight, it may seem slightly odd that the distinction between 'amateurs' and 'professionals' should have assumed such importance at exactly the time that cricket was supposed to be taking on the mantle of the 'national' game. But on closer examination it soon becomes clear that this was not a coincidence. The separation of amateurs and professionals was closely linked to the emergence of county cricket as a major spectator attraction. For many at Lord's and elsewhere, the presence of a largely working-class audience and a growing number of working-class players conjured up a prospect too unpleasant to contemplate. To prevent a return to the situation which had existed during the heyday of the professional XIs, a way had to be found of limiting the impact of this new working-class presence. The answer was to create a pair of roles, one of which reaffirmed the rights and privileges of the gentleman while the other defined the duties and obligations of the artisan. Provided this were done, cricket could become 'popular' without reneguing on its élitist traditions.

In its most extreme form, the separation of amateur and professional cricketers created two distinct worlds. Amateurs had their own dressing-rooms, ate apart and even entered the field of play by a separate gate. Their initials were placed before their names on the scorecard, while the professionals' came after. As well as playing, professionals were obliged to bowl to club members at the nets and to undertake a number of menial tasks around the ground. For example, before each match they helped roll the wicket and put out the boundary ropes or boards. On the field, particularly from the turn of the century, it was the same story. The individuality and flare of the amateur lent matches their spectacular appeal, while the application and consistency of the professional sustained their competitiveness. For the true amateur, cricket could never be more than an exciting and entertaining diversion, though this did not mean that he played any less hard. For the professional, however, it was his life. Every innings and every over were part of a career upon which his hopes and ambitions depended. Because of these pressures, professionals were held to be unsuited to the responsibilities of captaincy. At least, this has been the orthodox interpretation of Lord Hawke's famous plea, 'Pray God, that a professional should never captain England.'

Another way of looking at the traditional preference for amateur captains is to consider the background to the rise of the amateur-professional distinction. From 1900 onwards, most county cricketers were professionals and the majority of these came from a working-class background. This was also the period when labour (and Labour) first began to challenge the traditional authority of land and capital. Relationships between the working classes and the rest of society often reached the level of overt hostility. In industry, agriculture and even leisure, benevolent paternalism and the type of control it implied gave way to more rigid and often formal sanctions on the nature and frequency of inter-class relationships. In this atmosphere, the professional cricketer was affected more than any other sportsman. The triumphs of the touring XIs of the 1850s and 1860s were painfully fresh in the memories of those who had never appreciated that type of cricket, even less the popularity it had achieved. Players like Clarke, Parr, Jackson and Daft had become school-boy heroes; it was unthinkable that the county professional should be allowed to steal the limelight to the same extent. To prevent a recurrence of this situation, the relationship between amateurs and professionals in first-class cricket had to be reconsidered. Prince Ranjitsinhji, one of the greatest players of the day, pointed the way to a more appropriate definition of the professional's role in an article he wrote in celebration of Queen Victoria's Diamond Jubilee.

A professional in former times was entirely the servant of his club, and in a servant's position. In the exhibition elevens, he became a free member of a club with equal rights with other members, and also in a way a public character, supported by and responsible to the public. These two aspects of a professional's position are worth remarking on with reference to this position of modern professionals playing for counties. A modern professional who represents his county is partly a servant of a club, partly a servant of the public, and partly a skilled labourer selling his skills in the best market. He may or may not have a local interest in the club he represents: that is another aspect of his case.[1]

As Ranji suggests, the redefinition of the professional's role in first-class cricket had to embrace a return to something akin to the master-servant role of the eighteenth century, whilst at the same time paying lip-service to the demands of a free labour market and democracy. Once the desirability of a return to the pre-1846 *status quo* had been established, it was but a short step to argue that it was the amateur who, as captain, was best equipped to look after the interests of the game itself. Looked at in this light, any other justifications for amateur captains amount to self-fulfilling prophecies.

The ideals and values on which county cricket was founded bore the stamp of what has been described as the 'games-dominated tory-imperialism' of the late-Victorian ruling classes. Service in some far-off outpost of the Empire demanded self-discipline and obedience above all else. Cricket, contemporaries believed, encouraged the same qualities. The Hon. R. Grimston summed up the whole argument when he wrote,

> I claim for our cricket ground and football field a share, and a very considerable share too, in the formation of the character of the English gentleman. Our games require patience, good-temper and perseverance, good pluck, and above all implicit obedience. It is no bad training for the battle of life for a boy to be skinned at football, or even given out wrongly at cricket, and to be able to take the affliction quietly and with good-temper, and in a gentlemanly spirit.[2]

Nowhere has the relationship between cricket and qualities of character needed to succeed in the 'battle of life' been better expressed than Sir Henry Newbolt's oft-quoted poem, 'Vitae Lampada':

> There's a breathless hush in the Close tonight –
> Ten to make and the match to win –
> A bumping pitch and a blinding light,
> An hour to play and the last man in.
> And it's not for the sake of a ribboned coat,
> Or the selfish hope of a season's fame,
> But the Captain's hand on his shoulder smote –
> 'Play up! Play up! and play the game!'
>
> The sand of the desert is sodden red –
> Red with the wreck of a square that broke,
> The Gatling's jammed and the Colonel dead,
> And the regiment blind with dust and smoke.
> The river of death has brimmed his banks
> And England's far, and Honour a name,
> But the voice of a schoolboy rallies the ranks:
> 'Play up! play up! and play the game!'
>
> This is the word that year by year
> While in her place the School is set,
> Every one of her sons must hear,
> And none that hears it dare forget.
> This they all with joyful mind
> Bear through life with a torch in flame,
> And falling fling to the host behind –
> 'Play up! play up! and play the game!'[3]

When Kent won the Championship in 1906, a contributor to the *National Review* went so far as to claim that it was 'Because they were imbued that that co-operative and sporting enthusiasm, that superb playing for the side and not for the self, that sacrifice of the individual for the team's sake ... there is something Imperial both in the form of the Kent team and in the popular recognition thereof.'[4]

In an age less secular than ours, it was perhaps inevitable that someone would trace a relationship between success on the cricket field and entry to the most sought-after élite of all:

> Put your whole soul into the game, and make it your very life.
> Hit clean and hard at every loose ball. 'Steal a run' whenever

you safely can, for the least bit of work that helps anyone nearer to God is blessed work, and gladdens the Captain's heart. Be alert and ready, and you will keep up your end. Lay on hard, and you will run up a grand score. And when 'time' is called you will 'bring out your bat', your conscience will say 'Well done', and those you have cheered and helped will say, 'A good man! Thank God for such an innings!' Aye, and when on the resurrection morning you come out of the pavilion, leaving your playing clothes behind you, and robed like your glorious Captain-King, you and all the hosts of God will see and understand your score as you cannot now, and your joy will be full as you hear the Captain, 'the innumerable company of angels' and the whole redeemed Church of God greet you with the words, 'WELL PLAYED, SIR!'[5]

During the early years of county cricket, it was the ability to live up the highest moral and ethical standards which justified the automatic selection of an amateur as captain. By the end of the last century, however, this rationale had begun to change. Qualities of personality were gradually replaced by an emphasis on social stature. Thus one famous journalist of the day argued that 'County sides are best led by a man socially superior to the professionals.' One might have supposed that such a blatant assertion of class differences would have offended those who retained a belief in the inherently democratic properties of cricket. But the 'amateurs for captain' lobby easily dispelled any doubts on this score:

> Cricket will always be a gloriously democratic game, but in county cricket, the captain should always have some standing ... the Leicestershire committee have selected as their captain, Sir Arthur Hazelrigg, who has never participated in a first-class match in his life, and was not even in his school XI, nor yet in a university trial.[6]

For much of the last quarter of the nineteenth century, the argument over who should captain county teams continued alongside another, equally vitriolic, debate over the merits of county cricket itself. Its opponents were particularly active about the turn of the century. In 1902, for example, an anonymous author in *The World's Work* wrote, 'It will be an evil day for cricket when changes are made which are based upon the assumption that cricket depends more on gate-money than on the support of country gentlemen, more on its first-class fixtures than on the games at our country houses.'[7] The debates began to overlap as soon as questions were asked about whether or not county cricket should continue to be run as a business. Critics of this trend claimed that financial pressures were undermining the moral and ethical basis of the game. Mr C. E. Green, a county cricketer himself and later President of the MCC, was one of the many who felt that 'County cricket has become too much of a business, and too much of a money-making concern. There is, I am afraid, very little real sport in it now as a game, and the feeling of *esprit de corps* which ought to exist in conjunction with real county cricket is fast disappearing.'[8]

One aspect of county cricket worried Mr Green and his colleagues more than any other. By admitting the interests of a paying audience, they felt that it would not be long before the counties would be obliged to increase the numbers of matches they played and to field their best team as often as possible. At this point, much of the spontaneity of the game would be lost and, more seriously, many amateurs, finding that the game was occupying too much of their time, would be forced to withdraw completely. As it was, the true amateur, 'men like Lord Hawke, who have the taste and the means to go on playing first-class cricket strictly and purely as amateurs'[9] were rapidly becoming a rare breed. In many cases, the amateur's only recourse was to accept some form of payment for his services. Though this broke all the rules of amateurism, by 1900 at least four different ways of justifying these payments had been devised. The first of these, the payment of hotel and travelling expenses, was 'a custom that is perfectly recognised, and perhaps in no way lowers the status of those who receive this help'; the second involved receiving expenses in excess of those actually incurred; the third receiving compensation for losses incurred by the player's 'business' in his absence, and the fourth receiving a regular salary as payment for services which he did not perform and never thought of performing – for example, as an 'assistant secretary'. 'The fault', as contemporaries saw it,

> ... lies with the custom, the system approved by the custom ... and it is a system that is an almost necessary result of the immense, the all-embracing demands on a man's time that

first-class cricket makes . . . A man cannot make a decent pretence of attending to a business or a profession and yet play first-class cricket, excepting only in the case of professions like school-mastering and the law, with their long vacations, which nevertheless only give a man the necessary freedom at the latter end of the season.[10]

Even more trenchant opposition came from those who saw in the attention given to county cricket 'a disease characteristic of all sections of society', a threat to England's economic growth and, above all, to her national security. So much emphasis on cricket at school instilled a false idea of the relative values of work and play. The result, many feared, would be a generation ill-fitted to hold their own with others whose education had been conducted on 'sounder' lines. Certainly games had a value – 'when played in the right spirit, they are an admirable training for the more serious battles of life. They impress upon boys the necessity for patience, resourcefulness, and unselfishness as no other form of education could.' The danger was that in enjoying sport, boys tended to forget about work. And if the energies of the rich could be dissipated so easily, what was to stop the same malaise afflicting the rest of society? 'When the upper-classes thus magnify the importance of games it is not surprising that the lower class follow suit. It is obviously impossible for the great majority themselves to play games, but they can pay to look on – they cannot go to race-meetings, but they can bet in the streets.'[11]

These, then, were the main criticisms being levelled at county cricket at the beginning of the present century. In view of the dangers inherent in this type of mass entertainment, it is not surprising to find that the professional cricketer, the paid seducer of the masses, soon came under heavy fire. In the opinion of another anonymous writer, this time in the *Saturday Review*,

> They [the professionals] are for the most part a very well conducted and responsible body of men, and many of them would do credit to any station of life in which they were placed, but it must be remembered that cricket brings them into association with men of the best manners, and above all of impeachable character, whose traditions of the game, brought from school and college, make unfairness or even

sharp practice as impossible to them as cheating at cards. It is from these men that cricket takes its tone in this country, and that tone is sustained by their determination to have no pecuniary reward of any sort in the matches in which they play.[12]

To the bigots, and to those who were genuinely worried about the consequences of county cricket, a revival of country-house cricket seemed a much better idea. After all, it 'was truly amateur, people who wanted to play to win regardless of other aspects, would not find themselves again invited, nor again would fine exponents, but not so fine characters.'[13]

For a while it looked as though their wishes might be granted. In Edwardian England, the organization of country-house cricket matches was as elaborate and as widespread as county games. One who played in many of these matches, Mr C. K. Francis, described how,

> We used to stay in various country houses for about a week, playing two or three matches sometimes against very good teams. The cricket weeks at Preston Hall, Croxteth, Lees Court, Scarborough, Hothfield, Compton Verney, Wilton, Rood Ashton, Patshill, Northernwood, Escrick, Southgate, Vice Regal Lodge are only a few that I can remember out of the many.[14]

But like so much of Edwardian England, country-house cricket never really recovered from the Great War. The problem was not so much changing tastes as a lack of players and spectators; in many cases, entire teams had died in the Flanders' mud. There were many who, like Alec Waugh, saw in the post-war world a rejection of everything they had valued and believed in.

> It is sad to think how quickly that world has passed, and how effectively the machinery of our industrial system has already taken cricket for itself. Nyren's game is no longer entertained for a few. It is has become a part of the national life, and probably, if the Bolsheviks get their way with her, it will be nationalised with the cinema and the theatre and Association Football.[15]

While country-house cricket was enjoying an Indian summer, county cricket was slowly consolidating its position as a

popular, profit-making business. By the outbreak of war the
virtues of the Championship were accepted by all but a few
unrepentant diehards. Thanks largely to the efforts of no lesser
figure than the captain of England, Lord Hawke, even professionals were now viewed with only the mildest suspicion.
Rich and poor alike were now convinced of the value of the
entertainment provided by the combination of amateurs and
professionals in county cricket. When Ranji was asked 'What
excuse is there for the existence in the community of a class
that does nothing for the general welfare?', his answer summed
up the new feeling:

> Now I should be the last to say that a man of ability should
> give all his time to cricket. That would be quite absurd. But
> I do not think that the life of one who devotes himself to
> cricket is either altogether wasted or quite useless to his fel-
> low-men, for the simple reason that cricket provides a very
> large number of people with cheap, wholesome and desirable
> entertainment.[16]

The type of cricket envisaged by Ranji was far removed from
the elegance and privacy of the country-house. It was more
than a game, rather 'a huge institution, highly organised and
demanding the entire time of those actively engaged in it'. Its
home was a special arena, the county ground, its rationale was
profit, and its motif spectacle. 'The county clubs were no longer
glorified local clubs, but in addition business concerns. They
provided popular amusement and good cricket: in fact they
became what they are now – local in name and partly local in
reality, but also run upon exhibition or, as I called it, spectacular lines.'[17]

The factor that finally clinched the professional's place in
county cricket was expediency. Only professionals had the time
to acquire the skills and the consistency of application expected
by first-class cricket's audiences, and only they were in a position to play as often as required:

> The development of cricket has taught them [the audience]
> what the game can offer when played skilfully, and they
> would cease to come if matches were poor or if they sank
> to the average standard that can be attained by men who
> only played cricket occasionally and as a recreation. There

are players who can come into first-class cricket from other pursuits, and make centuries. But players like Mr W. H. Patterson and Mr D. C. Steel are very rare indeed ... I cannot see how cricket as a great institution for providing popular amusement, could, as things are now, exist without a class of people who devote themselves to it.[18]

The indispensability of professionals, however, was not seen as a reason for granting them any special privileges. Even their most ardent supporter would not have claimed other than that they were good workers, reliable and honest, and as such worthy of preservation. In the words of another president of the MCC, Lord Harris,

A more discerning body of men it would be difficult to find. Their work, especially among those who do not rise to the top of the ladder, is very hard; they are always expected to be keen ... It would be a distinct loss if such a body of men were to be withdrawn from our cricket fields ... Therefore, let us by all means encourage them to persevere in their profession, so they may do their part towards the welfare of the community.[19]

Others were less easily convinced. There was nothing intrinsically wrong in having professionals in a team: the danger was that they would carry the typically 'professional' approach to the game too far.

The skill with which Shrewsbury uses his legs upon a treacherous wicket is nothing short of miraculous. His comrade-at-arms, William Gunn, can also play the game very ably: so can Mr Stoddart and Mr Jackson – a fact not generally known. The difference between the play of the two amateurs and the two professionals is that the latter makes use of the method when it is not necessary to use it, where as Stoddart and Jackson only do so where there is no other course open save wild slogging. It is not the use of the method, but the abuse of it, that can with fairness be criticised.[20]

Off the field, the professional was treated rather in the same way as white emigrants to one of the colonies. Simplicity and honesty were the most sought-after qualities.

The cricketer is just a man with a clear eye, bronzed face, and athletic figure. He is usually somewhat lacking in general information, and is sometimes a poor conversationalist upon any but his own subject. He does not read much. On the other hand, he does not talk much about things he does not understand, which is a good trait. He gives the impression of having led a free, unconstrained life – he could be, in fact, anything from a trooper in the Rhodesian Horse to a Californian orange-grower. He is simple, frank and unaffected: a genuine person, with plenty of self-respect, and no desire to seem what he is not: on the whole, not a bad sort of man at all – quite the reverse.[21]

Between the heyday of the touring XIs in the 1850s and the end of the century, the world of the professional cricketer was turned upside down. Once he had been the master of his own destiny – even though gate receipts might not always have been shared out equally. Now he was back in the position of an artisan. The only compensation that he could derive from this reversal was the great increase in opportunity offered by a regular programme of county matches. Yet, as far as one can tell, professionals adjusted to their new station in county cricket with equanimity; where a grievance was voiced, it normally concerned rates of pay or earnings and not the question of the professional's status.

The most significant, and certainly the most publicized, example of a protest by professionals was the so-called 'Nottinghamshire Schism' of 1881. This event was described at length in James Lillywhite's *Cricketers Annual* the following year.

As a rule professional cricketers have borne themselves so respectably that the attitude taken by Alfred Shaw, Shrewsbury, Barnes, Morley, Selby, Scotton and Flowers in refusing to play for their county unless certain specified demands were granted by the committee was at first hardly credited ... The precise origin of the movement is difficult to trace, but indirectly the visits of the two Australian Elevens to England may be held responsible for the sudden and extraordinary change which took place in the bearing of professionals who had previously comported themselves most becomingly. The terms upon which the Colonial Players were accepted over here were utterly false to men like Shaw, who knew that the home *status* of some was certainly not above the level of professional cricket in England, and here no doubt was the first sign of a grievance. Then again, the readiness with which, in many cases, rather exhorbitant demands from the Australian managers were met by some of our chief clubs probably had some influence in encouraging Albert Shaw, who may be considered the leader of the movement, in believing that the withdrawal of seven most capable members of the Eleven might reduce the management of a county, even one so rich in cricketers as Notts., to accede to the imposition of new stipulations in the recognised contracts.

Lillywhite's account makes it clear that there were two major issues at stake. First, the professionals were seeking a formal contract of employment guaranteeing amongst other things an automatic benefit on completion of an agreed number of years with a county. Secondly, they demanded the right to organize their own matches. Of the two, the latter was probably the more serious. In the 1880s legally binding contracts for artisans were almost unheard of, and so it is unlikely that the professionals held out much hope in this direction. But the right to organize their own matches was another matter. The old professional XIs had organized all their matches, and Shaw had been a leading member of many of these teams. The withdrawal of this privilege would have been less disturbing had it been applied universally, but Nottinghamshire had already created a precedent by allowing a similar request from Richard Daft. For Shaw, this was the last straw. He had always been a staunch defender of the rights of professionals and in 1873, for example, he had refused to join W. G. Grace's team to tour Australia because professionals were to be allowed only second-class travel facilities. By 1881, as far as Shaw was concerned, the situation had become intolerable. It was no longer a question of professionals being prevented from making enough money to support them in retirement. Now it was a personal matter: he was being discriminated against because he was Albert Shaw.

No matter how justified Shaw's action may have been, the results were almost certainly other than he would have wished. The outcome of the 'schism' was to establish a pattern of control in first-class cricket which remained virtually unchallenged for eighty years. In deciding how to react, Nottinghamshire were strongly influenced by the widespread outcry that had greeted the professionals' demands. James Lillywhite, for example, was in no doubt about the seriousness of the 'schism': '[As] a deliberate combination against recognised administration ... it was not merely a question of the welfare of one county, but it involved a distinct and material alteration in the relations between paid cricketers and their employers which vitally affected the interests of every club of any importance.' The committee refused to accede to any of the requests, dropped the offending professionals from the eleven, and thereby surrendered the Championship to Lancashire. By the end of the season the 'schism' was over. 'After due submission had been made', five of the seven players were readmitted, and only Shaw and Shrewsbury 'whom the committee adjudged to be the prime movers in the conspiracy' were barred until the following season.

The 'schism' was the last occasion on which professional cricketers took collective action in support of a demand. Since 1881 many players have stood out for improvements in their conditions of employment, and some (particularly from Yorkshire) have tried to obtain a contract of employment, but there are no other examples of group protests. Against a background of industrial conflict this may seem unlikely, but it is not difficult to understand. Until 1945, and possibly even later, the annual earnings of a professional cricketer, and the conditions under which he worked, were better than any he was likely to find elsewhere. Then there was the prospect of a benefit and finally the intangible kudos of first-class cricket. As many players have since discovered, given the right contacts it is quite possible to convert the intangible into hard cash.

Besides these pecuniary advantages, there was another reason why professionals were by and large content with their lot. As the Championship became an established feature of the English summer, county cricket gradually acquired a set of values which incorporated a distinctive vision of the cricketer. According to this vision, professionals played cricket not for the money nor for the glory, but because they loved it. And, as Virgil once observed, 'Omnia vincit Amor'.

There is little doubt that most professionals were quite willing to accept this image of themselves. If it wasn't true, it was nevertheless comforting. For one thing, it helped to dispel any doubts about the wisdom of following such an unusual career or the adequacy of the rewards it promised. Not that many professionals at the turn of the century would have had second thoughts about either. From the young professional's point of view, the earnings of players like Hirst and Rhodes must have seemed more than attractive, and the gulf between potential earnings and the wages they actually received on joining a county – one pound a week, without a winter retainer – was bridged by their 'love of the game'. In his autobiography, Sir Jack Hobbs recalled how it was these considerations that persuaded him to try his hand at county cricket. After leaving the York Street Boys School in Cambridge, for which the fees were four-pence a week, he described how,

> I began to feel deeply that there was a career in front of me. Apart from the glamour, the earnings of professionals in those days (*c.* 1900) seemed to my mind very big. I had been told that they were getting five pounds a match. It seemed big money. But even the earnings paled in my imagination compared with the glory of playing for a county – say, for instance, for Surrey, the county of my hero Tom Hayward . . . Cricket had become with me an all-absorbing passion. It was my supreme ambition. It stuck out a mile in my mind before anything else. My father's occasional remarks about county players fired my hopes. Love of the game must have been bred in my blood.[22]

Hobbs' recollections, full of youthful enthusiasm and ambition, contrast sharply with the sober reflections of another professional test cricketer, Fred Root of Worcestershire.

> It is popularly supposed that there is quite a lot of money in first-class cricket. If there is, I have not found it. It is the worst paid of all professional games. With Worcestershire, the recompense for 1,500 overs a year, which yield an average crop of over 150 wickets a season, and 47 innings producing between 800 and 1,000 runs for twenty weeks' cricket, brought in under £300. During the period of depression it was suggested that the Worcestershire professionals should agree to a ten per cent reduction, and other clubs were circularised as to the amount of wages paid to their professionals. I was informed that at least four other counties paid less than

Worcestershire, and several other counties paid the same rate. Out of this, hotel accounts for away matches, taxi fares, flannels, and cricket equipment have to be paid by the professional.[23]

Root's opinion of the cricket career was undoubtedly influenced by the fact that, in his case, it involved a lot of hard graft and paid less well than he had anticipated. Even allowing for a slight element of bias, his account leaves one in little doubt that, between the wars, the average professional must have found it hard to make ends meet. Under these circumstances, many players must have considered the prospect of a benefit with a urgency born of despair. Yet Root goes on to quote examples of professionals actually turning down the offer of a benefit. One player, in what was to be his last year with Worcestershire, turned down the chance of a second benefit with the words, 'No, thank you, I can't afford it.' The truth of the matter, as Root went on to explain, was that risks involved in taking a benefit often outweighed the profits that might be expected.

A benificiary has to bear the whole of the expenses of both the home and away fixture of his club for the match he decides upon. He is not given an absolutely free choice of the fixture, the most profitable generally being denied him. Wages for players, umpires, gatemen, policemen, scorers, and so on, have to be paid, as well as the travelling expenses. It is not always possible to insure against the vagaries of the weather.[24]

The belief that, on retiring, a professional cricketer seldom found any difficulty in getting a good job was by the end of the nineteenth century firmly entrenched as part of the game's mystique. For many players, the prediction turned out to be true: for the county secretaries who were responsible for employing the budding professionals, it was always convenient. What had started as little more than a hopeful promise gradually acquired the mantle of inevitability.

A first-class cricketer, whose character is good, can rely with certainty upon obtaining on his retirement from county cricket a suitable and well-paid berth, which he will be capable of filling for many years. Frequently, too, their fame and popularity help cricketers to find good businesses upon their retirement, when usually they have a certain amount of money, gained from their benefit match, to invest.[25]

In general, the professional's own view of his prospects in county cricket and on retirement was noticeably more restrained than those of his employer. Sir Jack Hobbs, for instance, was under no illusion about the difficulties that a professional was likely to face: 'There is no royal road to success in cricket. It is a rough, hard road, and only a few can win through.'[26] His advice to young players contained a sobering reminder of the unpredictability of cricket:

Seek first a position in some business so that there may be something to fall back in the case of failure at cricket or dislike of it ... Cricket is too precarious. It is all right, if you can rise to the top and get the plums. Otherwise, it is a bare living for a few years, with nothing at the end; one saves a few pounds in the summer and spends them in the winter.[27]

Many people today might find it difficult to accept that Hobbs's forebodings were not just a trifle exaggerated. His contemporaries, however, knew only too well how realistic they were. Consider what Fred Root had to say on this score:

Many of the cricket heroes of the past are getting what consolation they can out of their memories – and an unskilled job at a pittance of a wage. During their innings they played life's game according to the rules of the circles in which, by unavoidable circumstances, they were compelled to enter. But dress suits are superseded by, in some cases, the corduroy of the pauper: and the presents and souvenirs have disappeared into the clutches of rich uncles owning shops denoted by the sign of the three brass-balls.[28]

It is an interesting comment on the professional's position in county cricket that so few publicly expressed their grievances during their playing days. By and large criticism was confined to Proust-like reflections in autobiographies, and even in this context it was often left to the reader to draw his own conclusions. Tom Dollery, a professional who captained Warwickshire shortly after the Second World War, was content for the most part just to describe the conditions under which professionals worked, but the implication cannot be missed:

At Edgbaston before the war the professionals were crowded into one small room and the amateurs – sometimes only one amateur – had the use of a dressing room twice the size. While accomodation was being wasted like that, the members of the professional staff who were not actually in the team for the match had to change in any nook they could find before they went out to bowl.[29]

The distinction between amateurs and professionals remained a feature of first-class cricket until 1962. Over the years many players, amateurs and professionals, had resented the separation that it fostered, though few had said so openly. On one famous occasion, Patsy Hendren contrived to ridicule the whole arrangement by refusing an invitation from the ten amateur members of an MCC team and walking alone through the professional's gate on to the pitch at Lord's. By 1950 many of the most abrasive aspects of the distinction had disappeared – at Lord's for instance, all players have lunched together since shortly after the end of the Great War – and by the time they were formally dropped 'amateurs' and 'professionals' belonged to history.

But when all is said and done, the most amazing feature of the distinction between amateurs and professionals was its durability. Created in a world of privilege and privacy, it survived the shattering effects of two world wars, the invention of the telephone, radio and television and the introduction of universal franchise and trade unionism. Nothing, it seemed, could upset the equilibrium of social relationships in first-class cricket. Nothing, that is, except the economic circumstances that finally led to the disappearance of the amateur.

11 Three Generations of Post-War Cricketers

In 1946 cricketers from the seventeen first-class counties prepared to resume their annual battle for the County Championship. On the surface, very little seemed to have changed. The last winners had been Yorkshire and, in the event, they were to retain the title. After six years of war, it was inevitable that some of the faces would have changed; some of the pre-war favourites had retired, while a few sadly had been killed or badly wounded on active service. But apart from the appearance of several new players, county cricket seemed to be starting from where it had left off in 1939. Depending on the size of their bank balances, the counties continued to employ between twenty-five and forty professionals in addition to a ground staff made up of promising young players. The traditional distinction between amateurs and professionals remained. Professionals were never appointed to the captaincy of the county side, though it was not unusual for them to deputise for the amateur skipper when he was ill or unavailable. The two sets of players inhabited separate changing rooms, and in some cases still came on to the field of play through different gates. The Gentlemen versus Players match at Lord's continued to be one of the high spots of the season.

Ten years later it may still have seemed as if first-class cricket was somehow shielded from the great political, economic and social changes that were at work in society at large. A second, consecutive defence of the Ashes was the most obvious and, for many, the most convincing measure of the well-being of English cricket. However, behind this comforting facade there were signs that the traditional structure of the first-class game was near to collapse. County cricket was plainly ailing, and many feared that the diagnosis would be terminal. The number of spectators at Championship matches was continually falling and county secretaries were experiencing the greatest difficulty in finding enough private benefactors and supporters to offset the resulting loss of revenue. It was also evident that the days of the amateur were numbered. In contrast with the pre-war situation, there were now very few people who could afford to devote all their time to cricket, and even fewer who wanted to. This shortage forced first the counties and then the England selectors to pick a professional as captain. In 1953 it fell to Len Hutton to show how misplaced Lord Hawke's fears had been.

By the early 1960s the ubiquitous 'wind of change' was poised to overturn much of the traditional frame-work of first-class cricket. In 1962 the separate statuses of the amateur and the professional were replaced by a single category – the player. This paved the way for a general improvement in the cricketer's lot. As well as more money and better conditions of employment, fundamental changes were made to rules governing the movement of players between counties. Under the new 'special registration' provisions, a player could transfer from one county to another without having to lose several years gaining a residential qualification. In 1967 another landmark was passed when cricketers formed their own 'union', the Cricketers' Association. But without doubt the most significant of all the post-war changes dates from 1963 – the year in which outside sponsorship in the form of the Gillette Cup was introduced into first-class cricket. More than any other single event, the inauguration of this annual competition marked the end of an era that had begun in 1894 with the MCC's reorganization of the County Championship.

From the beginning, the organization of county cricket had represented a subtle compromise between the forces of tradition and of business. Long before the first Gillette Cup match, it was evident that county cricket would have the utmost difficulty in surviving the rigours of the post-war economic climate. The simple truth was that tradition was no longer a marketable commodity, and the advent of sponsorship was merely a recognition of this fact. After 1963 there was no longer any doubt where cricket's future lay: henceforth, it would be organized and promoted as part of the entertainment industry.

Since then, the list of sponsored competitions has grown until today it includes not only the Gillette Cup, but also the John Player Sunday League (1969), the Benson and Hedges Cup (1972), the Prudential World Cup and Trophy (1975) and, most recently, the Schweppes County Championship (1977).

For the cricketer himself, the implications of sponsorship were scarcely less far-reaching. After the euphoria of the immediate post-war years, the 1950s had come as something of an anti-climax: attendances at county matches fell alarmingly; many counties seemed to be almost permanently on the brink of bankruptcy; real earnings never quite lived up to expectations; the problem of what to do when retirement could no longer be avoided loomed more menacingly every season. As the increasing competitiveness of domestic and international markets forced British industry to look to its margins, so good jobs for middle-aged men, often with little or no relevant expertise or experience, became more and more difficult to find. In the glare of the Wilsonian 'technological revolution', the cricketer found himself a far less marketable proposition. His skills and reputation counted for little in a labour market that echoed to the cry for formal qualifications and technical skills. The dawning realization that his future was much less secure than he had been led to believe was an unsettling influence on the best of players, and a profoundly depressing one on the run-of-the-mill county cricketer. Small wonder then that parents, schoolmasters and career advisers began to think twice before recommending a cricket career. The game, in short, was in danger of losing its mystique.

Within the last ten years, however, sponsorship has transformed the prospects of first-class cricket, and those of its players. The popularity of the one-day, 'instant' match has removed the threat of imminent bankruptcy and replaced it with a prospect of lasting prosperity which, only a few years earlier, would have seemed absurdly fanciful. But, at the same time, it has called into question the feasibility, or desirability, of retaining the County Championship in its present form. If cricket is supposed to be part of the entertainments industry, what justification can there be for retaining a competition that has largely lost its capacity to entertain? If, for the traditionalists, this question bordered on heresy, county treasurers knew only too well that it had to be faced up to in the near future.

The reorganization of the Championship in 1972 marked the first step in the process of modernizing what remains the competitive centre-piece of first-class cricket.

For the players, the most obvious attraction of sponsorship was the higher earnings that it promised. On the introduction of the John Player Sunday League in 1969, it became possible for a county cricketer to earn in one season a sum which, only twenty years earlier, would have taken him four years to amass. But there was another side to this picture – one which has received little or no publicity. As the spread of sponsorship has altered the rationale on which first-class cricket was based, players have found themselves confronted by several fundamental dilemmas. How were they, for instance, to reconcile the potentially conflicting demands of personal success, team loyalty and an audience? To what extent could the time-honoured techniques and tactics of a three-day county match be used in the totally different context of limited-over, league or cup matches?

At one level, it is very easy to sum up what has happened to first-class cricket since the war. A nineteenth-century game has become a twentieth-century business. The logistics of this process are faithfully recorded in the audited accounts of the MCC and the seventeen county clubs, in the records of attendances at test, county and one-day matches, in players' tax returns and in the marketing plans and budgets of firms like Gillette and John Player. But by themselves facts and figures like these do not adequately convey the enormity of the transformation that has overtaken cricket, nor do they give any idea of the effect that it has had on players and spectators alike. In 1949 the cricketing world was surprised to read that twenty-six professionals had been elected to Honorary Life Membership of the MCC. In 1977, twenty-eight years later, the captain of England caused an even greater shock by announcing that, instead of making himself available to lead the MCC party to Pakistan, he intended to spend the forthcoming winter in Australia playing in an 'international cricket circus' sponsored by a television magnate. In their own way, these two, apparently unconnected, events illustrate the distance that cricket has travelled in little more than a generation. In 1949 sponsorship was unheard of, and the captaincy of England was the greatest honour a player could receive – that is, assuming he was an amateur. Today, there are no amateurs. The captain of England is a player like everyone else. Sponsorship is the foundation of the game's new-found prosperity, and while players still love the game, most of them would be hard put to deny that money is now the great *desideratum*.

In many people's eyes, the image of the 'old pro' is giving way to one of the dynamic, media-conscious entrepreneur. The contrast may be exaggerated, but it highlights a basic truth. Of the professionals whose careers ended before 1960, the great majority belonged to the old school. By and large, their successors, the most recent generation of established players, have a different outlook on first-class cricket and their role in it. Their hopes and fears are more in tune with the realities of the modern world. They are less easily persuaded by well-rehearsed homilies on the virtues of a cricket career. There are signs too that the latest generation of 'young hopefuls' are even less enamoured of the traditional merits of a county cricketer's life. In their eyes, a cricket career is not so much an end in itself as a means of earning a lot of money and of setting up a prosperous future. They look upon the average county cricketer as something of a failure.

These are just a few of the ways in which the careers of the three generations of post-war cricketers can be contrasted. The following pages delve more deeply into their different expectations and experiences.

The Retired Cricketer

Cricketers tend to go on from one season to the next, thinking that it is going to last for ever.[1]

The cricketers of the immediate post-war era differed little from their predecessors. The basic fact was that they were still either amateurs or professionals. Even as late as 1950, it could be argued that these labels revealed much more about a person than just his status in a cricket team; they were signposts to two different social worlds. The typical amateur came from a prosperous, middle-class background. He had been educated at a public school and then at either Oxford or Cambridge. The first experience of county cricket came during the summer vacation, and this really summed up the amateur's outlook on the game. It was a means of enjoying himself before embarking on a career in finance, politics, public service or one of the professions. The thought of making a career out of cricket never crossed his mind. 'I had no intention of entering cricket as a profession – it was always my intention to play the game as an amateur.' Free from the pressures of a career, the amateur was in a position to play the game exactly as he wished. The result was what came to be known as the amateur approach to the game: 'Cavalier', 'spontaneous', 'devil-may-care' – each adjective captures something of his deliberate disregard for the more serious issues at stake. During Hampshire's run-up to the Championship in 1961, it was rumoured that their captain, Colin Ingleby-Mackenzie, used to get out quite frequently at about 2.55, the reason being that he wanted to back a horse in the 3 o'clock race. The story may be apocryphal; nevertheless, it makes the point.

Professionals were separated from amateurs by a centuries-old tradition of power and privilege which manifested itself in a deferential manner on and off the field, and a famous division of labour. The great majority came from working-class backgrounds, had not attended public or grammar schools, and had left school at the earliest possible opportunity. They had no doubts about the wisdom of becoming a professional cricketer. After all,

> When you think of 1934 and 1935, most youngsters leaving school were glad of any job. Those who had gone on to grammar school or who had got into technical school had probably come from a lot better families. I'm not saying I came from a bad family but we were just a working family. We were all interested in sport, but we weren't endowed with any money – I was the tenth child. Throughout the country, things were rough and you were glad of anything.

Contrary to popular legend, most professionals did not go straight from school to a county club. A few, it is true, were inducted in this way, and they then spent from three to six years working at the county ground, gaining valuable experience from watching and practising with the established players. But the majority spent several years working in other jobs before becoming full-time members of a county's playing staff. The decision to leave school had not been influenced by the prospect of becoming a county cricketer; at this time, working-class children generally left at the first opportunity, or before, if only because an extended education would have imposed a crushing financial burden on the rest of the household. The following is a description of how an ex-England wicket-keeper began his career.

I left school at the age of 14½ and went to work at an engineering firm on Southwark Bridge Road. I stayed for three months and then I went to another in the Westminster Road – my relations worked there and got me the job. Jobs weren't easy to come by at that time. I stayed there for nearly two years, then I had a letter from my schoolmaster, asking me whether I would like to go for a trial for the county ground staff. I got the job and started playing for the Surrey Colts and from there, having done well with the Colts, I eventually went on to the staff.

Listening to retired professionals talking about their early years in the game, it is impossible not to be struck by the number of references to chance and luck. Rather than seeking the comparative security of an apprenticeship or a white-collar job, they had opted for a career which offered an outside chance of national and international fame as collateral against a depressingly high failure rate. As one player put it, 'Like most other people in the 1930s, my idea was to get security, but looking back, if I had stuck to security, I would still have been a solicitor's clerk.'

Once a member of a county, the professional continued to live in a different world from the amateur. The emphasis during these early years was on practice. It was not that the professional lacked faith in his own natural talent; the point was that to be successful he had to tailor this ability to the peculiar demands of the role he had to play. He was in the team to provide reliability and consistency, while it was left to the amateur to supply the fireworks. Occasionally, an exceptional individual, like Dennis Compton for example, managed to transcend this traditional division of labour, but usually practice was the only protection that a young player had against the threat of a premature termination of his career.

You have got to have natural ability before you can be coached. But when you start playing cricket you have to practice, practice, practice – which unfortunately today they don't seem to do. The more you play, the better you become. It is true of any profession, whether you are a doctor, snooker player or footballer – it must be lots of practice to make perfection.

All the practice in the world, however, could not totally eliminate that nagging doubt always in the back of the professional's mind that somehow he might not make the grade. Intense competition from other young players, injury and temperament were all potential barriers to a county cap and relative security. This doubt was reflected in the way professionals tended to play down their chances of success. Few were prepared to admit that they had always wanted to be cricketers until it seemed more or less certain that this ambition would be satisfied. One player, for example, confessed that, 'I had always hoped that I had the ability to take up sport, but I never really thought that I was going to be good enough. My headmaster told me that I would play for Surrey one day, but I never believed him.'

The suspension of the County Championship between 1940 and 1946 and the post-war National Service obligation were two major problems that the first generation of post-war professionals had to contend with. The cessation of first-class cricket during the war years only aggravated the doubts that the young player was already susceptible to. With the length of his career cut by seven years, he had even less time to make the reputation that would safeguard his future. Before the war, the majority had been young enough to think of little more than enjoying themselves. Seven years later, the same players, many now with a wife and family to support, were understandably more concerned about what the future had to offer. Most, it must be said, did not view the revival of county cricket with absolute confidence.

I think my greatest worries came during the war. Although I managed to play some cricket in the meantime, it was difficult to know what was going to happen in 1946. Would I still be good enough? There was no way of knowing whether another one hundred good players would suddenly spring up. But because it was wartime, there was nothing to do but wait and see.

The problems were clearly most acute for those professionals with least pre-war experience. One recalled how,

In 1945 I was very worried whether I would be retained after the war. It was at this time, during a conversation with the Bedsers, that I was advised to take up wicket-keeping – originally I had been a bowler. I wrote to the club telling them that I also kept wicket (the thought at the back of my mind being that they were not going to retain me).

Like the war, National Service was an important influence on the lives of professionals in the 1940s and 50s. Providing they were judged to be physically sound, it meant the loss of at least two seasons' cricket. Unlike the war, however, this interruption was not without its advantages. Between leaving school and joining Her Majesty's Armed Forces, the young player had about three years in which he could do almost what he liked because no firm decisions about his future could be taken until after National Service had been completed. Many chose to spend their time playing cricket: 'What decided me to go into county cricket was the fact that I had two years of National Service in front of me. I thought I'd try county cricket for two years and then go in the army on the basis of "nothing lost, nothing gained".'

Once the retired professional had secured his place in the 1st XI, most of his initial doubts and anxieties disappeared. Cricket was now a way of life rather than a job of work. His commitment to the game revealed itself in a number of ways. He was immensely proud of being thought of as a cricketer, and remained so long after retiring from the game. When one ex-player was asked whether he would prefer to be known as a cricketer or as a member of the occupation he belonged to now, he replied without hesitation, 'A cricketer, naturally – I wouldn't like not to be connected with it somehow.'

What was the source of this attachment to the game? It was largely a product of the amount of effort and energy that the cricketer had put into making a success of his career. To survive in the game, a professional needed more than technical ability alone. He had to have, or to develop, an acute tactical aware-ness, based on a feeling for the dynamics of the game and a detailed knowledge of the strengths and weaknesses of the other players in it. For many players, this was as much, if not more, of a challenge than the perfection of a cover drive.

> I used to enjoy thinking things out and watching them work. It was only a matter of application to the job. Jack Robertson once scored three hundred in a day against us. The next time I bowled against him, he got eight. He used to hook in front of his face, so I decided to give him a bouncer fourth ball in the first over, and move up the fine-leg fielder forty yards. This we did, but the fielder dropped the catch. We tried it a few overs later and got him.

The early post-war professional's pride in his own ability was matched only by his scepticism for the present generation of players. In recent years changes in the game, particularly in the preparation of pitches, had favoured bowlers to the extent that now even moderate 'seamers' could achieve figures which equalled or bettered the performances of the giants of the past.[6]

> I think the game is farcical compared to what it used to be. I was brought up on the finest ground in England – they played bowls on the outfield – and I had to learn my craft on it. In those days, county clubs weren't supported by foot-ball pools and that kind of thing. They relied upon getting three days' cricket, and it was up to the groundsman to pre-pare a wicket that would last three days. Today, there is so much fiddling of wickets that a lot of good bowling perform-ances are fictitious. When they come to play on good test wickets, they haven't learned their craft. Before the war, there were better wickets for people to play cricket on. Since the war, counties have prepared wickets to suit their bowlers. The celebrated story on one ground during the 1950s was of a visiting captain who, on being asked which roller he would like, replied, 'I don't want a b***** roller: I need a s****** vacuum cleaner.'

Almost on a par with the professional's commitment to cricket was his loyalty to the county he played for. It was not just a question of maintaining standards on the field; appearances off the field were equally important.

When I played, we had a great pride in playing for the county, and we were very strict about not letting the side down, both on field and off it. Everybody had to be turned out perfectly on the field – and everybody had to come to breakfast dressed properly. The last year I was captain, some of our side came down to breakfast in casual clothes – I sent them back to put collars and ties on.

In the face of such loyalty, the merest mention of 'transferring' to another county was enough to send accusations of betrayal reverberating around the changing room. The traditional view was quite simple: 'If you contract to play for a county, you stay playing for it.' It was not a question of jealousy; transfers could only weaken and eventually destroy the individuality of the counties: 'If you call a side a county side, you have got to keep it a county side. It has a dampening effect on appeal if you don't – especially for the local people. The wealthiest clubs, those with the best football pools and the like, would get all the best players. It puts off the youngsters in your own county.'

It was not until the late 1950s that this more-or-less universal hostility to transfers began slowly to give way to a less dogmatic approach. Players began to question whether an unshakeable loyalty to their counties, often at the expense of their own careers, was justifiable, or really necessary. Provided that a system as extensive as that found in the Football League was not introduced, many came round to the view that a professional had a clear obligation to his own career, and that in the event of a clash of interests, his future must take precedence over considerations of loyalty.

I think players should be allowed to move. I don't agree with the transfer system, because some counties are a lot richer than others – Warwickshire, for instance – and can therefore buy just what they want. Other sides, like Essex, would go out of existence if this did take place. I don't see any reason why a chap who is fed up with one county, or whose career is blocked by a test player, shouldn't move to another one – but not transfer fees.

Thus far there has been little indication that the first post-war generation of professionals regretted having chosen cricket as a career. But when the subject of retirement is raised, a different picture begins to emerge. Universal acceptance of the virtues of a county cricketer's life gives way to a sharp division of opinion between those who believed that having been a cricketer enabled them to get a good job on retiring, and those who thought otherwise. In other words, for those professionals whose careers ended in the 1940s and 1950s, it was not the demands of the game but the problem of what came after that caused the most concern.

A professional's opinion of cricket as a career depended to a large extent on how successful he had been. The outstanding player understandably rated cricket very highly. He believed that providing a young professional 'had what it takes', there was nothing to stop him reaching the top. Or almost nothing. One famous player believes to this day that the only reason he never toured Australia was his inability to play bridge. The selectors, he has been heard to say, were looking for a good 'school' to help them while away the hours during the less exhilarating up-country matches. When it came to the subject of retirement, the most successful players were united in their praise for cricket's job-creating properties. If the lavishness of their tribute is any guide, the war and the profound social changes that followed in its wake had had little effect on this aspect of the cricketer's beliefs. Consider, for example, the following assessment:

> It is quite remarkable how well cricketers do when they retire. There are charities in existence designed to provide assistance for cricketers who find themselves in difficulties. Today, the number of applications for assistance has reached almost rock-bottom. I can't think of one successful cricketer who didn't get a good job when he retired – because of the sort of chap he is. Having met people, and perhaps travelled the world, his outlook is fairly broad, and he is a very employable person.

Very few of the great players of the past would quarrel with this judgement. After all, their experiences tend to confirm its accuracy. But it is interesting to note how many were much less enthusiastic about the prospects of their would-be successors today. In fact, there was a general reluctance to recommend a cricket career to persons who had no alternative source of income. As one retired professional explained, 'I'd advise a relative or friend of mine to learn a profession first – and then give cricket a go.'

Amongst the less successful of the immediate post-war professionals – the run-of-the-mill county cricketers – this lone *caveat* was transformed through sustained self-doubt into a comprehensive re-appraisal of the value of a cricket career. Because he had failed to live up to his own expectations, many of the sacrifices he had made as a young player now seemed unjustified. As the prospects of an England cap faded, so the famous 'love of the game' appeared to be more and more expensive. Yet, ironically, at the same time it became the only justification for continuing as a professional. If dedication functioned to minimize the burden of financial sacrifice, it also masked many of the less attractive features of the career. Even so, the disappointment suffered by the average county cricketer was often enough to make him doubt the wisdom of devoting twenty years of his life to cricket.

> Looking back, I don't know whether I would choose the same occupation. I loved cricket, and I still do, and it was something I wanted to do all the time. But when you get older, you look back and ask, 'Where has it got me?' If you could think that when you've finished with cricket, you were going to be financially secure, that would be O.K. But when you have got to start looking for another job, it is not so easy. You have a great life and meet some great people, but you have to think of security. Perhaps in another job, you mightn't have enjoyed life so much, but you would have been secure until retiring age.

But one of the most intriguing features of the retired professional's relationship with cricket was that he never lost complete faith in the game. Even the most disillusioned and embittered still clung on to the belief that, 'It must provide the odd opportunity which would not occur in other jobs, because even if you are just a county player, and don't reach test standards, you are in the public eye and you are known. This can open doors when otherwise you wouldn't have a chance.'

The inconsistency between these two statements is striking,

but not completely inexplicable. Until very recently, cricket's lasting appeal depended largely on the player's willingness to 'suspend disbelief'. The two factors which did most to encourage this approach were his apparently unquenchable 'love of the game' and the promise of a 'good job' on retirement. This combination surrounded the career with an aura of credibility which helped to sustain the player through those dark periods when success seemed an elusive quality. In a strange way, it also helped to maintain the career in its traditional form. By the time the average cricketer finally faced up to the fact that he was not going to win an England cap, he had become so thoroughly steeped in the traditional beliefs associated with the career that any grievances which he might have held against the game were expressed instead as criticisms of his own inadequacy. If he failed to play for England, it was either because he wasn't good enough or because he hadn't made the best use of the opportunities that had come his way. No blame was attached to the organization of the game or the career.

This reluctance to question many of the assumed virtues of a cricket career meant that most of the first generation of post-war players gave little thought to the subject of retirement. Like Mr Micawber, they were convinced that something would turn up. It was no accident that the most popular option, 'getting a business', was also one of the vaguest. The idea of trying to acquire an alternative set of skills, be they professional, commercial or craft, which would guarantee a reasonable income when age or injury terminated the cricket career, was notable only by its absence. The same disregard for the future manifested itself in the retired professional's attitude to winter jobs. These were looked upon solely as means of sustaining an acceptable standard of living; no-one seems to have thought of trying to turn them into permanent jobs. Typical of this short-sighted approach, and the regret which it gave rise to later, was the following comment: 'When I was playing I had various jobs in the winter – none really directed at providing some durable experience and prospects. Now I am coach here, I insist that the youngsters I see further their education. They learn from my mistakes.'

To conclude that most of the first generation of post-war cricketers spent the second half of their working lives ruing the day that they had decided to make a career out of first-class cricket is to misinterpret the tenor of their own observations. Retirement had rarely turned out to be as disturbing an experience as expected. Indeed, many found themselves to be financially better off in a different job. But it would be equally wrong to pretend that the intense anxiety and doubt to which all had succumbed at some stage of their careers had not left its mark. Very few retired professionals were prepared to recommend the cricket career unconditionally. Almost without exception, they felt that the young player today should try to ensure that he had something to fall back on before contracting to play for a county. One player spoke for everyone when he said that given the opportunity to relive his life, he would still play cricket, 'but I would make sure that I had learnt something other than being able to play cricket. When I was starting, no-one gave you this advice.'

The Established Cricketer

The bowler has a job to do; the batsman has a job to do; and somewhere down the line, we have to entertain the public.

The careers of the present generation of first-class cricketers started at a time when the immediate post-war boom in the game's popularity seemed a distant memory. The first decade of peace had seen a sport-starved population flocking into county grounds all over the country. Not yet distracted by an ever-increasing range of alternative leisure activities, nor lured away from the cities by 'areas of outstanding natural beauty' and yachting marinas, the cricket-loving public, measured in terms of the numbers who passed through the turnstiles, exceeded two million. Yet even this figure, miraculous though it may seem today, gives little idea of the symbolic importance of the game. When England regained the Ashes in 1953, and hence laid claim to the title of world champions, it was widely held to be the event which set the seal upon an *annus mirabilis* which had already witnessed a coronation, a British-led conquest of Everest, a first Derby victory for Gordon Richards and a Cup-winners medal for Stanley Matthews. Between 1953 and 1956 cricket enjoyed as great a prestige as it had at any time since the 'Golden Age' at the beginning of the century. A string of successful performances in test matches won a halo, and even a knighthood, for the most illustrious performers. To play for England was now the ultimate dream, treasured equally by youngsters on the playing fields of Eton and the local recreation ground.

Many knowledgeable figures were inclined to accept that at last cricket had triumphed over the incessant crises which seemed to have plagued its existence since the inauguration of the Championship. One of the most encouraging features of this revival – one which certainly recalled memories of the Golden Age – was the appearance almost simultaneously of a group of young amateurs – including Peter May, Colin Cowdrey, David Sheppard and Trevor Bailey – whose talents triggered off thoughts of Fry, Ranji, Jackson and MacLaren. For those who secretly (or publicly) yearned for a return to those palmy Edwardian days, what was so encouraging about this new generation – apart from their ability – was their public school and Varsity background. They re-invigorated the amateur tradition at a time when every indication pointed to its imminent demise, not least the fact that a professional now captained England.

This euphoria was short-lived. Prestige and glamour are not the only, or even the most reliable, indices of an institution's well-being. Though they succeeded in concealing from both players and supporters for nearly a decade the desperate financial straits into which cricket had sunk, the reprieve was only temporary. Many tried to deny the gravity of the situation by arguing that since county cricket had always been financially unstable, there was no reason to believe that this was more than a temporary hiccup. Excessive gloom based only on statistics was always unjustified since, as in the case of the national economy, the latter failed to take account of 'invisible' assets. In the context of county cricket, these came in the form of wealthy benefactors who were prepared to guarantee overdrafts. By the end of the 1950s, however, there were unmistakeable signs that cricket was sliding inexorably towards a state of bankruptcy. One was the continuous decline in attendances at county matches. Between 1949, when cricket's popularity was at its peak, and 1965 the total annual 'gate' at championship matches fell from 2,126,000 to less than 750,000. To the county clubs on whom the growing burden of insolvency weighed most heavily, the message contained in these figures was obvious. In order to survive, first-class cricket needed to be re-organized and its rationale reconsidered. It could no longer be treated as an élite pastime; economic viability depended on the game being redefined as part of the entertainments industry. The 1956 Political and Economic Planning report reached precisely the same conclusion: 'The first-class counties play six days a week and are thus definitely part of the business of public entertainment. If they relied on gate money as their sole source of income, however, few would escape bankruptcy.' (p. 14.)

The counties did not adjust to this new situation in the same way or at the same time. Some found the implications of re-organization too difficult or too unpleasant to grasp all at once. Others, because they were richer, could afford to put off the evil day when they too would have to face up to the prospect of insolvency. Though the majority had promoted fund-raising schemes like football pools for several years, it was not until 1963 that the decision to allow sponsorship was finally taken. By this act, the game's administrators finally conceded that cricket was no longer played for its own sake, nor for the good of its players, but for the entertainment of an audience.

By admitting the indispensability of an audience, cricket in effect became a service occupation. For the cricketer, this meant a new identity and new obligations to his public; he was now a paid entertainer, and the crowds that came to matches were his clients. The consequences of this transformation were profound. One of the distinctive features of working in a service occupation is that, 'the client is able to direct or attempt to direct the worker at his task and to apply sanctions of various kinds, ranging from informal pressures to the withdrawal of his patronage and the conferring of it on some other of the many people who perform the service'.[2]

Thus the introduction of sponsorship provided the spectator at a first-class match with every justification for exercising his critical faculties. This was particularly true of the one-day match which had been deliberately designed to entertain the public. If the spectator felt that he was not getting value for money, he was entitled to question the techniques or the temperaments of the players on view. Moreover, as a client, he had every right to expect that steps would be taken to improve the service he had paid for. In this unprecedented situation the cricketer found that his judgement was challenged by persons who were not as capable as he, nor as concerned to make a living out of the game. The one-day match 'brings together a person whose full-time activity is centred around the occupation and whose self is to some degree deeply involved in it and another person whose relation to it is much more casual, and it may be expected that the two should have varying pictures of the way the occupational service should be performed.'[3]

In adapting to this new role, the cricketer has been hampered by the tradition which he represents. Over a period of fifty years or more his predecessor, the professional, perfected a style of performance which was based essentially on the minimization of risk. To use a modern idiom, it was 'percentage' cricket. While this style helped the professional to achieve the consistency and reliability expected of him, it was rarely exciting and often difficult to appreciate. So long as the amateur survived, his presence guaranteed an element of eccentricity and excitement to complement the consistency of the professional. But as the Political and Economic Planning Report pointed out,

> Today amateurs are fast disappearing from the county sides as the numbers of young men who can afford to devote six days a week to cricket without pay is declining. Many clubs pay travelling expenses to amateurs, and in some cases, paid jobs as secretaries are found for the most proficient. Even so, many counties cannot find an amateur good enough to captain the side. (p. 18)

The demise of the amateur was a fatal blow to the traditional structure of first-class cricket because it destroyed the critical balance of styles from which so much of the game's appeal derived. It was left to the professional (or the contract player as he became known in 1962) to supply not only the consistency but also the excitement, flair and personal magnetism which a modern audience seeks.

Pushed into the limelight by circumstances over which he had no control, the player soon found himself faced with a double problem. He has had to come to terms not only with a new role but also with a new game. For this, sponsorship has been largely responsible. While the extra money that it has brought into the game has undoubtedly enhanced the appeal of the cricket career, at the same time it has created a situation in which the player finds the greatest difficulty in deciding what is required of him. His uncertainty stems at heart from the conflicting demands that are typically made of members of service occupations. Somehow, they have to try and reconcile their own ambitions with the more immediate requirements of their audiences. For the cricketer, this means deciding how far he can observe the traditional standards of his profession in the face of what are often the conflicting expectations of his public. In the words of one famous player, 'the bowler has a job to do, the batsman has a job to do, and somewhere down the line we have to entertain the public'.

Some idea of the stress generated by this dilemma can be gained from the growing number of players openly criticizing spectators and, more particularly, members of the Press for their ignorance and insensitivity. If there is any consolation to be offered to the cricketer, it is that he is not alone in this respect. At first sight, jazz musicians may not appear to have much in common with cricketers, but in fact there are several respects in which they can be compared. Many feel that the only music worth playing – what they call jazz – is produced without reference to the demands of outsiders. Yet, like cricketers, they are obliged to endure frequent interference with their playing from their audience.

> The most distressing problem in the career of the average musician is the necessity of choosing between his 'artistic' standards and their demands. In order to achieve success he finds it necessary to 'go commercial', that is, to play in accordance with the wishes of the non-musicians for whom he works: in doing so, he sacrifices the respect of other musicians and thus, in most cases, his self-respect.[4]

As far as the cricketer is concerned, the importance of spectators' interests is a new phenomenon. Before the Second World War it was rare to find spectators out of sympathy with the players. While the amateur bestrode the wicket, the working classes' traditional deference to the 'gentleman' guaranteed the inviolability of established standards, and so long as counties remained solvent and convinced of the value of his services, the professional enjoyed the unusual privilege of being able to define the standards by which his own performances were to be judged. Since these were inevitably based on an understanding of cricket normally confined to players themselves, it followed that the great majority of spectators were in no position to criticize. Since 1950 the gradual loss of this privileged status has left the cricketer in a position similar to that of the jazz musician. As the survival of first-class cricket comes to depend more and more on its popularity as a form of mass entertainment, he is forced into a position of subordination *vis-à-vis* his audience. Paradoxical though it may seem, the more the erstwhile spectator stays away from matches, the greater becomes the player's dependence on him. If the crowd is small, the entertainment must be unpopular. This dependence is the source of many of the modern player's difficulties. The skills which were once the hall-mark of his profession are no longer guaranteed to satisfy spectators. In short, the MCC Coaching Manual is not necessarily compatible with the demands of 'brighter cricket'. At this point the cricketer's artistic and technical integrity is called into question and, as Geoffrey Boycott discovered in 1967 when dropped from the England team after scoring 246 not out too slowly, there is now no answer to the charge of failing to entertain.

However, there is one vital respect in which the positions of the cricketer and the jazz musician differ. The cricketer cannot assume that a favourable audience reaction or a display of technical perfection will necessarily improve his career prospects. The organization of the County Championship and the various one-day 'cups' and 'leagues' precludes this. Unless an extraordinarily talented individual, his performances cannot determine the outcome of a match by itself. It is but one contribution out of eleven, and the decision as to how and when it should be made is taken not by the player, but by his captain. And the principle which the captain must follow in taking these decisions is not individual glory but team success. If a player, no matter how famous or talented, gains a reputation for being eccentric or a bad 'team-man', he is likely to find that his long-term prospects have been seriously damaged. Witness the case of John Snow, whose 'maverick' character was widely believed to be the reason for his omission from the England XI on more than one occasion.

Thus the modern player finds himself in an unenviable position. His immediate security depends on his playing as a member of a team in a way which may endear him to neither spectators nor reporters. But in the process he often has to compromise many of the standards which are the basis of his 'professional' identity, and to forgo the style of performance which gives him the greatest pleasure. In the face of these challenges to his integrity, the player's first reaction is generally to denounce the ignorance of 'outsiders', in the following case spectators and reporters.

Cricket has been criticized so much over the years that this must have done something to the public who would normally come to watch the game. Sportswriters, many of whom have never played the game at a very high level, which means that they don't appreciate what it means to face a ball coming down at 90 m.p.h., find it easy to sit down and say what you have done wrong. It is a different matter to go out there and do it. They don't get it over to the public that this is an art, that it is a battle between bat and ball, that the bowler isn't coming up specifically for the batsman to hit sixes. He is trying his hardest to get him out, and if he can't do this then he is going to try and stop him scoring runs. That is his job, that is what he is paid to do. If this was put over to the public in a better way, I think they would accept that the game is a hard game. The public loves to see fours and sixes – who doesn't? The batsman loves to hit fours and sixes. You do find occasions when he fails to take the initiative – I've done it myself. But I have also faced many bowlers on wickets which are helping them, who have continued to bowl to a defensive field. But there again, the people who write about the game should appreciate that on a bad wicket, they [the bowlers] cannot afford to turn in bad figures, and that the only way of avoiding this is to bowl to a tight field, and eventually you will probably get a wicket.

Irrespective of how much they would like to entertain their audiences, more often than not players feel bound to play in a 'professional' manner by the state of the contest and by the need to maintain the integrity of their own image. Since the majority no longer see themselves as playing a sport, it would be irrational for them to adopt any other approach. But this is not to say that rationality isn't often tinged with regret.

Let's face it, it is no longer a sport as it was known twenty years ago. Cricket has got to become the same as football has become, and many other sports like golf – a business. It is lovely to play with a 'don't care' attitude, but when you are paid, and my county pays me to score runs, whatever happens I will do my utmost to justify their faith in me. So you see that I could not go out on the field and not give 100 per cent – and I think there are very few players who could. I feel that it has become a job of work. The game has now become so technical that every strong part of every batsman is now blocked off immediately. Jack Robertson once made three hundred runs in a day – now I don't believe that batsmen of today are any worse than they were, in fact they are probably better equipped than they were then – but no batsman will score three hundred in a day now. (If anybody does, come back and see me and I'll buy you the best drink in the house.) Bowlers don't attack the wicket as they used. I have had days when they deliberately aimed a foot outside the off-stump, and going even further. They think of their figures, and say 'if you want runs, get them'.

Besides the general public and the other members of his team, the player also has an obligation to his own career. Few county cricketers today possess the sublime self-confidence needed to believe that their own success is necessarily in the best interests of their team, nor the naïvety to accept the reverse. Despite their unhesitating avowal of the principle of team loyalty, players are all too aware of the sacrifices that this might entail. At worst, it could cost them the chance of playing for England with all its attendant benefits. No player can afford to miss such an opportunity, yet short of deliberately disobeying orders there is very little he can do.

It is difficult, you know. You always feel there is a chance you might miss the boat by playing to orders. If the selectors are there, and you get out chasing a few quick runs, or bowl wide to stop the others getting them, they aren't going to be very impressed. It is like that these days – almost every time you go in, it is either a crisis and you have got to dig in, or a declaration's near and the skipper needs a few quick runs. You need a lot of luck – being in the right place, doing the right thing at the right time.

Being a first-class cricketer these days necessarily involves a degree of masochism. In addition to all the uncertainties of the early years, the player has to face up to the fact that the winning of his county cap (traditionally the sign that he has made the grade as a cricketer) is as much the beginning as the end of his difficulties: spectators have to be entertained; his team has to win; he has to make a success of his own career. As far as the present generation of players is concerned, the mark of a great cricketer is his ability to reconcile these potentially conflicting demands. The events surrounding the recent dismissal of Tony Greig from the England captaincy provide a graphic illustration of how intractable a problem this can be.

In the course of searching for this magic formula, players gradually acquire a distinctive set of attitudes to their job and their colleagues. The key to these lies in the cricketer's celebrated love of the game. It is his life, and despite the anxiety and stress that it often causes, not even a win on the football pools would persuade him to retire early. 'Yes, I'd go on playing the game. I'm a bit of a masochist at heart. You put thirty overs down in a day and come off shattered, but you have got that inner glow of a job well done.'

What is it about cricket that inspires such extraordinary dedication and devotion? Part of the answer lies in the companionship, sometimes amounting to an almost mystical communion, that the game provides. To help understand this, it is useful to return to the comparison with the jazz musician. The latter's standard reaction to the challenge of 'squares' (outsiders) involves segregating himself from his audience and, in some cases, the rest of the community in which he lives. In this way he is able to retain his artistic and personal integrity. Unlike the jazz musician, the cricketer cannot resolve the conflicting demands made of him by withdrawing into an isolated, protected world, populated only by persons subjected to the same pressures. Cricket exists only as a business or a game. It has no underworld capable of providing emotional and even financial support for the individual who refuses to compromise his standards.

Moreover, it is based on competition and rivalry. For one player to succeed, another must fail. Faced by the twin challenge of opponents and spectators, the cricketer looks to the other members of his team for sympathy, understanding and encouragement. Since they are equally as conscious of the closeness of failure, he is unlikely to be disappointed.

> The great thing about cricket, especially about batting, is that failure is at your right elbow. There is no shadow of doubt about that. You can have a bad day at the office, but you can still make a come-back at 4.50 pm and do something right. But cricket is so final – if you get a good ball early, or you are in bad form and get out to a bad shot, you are irretrievably lost. You sit down and watch everybody else for the rest of the day. That is not only frustrating, but it is very hard to get going again. It is a great worry – you take it home with you which is bad for the family. This is why cricketers have this tremendous feeling of togetherness. They create it themselves because it is the only thing which can give them security. You feel part of a team, and you almost forbid anybody else to come in. It works that way only because you feel so unsafe.

The Young Cricketer

> I like to make money out of the game, otherwise I feel I am not so much marking time as wasting time.

The prospect of first-class cricket which greeted the young player in the early 1970s was, to put it mildly, uninspiring. Most of the counties were near to bankruptcy; few, if any, prospered. Newspaper columnists hovered over the the game like vultures anticipating death, occasionally dropping a wounding article to hasten the process. In reviewing the state of county cricket in 1971, one journalist, himself an ex-county cricketer, summed up the situation in a few bleak sentences: 'Half a dozen bank managers could kill county cricket tomorrow morning. The figures are well enough known. The seventeen first-class counties made a loss of £175,000 last year. Only two, Worcestershire and Leicestershire made a profit, and that was counted in hundreds, not thousands.'[5] Later in the same article, he revealed some of the major points to emerge from a survey of county clubs' finances.

> Six counties – Derbyshire, Gloucestershire, Hampshire, Middlesex, Nottinghamshire and Somerset – will collapse unless something quite unforeseen occurs.... Income from membership, traditionally between a third and a half of revenues, is declining against the rising trend of costs. The average daily attendance at championship matches last year was 581 and that includes a near 30,000 crowd for the Saturday of the second Roses match. Supporters' clubs, cricket's props in the fifties and sixties, are declining. They depend on membership enthusiasm for sales and last year's revenue dropped by £46,000 to £92,000.[6]

No doubt, the accuracy of some of these statements could be questioned. Surveys, after all, have been known to err. But the exact financial position of the counties is not the point at issue here. Few prospective employees feel obliged to precede their application with a detailed analysis of their potential employer's financial credibility, yet for the budding cricketer in the early 1970s, such a precaution would have been more than justified. Even a cursory check would have revealed how close county cricket was to disaster. The headlines of an *Evening Standard* article which compared the average annual earnings of British sportsmen proclaimed, 'Don't play cricket ... if you want to turn your sport prowess into cash.'[7] The final paragraph of the same article reads ominously like a valedictory address for cricket: 'Today a schoolboy's dream is of scoring a soccer hat-trick at Wembley. Few dream of playing at Lord's or the Oval. The wealth and the glamour of the modern footballer – indeed a jockey, golfer, and a tennis player too – makes cricket the poor relation in British professional sport.' The facts contained in such articles may be suspect, the arguments frequently illogical, but they all came to the same conclusion – that a cricket career these days is not nearly such a desirable prospect as it had been before 1950.

The same message is hammered home in several career guidance publications. The Central Youth Employment

Executive's booklet, *Professional Sport*, included the following assessment:

> Although the county cricketer has seen a financial improvement in the post-war years, he is still not highly paid when compared to professionals in some other sports. There are a few exceptions, mainly well-known and well-established players, whose reputations as cricketers have gained them financial rewards above the average. (p. 18.)

As if this wasn't sufficiently damning, the author then proceeds to describe the difficulties that the young player faces when he joins a county club. The final advice does not enhance the attractiveness of the occupation:

> It is important to note that only a few of the hundreds of boys given trials by their counties show enough promise to be offered an engagement and the proportion of failures amongst those engaged is high.
> For the first few seasons, the young player gains experience in club and 2nd XI cricket ... if at any time his performance fails to maintain its early promise he could be well advised to seek another career. He would be wise to do so, in any case, if he has not secured a regular place in the county side by the age of twenty-five, as the successful player usually achieves this in his early twenties. (p. 19)

A recent report, prepared by the Industrial and Professional Careers Research Organization Ltd (1971), offered not only the same graphically unfavourable comparisons with the golfer, the tennis player and the footballer, but also ventured the conclusion that the cricket career could only regain its former appeal if the entire structure of the game were reorganized.

> Unlike the other three sports [golf, tennis and football], cricket must be classed as a declining occupation. Around 200 English-born professionals play for 17 counties, earning low wages, playing before largely empty stands, and taking second jobs in the winter to make ends meet ...
> Assuming fair progress, the average county player now earns £1,500 for a six-month season. Even Test match players seldom earn more than £2,500 in a season and one or two international performers find it possible to earn more from broad-

casting and other ancillary activities than from actually playing.

Playing professional cricket, therefore, puts a higher premium than most other sporting careers on love of the game and a certain disinterest in material rewards. In the 1970s it is hardly surprising that fewer and fewer schoolboys seem attracted by a career in cricket, coupled as it is with a disjointed family life, seven days a week commitment during the summer, uncertain future and fading glamour.

For those still enraptured by the most English of all sports, perhaps it is best at this time to concentrate on another full-time career and hope that before long the cricket administrators decide to copy Australian practice, cut the amount of first-class cricket and depend on part-time professionals paid only on a match-fee basis.

If these reports are taken literally, the attractions of a cricket career have dwindled to the point at which it is surprising that anybody seriously considers taking up the game. Yet they do – not perhaps in the same numbers as before, but enough, nonetheless to satisfy the immediate requirements of county cricket. Within the last two or three years in fact, a new optimism has been evident amongst cricket's senior administrators. As far as recruitment is concerned, many are now daring to suggest, albeit in whispered monosyllables, that the worst may be over. The feeling seems to be that the game is regaining much of its old appeal amongst the 'better educated' young men. How much this may be a consequence of the present high rates of unemployment amongst school-leavers, it is too early to say. But at least there is now some encouragement for those who want to believe that the age of miracles is not dead.

Leaving aside for a moment the question of numbers, there is no doubt that the present generation of 'young hopefuls' have a very different outlook on the game from their predecessors. The spate of adverse commentary directed at cricket over the past decade has left its mark in the form of a more pragmatic, less enraptured approach to the prospect of a cricket career. Young players today still love the game, but they are also aware of what it might cost them. The career's break-even point is now calculated to a number of decimal points. The word 'mercenary' was recently used to describe a particular group of cricketers who, it was felt, had put their own well-being before that of the game. In fact, all cricketers these days are to some extent mercenaries. They have to be. In business, the opposite of the mercenary tends to be the lame duck.

Today, the young cricketer is advised of the dangers of the career at the same time as, or even before, he is offered a contract. The secretaries of the county clubs make a point of stressing all the risks involved, and even go so far as to suggest that he should try to further his education before coming into the game, or at least during his early years with the club. Thus, instead of trying to instil in the young cricketer a sense of loyalty and commitment, authorities nowadays go out of their way to make sure that he appreciates all the pitfalls that lie between him and an England cap. 'When we have a promising young boy come down to the county ground, we always suggest to him and to his father the precarious nature of county cricket. If the boy can take an apprenticeship or go to university before he tries his hand at cricket, he would be well advised to do so.'

How many of the new recruits take any notice of the advice they are given is another matter. Only comparatively few seem to be able to combine work and study for any length of time. It is not that the rest doubt the value of paper qualifications, but that they find it impossible to devote enough time to studying for them. It is a question of, 'I was going to, but it has been a bit difficult what with cricket and having to find a winter job as well', or, 'I play a lot of football which takes up three nights a week and what with being married as well, it doesn't leave much time for anything else.'

Thus, the latest generation of young players is confronted at a much earlier stage than their predecessors with one of the great drawbacks to a cricket career. They are warned that the mere fact of having been a first-class cricketer no longer carries with it the guarantee of being snapped up by eager employers as soon as the proverbial boots – or whatever – are hung up. More than likely, they will find it very difficult to get another job which measures up to their expectations. Today, a cricket career is a gamble and there is no disguising the fact. Earnings may be higher, but so are the consequences of failure.

The young cricketer's approach to the game is consistent with a realization of the risks he is taking. Far more than either the retired or the established player, he looks upon cricket as a means to an end rather than an end in itself. Although in taking the initial decision to join a county he is strongly influenced by his love of the game, once under contract cricket is treated essentially as a job of work and a source of money. When asked why he adopts this approach, the young player provides a disarmingly simple answer: 'I have to, because I know that I have to do well in order to stay in the side, and to be successful for myself. You also have to think about the win-bonus and appearance money – you must do, it is your bread-and-butter.'

This concern with earnings is inextricably linked with the young player's conception of success. The intrinsic satisfactions to be gained from playing cricket come nowhere near to justifying his choice of career. Neither does he find it easy to accept the argument that cricketers have to make do with low wages because the counties can't afford to pay any more. The young cricketer's eyes are set firmly on test cricket, not just because of the honour and glamour that goes with it, but also because a test cricketer earns most money and has the greatest opportunity to make potentially useful contacts.

With his ambitions firmly established, the young player subjects himself to a process of self-evaluation more rigorous than anything his predecessors ever inflicted on themselves. The following assessment is a superb example of the levels of introspection that are often involved.

At the stage I'm at, I should say that this is the season that will make or break me. I have had, so far, one very good season in the 1st XI, and one disastrous one. The first one probably kept me on the staff, because potentially I have still got it – having already done it once. All the senior players you talk to say that in the first year in the game you do a bit better than you are really capable of at this stage because nobody knows how you play and how you get your runs. By the second year, they will have sorted you out and, in fact, you will find it very difficult. You won't get the type of bowling you play best. In the third season, you tend to hit a happy medium and develop whatever ability you have got. So this season should decide it for me, one way or the other. If the county signs a lot of new players in the winter and I don't get in the team, I don't think I'll be sacked – I'll have a chance to see whether I can get back in first.

But a regular place in the county team is only one step on the road to test cricket. It is never an end in itself. In fact, the young player makes it quite clear that he has no time for the idea of a career in county cricket alone. '[I want] to get into the side regularly and then to do well enough to play for England. Without these ambitions I would be wasting my time as an ordinary county cricketer – there is not enough in it financially. I like to make money out of the game, otherwise I feel I am not so much marking time as wasting time.'

Perhaps the most extreme manifestation of the budding cricketer's dedication to his own future is his willingness to accept the relatively short-term contracts offered by counties. At first sight, this smacks of masochism, but in fact it is strictly consistent with his determination to succeed. Again, his argument is simple and direct: 'The less time I have to prove myself, the less the temptation to relax and the sooner I can leave the game if I am not going to make it.'

At this point, sociologists might be tempted to argue that the latest generation of cricketers are in danger of becoming alienated from their work. Be that as it may, there is no doubt that the pressures on the cricketer these days are sufficient to deprive the game of most of its intrinsic satisfaction. Only a privileged few remain impervious to these pressures, or at least manage to appear so. By common consent, theirs is the ideal situation, for the fewer the pressures on a player, the greater is the likelihood that he will make full use of his ability, and thereby derive most pleasure from the game. Naturally enough, the majority of young cricketers believe that they would be better players if they weren't dependent on the game for a living.

It is very difficult to explain but, like anything else, if your living depends on something, you'll be cautious and probably try too hard at one particular aspect of it. Older players tell me that Bob Barber was the best example of this. Although he was always reasonably secure, cricket was something he became very engrossed with, and so he did not look a particularly good player – in fact, he was a very stodgy, head-down batsman. Then he changed clubs, went into business – cricket became his second love – and he played virtually a shot a ball and played for England.

Reactions to latter-day amateurs like Barber are strangely ambivalent. On the one hand, the young player tends to resent the presence of players who are in the happy position of being able to choose the matches they are going to play in, and so avoid what becomes the drudgery of playing cricket seven days a week. 'Although we are all supposed to be "cricketers" now, you still find the amateur-professional distinction. The amateur can always take a break when he is getting stale, but the "pro" can't – unless he wants to be dropped.' On the other hand, he knows only too well that, given the chance, he would probably act in exactly the same way. The prospect of escaping the burden of responsibility would prove too great an attraction. This mixture of resentment and admiration creates a further source of tension to add to the burdens already weighing on the young cricketer.

I don't regret playing cricket, but at the same time I wish I could have been in a position where I had the kind of job which let me look at cricket as real relaxation – someone like Ted Dexter. I don't particularly admire him for leaving cricket at his peak. I thought he got a tremendous amount out of the game and he ought to have put something back in it. But I admire someone who has got the brains and money to do something outside cricket, and play purely and simply for relaxation. If you do badly, then it is not going to get you down; you are naturally disappointed, but you don't worry about it. But you do if you are playing cricket and depend solely on it.

Among retired and established players, the most revealing indication of the stresses and strains present in first-class cricket was their reluctance to recommend the career to anyone else, except as a last resort. The fact that the young players of today are just as reluctant, even though they have been in the game for no more than five years, suggests that the pressures involved now are even more severe. When he was asked whether he would recommend a career in cricket to a friend or relative of his, one young player replied, 'I would say no, if they have got brains. If they had done well at school I would tell them to do something else – to get something else behind them. Because I didn't have much of a brain at school, I had to take what I could do best.'

Paradoxically, the young cricketer's concern for others is not matched by a similar concern for his own future. Despite being bombarded with warnings and advice, he seems incapable of coming to terms with the dangers of retirement. Up to a point, this can be put down to his youth and the fact that retirement seems a long way off. But thereafter, the only explanation seems to be that this is, and always has been, a genuine blind-spot for cricketers. Very often, all that stands between the young player and retirement is a blind faith in the job-creating properties of cricket. Witness the comment, 'All players who make the grade find themselves fairly comfortable after their playing days. If I make the top-grade at cricket, I think the job which I would like to do will come my way quite easily.'

It is almost as though the emotional content of cricket makes rational thought impossible. But not completely so. For if he is pushed to explain this cavalier disregard for his own future, the young player produces his trump card – an assertion of the uniqueness of the cricketer's life which puts him totally beyond the range of such mundane considerations as career guidance. 'I don't think of the end – I try to think of now. You can't afford to think of finishing until you get to the top, and if you think too much about it, you won't reach the top. When you are there, then you can think, "Who shall I chat up for a good job now?"'

12 The Beginning or the End?

During the 1977 season the question of cricket's future, and of the future it offers to players, has been highlighted by the activities of Kerry Packer, the Australian television magnate. By offering over fifty of the world's best players five times what they could be certain of earning elsewhere, Packer has mounted a strong challenge to the existing structure of competition between the cricketing nations, and, by implication, to the sovereignty of the International Cricket Conference and the various national governing bodies. The rights and wrongs of the proposed 'circus' do not concern us here. Of far greater relevance is the impact that Packer's activities have had, and will have, on the present generation of first-class cricketers. In a recent article in *The Times* (15 August 1977), David Lloyd, then captain of Lancashire, made the following observation on cricketer's earnings: 'Whichever way you look at it, the players are very badly underpaid. In the old days, in Eddie Paynter's time, it used to be said that cricket was better than working down the pit. Now you would be far better off financially staying down the mine.'

Today, first-class cricket is big business: its players are paid entertainers. As Lloyd's remarks indicate, there is now a feeling amongst players that their earnings should be related more closely to the value, measured in gate receipts, TV contracts and advertising revenue, of the service they provide. Not only do the majority believe that they are badly paid in comparison with other professional sportsmen, but, more important, they also feel that players in general are not receiving their fair share of cricket's new-found riches. The former England captain,

Tony Greig, was evidently well aware of this growing dissatis-
faction when he sought to justify the Packer 'circus' on the
grounds that it would lead to an improvement in the average
first-class cricketer's lot.

In one sense, Greig was probably right. From the player's
point of view, Mr Packer's intervention could not have come
at a better time. In the first place, his activities have presented
and publicised their own case for higher earnings. Previous
generations of cricketers, and other species of sportsmen, were
not so lucky. In 1846 the professionals' leader, William Clarke,
had to form his own team, the All-England XI, and arrange
his own matches to break the 'establishment's' stranglehold on
the organization of the game, and to capitalize on its growing
profit potential. In 1962 George Eastham had to have recourse
to the law to remove the maximum earnings rule which hitherto
had drastically restricted the professional footballer's capacity
to negotiate his own earnings.

Secondly, Mr Packer's initiative in organizing his 'circus' has
alerted others to the commercial potential of cricket. Irrespective of the success or failure of the 'circus', first-class cricketers
in England have already benefited by £10,000 a year from the
introduction of an incentive scheme sponsored by Bonus-plan
Ltd in association with the Cricketers Association. In addition
the Cornhill Insurance Company has agreed to invest £200,000
in the game in 1978 in return for having some international
matches called the Cornhill Tests. Thus, instead of finding
themselves in another monopsony situation, cricketers now
have the chance – through shrewd manipulation and hard bargaining – to reap the benefit of competition between potential
sponsors. As a recent article in the *Economist* (6 August 1977)
put it, 'What the cricketing authorities should want is lots of
competing Packers, running various tournaments all over the
world.'

Despite the enormous promise of the present situation,
cricket's ruling bodies, and the players themselves, would do
well to remember Thomas Gray's advice to a favourite cat:

> Not all that tempts your wand'ring eyes
> And heedless heart is lawful prize,
> Nor all that glisters, gold.

Like another current bonanza, North Sea oil, the blessings of commercial sponsorship are not limitless. Cricket's popularity, and hence its prosperity, depend to a large extent on the continuation of international competition. Test matches and test cricketers remain the major spectator attraction despite the current popularity of one-day cups and league matches. If the Packer circus undermines the appeal of test matches, ultimately it may become the cause of its own downfall. Mr Packer, other potential sponsors and the players themselves would be well advised to reflect on the fate of a previous players' circus – the professional XIs of the mid-nineteenth century. On that occasion it was the overwhelming superiority of the All-England XIs and United XIs of England, coupled with their lack of local, regional or national identity, that eventually cost them the support of the general public. Will the position of an Australian XI, divorced from the rest of Australian cricket, and a Rest of the World XI be so very different?

In defending the idea of 'super tests', supporters of the principle of an international circus often point to the success that international tennis has enjoyed since the advent of large-scale, commercial sponsorship. Up to a point, this comparison is appropriate. The present generation of tennis stars – Connors, Borg, Vilas and the like – are amongst the most highly paid sportsmen in the world. Whether, however, an equally large injection of sponsorship into cricket would enable the leading players to achieve a similar degree of *lasting* prosperity is another question.

There is little doubt that the introduction of 'team tennis' and the international, 'grand prix' circuit has led to the decline of the Davis Cup, the premier team competition in international tennis. But tennis is basically an individual's game. Its popularity is based on the rivalry between individuals, and that will survive regardless of the fate of the Davis Cup. Cricket, on the other hand, is a team game. The great stars – Richards, Chappell, Proctor, Boycott and the like – made their names not as free-lance players, but as representatives of provincial and national teams. Once established as stars, their identities serve to sharpen and focus the rivalries between the teams they represent. In other words, they are not just test players, but West Indian, Australian and English test players. The complex balance between ability and representative identity lies at the heart of cricket's popularity as a spectator sport. If sponsors, intentionally or otherwise, disturb this balance by diluting the representativeness of test matches, they run the risk of losing the mass following that makes cricket such an attractive commercial proposition.

Notes

1 Myths and Mysteries

1 N. Cardus, *English Cricket* (1945), p. 9.
2 'The Cricket Industry', *Political and Economic Planning*, Vol. XXII, No. 401 (1956), p. 3.
3. A. Haygarth, *Cricket Scores and Biographies* (1862), p. xiii.
4 H. Squire, *Henfield Cricket and its Sussex Cradle* (1949), p. 22.
5 H.P-T, 'Cricket's Cradle', *Old English Cricket* (1922–9), p. 13.
6 Rowland Bowen, *Cricket: A History of its Growth and Development throughout the World* (1970), pp. 28–9.

2 Cricket: the Folk-Game

1 Philip Stubbes, *The Anatomie of Abuses* (2nd edition, 1583), quoted in J. Dover Wilson, *Life in Shakespeare's England* (2nd edition, 1913), pp. 18–19.
2 The following analysis of folk-games draws heavily on the work of Eric Dunning and Norbert Elias. See, for example, 'Folk Football in Medieval and Early Modern Britain' in Dunning, *The Sociology of Sport* (1971), pp. 116–32.
3 Quoted in H. S. Altham, *A History of Cricket: From the Beginnings to the First World War* (5th edition, 1962), p. 20.
4 L. Humphrey, *Of Nobilitye* (1563), p. 57.

5 J. C. Jeafferson (ed.), *Middlesex County Records* (1886–7), quoted in Dunning, *Sociology of Sport*, pp. 118–19.
6 Quoted in W. Haller, *The Rise of Puritans* (1938), p. 59.
7 Richard Baxter, *A Christian Directory* (1678), quoted in Dennis Brailsford, *Sport and Society; Elizabeth to Anne* (1969), p. 147.
8 *Sussex Record Society* Vol. XLIX (1947–8), p. 27.

3 The Adoption of Cricket

1 J. Thirsk, 'The Sale of Royalist Lands during the Interregnum', *Economic History Review*, 2nd series, No. 2 (1952), p. 206.
2 J. Thirsk, 'The Restoration Land Settlement', *Journal of Modern History*, Vol. XXVI, No. 4 (1954), p. 327.
3 Dorothy Marshall, *The English Domestic Servant in History*, Historical Association, No G. 13 (1949), p. 9.
4 M. Misson, *Memoirs and Observations in his travels over England*; trans. (1711), p. 142.

4 'Gamesters, Jockeys and Cricket Players'

1 Quoted in J. Marshall, *The Duke Who Was Cricket* (1961), p. 40.
2 J. R. Sutherland, 'The Circulation of Newspapers and Literary Periodicals, 1700–1730', *Library* Ser. 4, Vol. XV (1934), pp. 110–24.
3 Quoted in Lord Harris, *The History of Kent County Cricket* (1907), p. 15.
4 W. Marshall, *On the Landed Property of England* (1804), p. 1.
5 J. Boswell, *London Journal, 1762–1763* (Yale Edition, 1950), p. 320.

6   H. J. Habakkuk, 'English Landownership', *Economic History Review*, Vol. X, No. 1 (1940), pp. 1–17.
7   G. M. Trevelyan, *English Social History* (1946), p. 404.
8   E. G. Bulwer-Lytton, *England and the English* (1883), p. 30.
9   Quoted in Sir Pelham Warner, *Lord's, 1787–1945* (1946), p. 21.
10 E. B. Perkins, *Gambling in English Life* (1950), p. 11.
11 'In Certamen Pilae', translation by H. A. Perry (1922), quoted in R. S. Rait-Kerr, *The Laws of Cricket* (1950), pp. 4–8.
12 Rait-Kerr, *Laws of Cricket*, p. 22.
13 Ibid., p. 23.
14 Ibid., p. 19.

5 The Organization of Eighteenth-Century Cricket

1   Quoted in Harris, *Kent County Cricket*, p. 28.
2   Ibid., p. 29.
3   Ibid., p. 80.
4   H. P-T, *Old English Cricket*, p. 54.
5   G. B. Buckley, *Fresh Light on Pre-Victorian Cricket* (1937), p. 39.
6   Ibid., p. 40.
7   H. T. Waghorn, *The Dawn of Cricket* (1906), p. 20.
8   Gregory King, *Scheme of the Income and Expense of the several families of England* (1699); in Charles Davenant, *Works*, p. 89.
9   D. Defoe, *The Complete English Tradesman* (1726), p. 376.
10 Quoted in P. Laslett, *The World We Have Lost* (1965), p. 41.
11 Waghorn, *The Dawn of Cricket*, p. 9.
12 Ibid., p. 10.
13 Harris, *Kent County Cricket*, p. 12.
14 J. Marshall, *Sussex Cricket: A History* (1959), p. 42.
15 F. S. Ashley-Cooper, *The Hambledon Cricket Chronicle* (1924), pp. 143–76.

16 John Nyren, *The Young Cricketer's Tutor*, ed. F. S. Ashley-Cooper (1902), p. 71.

17 John Nyren, *The Cricketers of My Time* (1833), quoted in J. Arlott, *From Hambledon to Lord's* (1948), pp. 26–7.

18 Harris, *Kent County Cricket*, p. 13.

19 James Love, *Cricket: An Heroic Poem* (1744), Book III (1.9–20).

20 Nyren, *Cricketers of My Time*, p. 18.

21 Ibid., p. 32.

22 Ibid., p. 24.

6 The Early Years of the Marylebone Cricket Club

1 Warner, *Lord's, 1787–1945*, p. 25.

2 Anon, *The Devil and the Peers, or a Princely Way of Sabbath Breaking* (1712), p. 5.

3 Quoted in Altham, *A History of Cricket*, p. 37.

4 Harris, *Kent County Cricket*, p. 23.

5 Revd J. Pycroft, *The Cricket Field* (1922 edition), p. 34.

6 Altham, *A History of Cricket*, pp. 58–9.

7 Revd J. Pycroft, *The Cricket Field*, p. 134.

8 Quoted in Altham, *A History of Cricket*, p. 71.

7 The Second Transformation

1 Mary Russell Mitford, *Our Village Sketches of Rural Character and Scenery* (1879), p. 171.

2 T. B. Bottomore, *Early Writings of Karl Marx* (1964), p. 172.

3 T. Carlyle, *Chartism* (1889), Ch. vi.

4 A phrase used by H. A. Perkin in his *The Origin of Modern English Society* (1969).

5   'The Warder, No. VII', *Blackwood's* (1820) Vol. VII, pp. 93–4.

6   J. Schumpeter, *Capitalism, Socialism and Democracy* (1947), pp. 136–7.

7   S. T. Coleridge, *On The Constitution of Church and State* (1838), p. 27.

8   F. M. L. Thompson, *English Landed Society in the Nineteenth Century* (1963), p. 20.

9   W. L. Burn, *The Age of Equipoise* (1964), p. 264.

10   *Report and Evidence of the Royal Commission on the Public Schools* (1864), quoted in W. L. Guttsman, *The English Ruling Class* (1969), p. 201.

11   Thomas Hughes, *Tom Brown's Schooldays* (1958), pp. 301–302.

12   Anon, 'Cricket at Lord's', *Belgravia* (September 1871), p. 219.

13   F. S. Ashley-Cooper, *Nottinghamshire Cricket and Cricketers* (1923), p. 20.

14   Ibid., p. 29.

15   *Bell's Life*, Saturday, 8 May 1875.

16   Anon, 'Cricket at Lord's', p. 216.

17   'Lord's and the Players', *Temple Bar* (Nov. 1862), p. 272.

18   Revd J. Pycroft, *Oxford Memories*, quoted in Arlott, *The Middle Ages of Cricket* (1949), p. 122.

19   Rait-Kerr, *Laws of Cricket*, p. 62.

20   Arlott, *Middle Ages of Cricket*, p. 122.

21   Rait-Kerr, *Laws of Cricket*, p. 65.

22   A. V. Pullin, *Talks with Old English Cricketers* (1900), p. 10.

23   F. Gale, *Echoes from Old Cricket Fields* (1871), p. 59.

8 William Clarke and the Professional XIs, 1846–70

1   Revd J. Pycroft, *Cricketana* (1862), p. 139.

2   Pycroft, *The Cricket Field*, p. 20.

3   R. Daft, *Kings of Cricket* (1893), p. 76.

4   Ibid., p. 77.

5　A. V. Pullin, *Talks with Old Yorkshire Cricketers* (1898), p. 8.

6　Ashley-Cooper, *Nottinghamshire Cricket*, p. 64.

7　Pullin, *Old English Cricketers*, p. 35.

8　W. Denison, *Sketches of the Players*, quoted in Arlott, *The Middle Ages of Cricket*, p. 60.

9　Albert Shaw, *Reminiscenses of a Cricket Career* (1902), p. 10.

10　J. F. Sutton, *Nottingham Cricket Matches* (1853), p. XV.

11　Pullin, *Old English Cricketers*, p. 89.

12　Ibid., p. 28.

13　Ibid., p. 61.

14　Altham, *A History of Cricket*, pp. 121–2.

15　W. G. Grace, *Cricket* (1891), p. 128.

16　Rait-Kerr, *Laws of Cricket*, p. 38.

17　Altham, *A History of Cricket*, p. 129.

18　H. Silver, 'Our Critic upon Cricket', *Once a Week* (June 1861), p. 665.

19　Anon. 'The Siege of The wicket', *Once A Week* (August 1867), p. 225.

20　Silver, 'Our Critic upon Cricket', p. 666–7.

21　Pullin, *Old English Cricketers*, p. 153.

22　Daft, *Kings of Cricket*, p. 167.

9 The County Championship, 1873–94

1　Viscount Alverstone and C. W. Alcock, *Surrey Cricket: Its History and Associations* (1902), p. 97.

2　Revd R. S. Holmes, *The County Cricket Championship* (1894), p. 32.

3　Ibid., p. 33.

4　A. D. Taylor, *Annals of Lord's and the History of the M.C.C.* (1903), p. 103.

5　Rowland Bowen, 'The Early County Championship', *Wisden* (1959), p. 92.

6　Ibid., p. 93.

7　Holmes, *The County Cricket Championship*, p. 32.

8　Alverstone and Alcock, *Surrey Cricket*, p. 104.

9   Prince Ranjitsinhji, *The Jubilee Book of Cricket* (1897), p. 213.

10 Altham, *History of Cricket*, pp. 123–4.

11 W. Bagehot, *The English Constitution* (1958), p. 235.

12 E. J. Hobsbawm, *Industry and Empire* (1967), p. 170.

13 Perkin, *Origins of Modern English Society*, p. 431.

14 Hobsbawm, *Industry and Empire*, p. 137.

15 Warner, *Lord's, 1787–1945*, p. 69.

16 *Bell's Life*, Saturday, 8 May 1875.

17 Warner, *Lord's*, p. 71.

18 R. E. Pumphrey, 'The Introduction of Industrialists into the British Peerage', *American History Review*, LXV, No. 1 (October 1959), pp. 1–16.

19 Anon, 'Chaos in Cricket', *Belgravia* (August 1890), p. 104.

20 Holmes, *The County Cricket Championship*, p. 67.

10 Amateurs and Professionals, 1873–1962

1   Prince Ranjitsinhji, 'Cricket and the Victorian Era', *Blackwood's Edinburgh Magazine* (July 1897), pp. 15–16.

2   Hon. R. Grimston in *Fifty Years of Sport at Oxford, Cambridge and the Great Public Schools* (1913), p. 113.

3   Sir Henry Newbolt, 'Vitae Lampada', *Selected Poems* (1940), p. 87.

4   Home Gordon, 'First Class Cricket', *National Review* (1906), p. 659.

5   Revd Thomas Waugh, *The Cricket Field of the Christian Life* (1894), p. 148.

6   Home Gordon, 'First Class Cricket', p. 660.

7   Anon, 'Cricket', *The World's Work* (1902), p. 216.

8   Mr C. E. Green, in W. A. Bettesworth, *Chats on the Cricket Field* (1910), p. 183.

9   H. G. Hutchinson, 'The Parlous Condition of Cricket', *National Review* (1900), p. 32.

10 Ibid., p. 42.

11 Ibid., p. 47.

12 Anon, 'Professional Cricket, *Saturday Review* (14 July 1883), p. 83.

13 Rowland Bowen, *Cricket: A History of Its Growth*, p. 117.
14 Mr C. K. Francis, in Bettesworth, p. 207.
15 A. Waugh, 'Lord's and Its Literature', *London Mercury* (1922), p. 78.
16 Ranjitsinhji, 'Cricket and the Victorian Era', p. 9.
17 Ibid., p. 16.
18 Ibid., p. 10.
19 Lord Harris, 'The Development of Cricket', *National Review* (1883), p. 172.
20 P. C. Standing, *The Hon. F. S. Jackson* (1906), p. x.
21 Ranjitsinhji, 'Cricket and the Victorian Era', p. 10.
22 J. B. Hobbs, *My Life Story* (1935), p. 32.
23 F. Root, *The Cricket Pro's Lot* (1937), pp. 43–4.
24 Ibid., p. 45.
25 Ranjitsinhji, 'Cricket and the Victorian Era', p. 10.
26 Hobbs, *My Life Story*, p. 47.
27 Ibid., p. 47
28 Root, *The Cricket Pro's Lot*, p. 50.
29 H. E. Dollery, *Professional Captain* (1952), pp. 161–2.

11 Three Generations of Post-War Cricketers

1 All the quotations included in this chapter, except where otherwise stated, were made during recorded interviews with players.
2 H. S. Becker, 'The professional Dance Musician and his Audience', *American Journal of Sociology*, Vol. 61 (1956), p. 146.
3 Ibid., p. 147.
4 Ibid.
5 Robin Marlar, 'Cricket's Poor get poorer', *Sunday Times* (2 May 1971), p. 26.
6 Ibid.
7 'Sporting salaries', *Evening Standard* (24 October 1969).

Bibliography

Except where otherwise stated, all works listed below were published in London.

Altham, H. A. *A History of Cricket*, Volume 1. 1962
Arlott, J. *From Hambledon to Lord's*. 1948
Arlott, J. *The Middle Ages of Cricket*. 1949
Ashley-Cooper, F. S. *Nottingham Cricket and Cricketers*. Nottingham, 1923
Ashley-Cooper, F. S. *The Hambledon Cricket Chronicle: 1772–1796*. Nottingham, 1924
Bagehot, W. *The English Constitution*. World's Classics, 1904
Bettesworth, W. A. *Chats on the Cricket Field*. 1918
Bottomore, T. *Karl Marx, Early Writings*. New York, 1964
Bowen, Rowland. *Cricket: A History of Its Growth and Development throughout the World*. 1970
Brailsford, D. *Sport and Society: Elizabeth to Anne*. 1969
Buckley, G. B. *Fresh Light on Eighteenth-Century Cricket*. 1937
Buckley, G. B. *Fresh Light on Pre-Victorian Cricket*. 1937
Burn, W. L. *The Age of Equipoise*. 1964
Caffyn, W. *71 Not Out*. 1899
Cardus, N. *English Cricket*. 1945
Carlyle, T. *Chartism*. 1889
Central Youth Employment Executive, *Professional Sport*. 1969
Chamberlayne, J. *Magnae Britannicae Notitia*. 1698
Croome, A. C. M. (ed.) *Fifty Years of Sport at Oxford, Cambridge and the Great Public Schools*. 1913
Daft, R. *Kings of Cricket*. Bristol, 1893
Dahrendorf, R. *Class and Class Conflict in an Industrial Society*. 1959
Denison, W. *Sketches of the Players*. 1848
Dollery, H. E. *Professional Captain*. 1952
Dunning, E. G. (ed.) *The Sociology of Sport*. 1971

Elton, G. *England Under the Tudors*. 1961

Gale, F. W. *Echoes from Old Cricket Fields*. 1871

Giddens, A. *Capitalism and Modern Social Theory*. Cambridge, 1971

Haller, W. *The Rise of Puritanism*. New York, 1938

Harris, Lord. *A History of Kent County Cricket*. 1907

Harris, Lord and Ashley-Cooper, F. S. *Lord's and the MCC*. 1914

Haygarth, A. *Cricket Scores and Biographies*. 1865

Hill, C. *Society and Puritanism*. 1964

Hobbs, J. B. *My Life Story*. 1935

Hobsbaum, E. J. *Industry and Empire*. 1968

Holmes, Revd R. S. *The County Cricket Championship*. 1894

Hughes, E. C. *Men and Their Work*. New York, 1958

Huizinga, J. *Homo Ludens*. 1949

Hunt, B. C. *The Development of the Business Corporation in England: 1800–1867*. Cambridge, Massachusetts, 1936

Laslett, P. *The World We Have Lost*. 1965

Lockwood, D. *The Black-Coated Worker*. 1958

Marshall, D. *The English Domestic Servant in History*. 1949

Marshall, J. *The Duke Who Was Cricket*. 1961

Marshall, J. *Sussex Cricket: A History*. 1959

Marylebone Cricket Club. *A History of Lord's and the MCC*. 1968

Mitford, Mary Russell. *Our Village*. 1879

Moore, Jnr, Barrington. *Social Origins of Dictatorship and Democracy*. 1971

Newbolt, Sir Henry. *Selected Poems*. 1940

Perkin, H. A. *The Origins of Modern English Society, 1780–1880*. 1969

Pycroft, Revd James. *The Cricket Field*. 1851

Rait-Kerr, R. S. *The Laws of Cricket*. 1950

Ranjitsinhji, Prince K. S. *The Jubilee Book of Cricket*. 1897

Root, F. *The Cricket Pro's Lot*. 1937

Squire, Dr H. *Henfield Cricket and Its Sussex Cradle*. 1949

Stone, L. *The Crisis of the Aristocracy*. 1965

Strutt, J. *The Sports and Pastimes of the Peoples of England*. 1801

Tawney, R. H. *The Agrarian Problem in the Sixteenth Century*. 1912

Taylor, A. D. *Annals of Lord's and the History of the MCC*. 1903

Thomas, P. (H. P-T) *Old English Cricket*. Nottingham, 1922–9

Thompson, E. P. *The Making of the English Working Classes*. 1963

Thompson, F. M. L. *English Landed Society in the Nineteenth Century*. 1963

Thomson, A. A. *Cricket, The Golden Age*. 1961

Waghorn, H. T. *The Dawn of Cricket*. 1906

Warner, Sir P. *Lord's, 1787–1945*. 1946

Weber, M. *The Protestant Ethic and the Spirit of Capitalism*. 1920

Wodehouse, P. G. *Mike*. 1906

Index

Aburrow, Edward, 63
Advisory County Cricket Committee, 125
Aisalbie, Benjamin, 70, 87
Albemarle, Duke of, 56
Alcock, C. W., 120
All-England XI, 57, 101–3, 106–15, 118–19, 188, 189
Allsop Arms, St Marylebone, 73
Altham, H. S., 1, 69, 74; quoted, 14, 30–1, 68, 78, 93–4, 109, 112, 125–6
Alverstone, Viscount, 120
amateur players: abolition of separation from professionals, 154, 156, 172; batting qualities, 92; 1873–1962, 138–54; modern equivalent, 185; origins, 87; payment, 143; post-war, 154, 155; pre-war, 159–60
Amherst, Stephen, 47, 61, 66
Anderson, George, 103, 108, 112
Andrews, 35
Ardingley, 105
aristocracy: adoption of cricket, 24–33, 51; and county cricket, 127; effect on the game, 41–4, 45, 60–1; growing distaste for 'great matches', 75–7; hostility towards cricket, 21–3; as members of MCC, 87, 134–5; take up playing cricket, 34–6
Arlott, John, 1
Articles of Agreement (1727), 41–2, 43

Artillery Ground, 49, 50, 53–4, 75, 77
Ash Street, 24
Ashby, 93
Ashes, 155, 169
Ashford, Kent, 47
Ashley-Cooper, F. S., 56, 60, 64
Atkinson, G., 112
Australia: English tour of (1861), 112; English tour of (1873), 149; first 'tests' with England, 124; and the 'Nottinghamshire schism', 148–9; Packer's 'cricket circus', 158, 187–9
Aylward, 61

Bagehot, Walter; 128
Bailey, Trevor, 170
bails: etymology, 15; specifications, 43
Baker family, 98, 99
Baker, John, 98
Baker, William de, 98
balls: new ball rule, 125; 'specifications, 43
Baltimore, Lord, 36
bandy, 11
Barber, R. W., 184, 185
Barber, William, 58, 59, 63
Barker, 97
'Barn Door' match (1837), 73
Barnes, W., 148
Bartrum, 62, 63
Bat and Ball, Broadhalfpenny Down, 59

bats: curved, 42; etymology, 15; specifications, 43
Bayley, James, 59
Beagley, Thomas, 79–80
Beauclerk, Lord Frederick, 70, 71, 77, 89
Bedser family, 163
Beldham, George, 64
Beldham, William, 59, 64, 72, 78
Belgravia, 87
Bell Inn, Nottingham, 106
Bell's Life, 131–2
benefit matches, 152
Bennet, Thomas, 98
Benson and Hedges Cup, 157
Bentinck, Lord George, 71
Bently, 95
Bethersden, 47
Beverley Club, 98, 99, 105
Birrup, W., 112
Bishopbourne, 46
Bisse, James, 19
Blackwood's Edinburgh Magazine, 83
Bligh, E., 60
Bonus-plan Insurance Ltd, 188
Boswell, James, 37
boundaries, 11, 51, 125
Bourne Paddock, 47
Bowen, Major Rowland, 5–6, 123
bowling: no-ball rule, 43, 87, 95–6; over-arm, 95–6, 109; professional bowlers, 92, 93–5; round-arm, 93–5
bowls, 22
Bownde, Nicholas, 18–19
Box, Thomas, 105
Boxall, 61, 66
Boxgrove Deanery, 21
Boycott, Geoffrey, 174, 189
Brenchley, Harman, 98
Brenchley, Henry, 98, 99
Brett, Thomas, 63
Brighton, 105
Broadhalfpenny Down, 58
Broadridge, James, 72, 93, 94–5
Broderick, Alan, 35, 39, 41–3
Bromley, 54
Bromley Common, 36
Brompton, 36, 53

Brown (Kent), 61
Brown (Leicester), 69
Buckinghamshire, County Championship, 123
Budd, E. H., 71, 89
Budd, Joseph, 61
Bunbury, 69
Burbage, Frederick, 121
Burton, Robert, 22
Bury and Norwich Post, 95
Bury St Edmunds Club, 105

Caesar, Julius, 112
Caffyn, 112
Caldecourt, William, 95
Cambridge, 103
Cambridge University, 71, 90, 91, 112
Cambridgeshire, early 'county' matches, 97
Campden, 19
Canada, tours of, 113
Canterbury, 47, 98, 102, 114
captaincy: amateurs *v.* professionals, 139, 140, 141, 155, 156; effect of sponsorship on England's captaincy, 158–9
Cardus, Neville, 1, 2
Carlyle, Thomas, 83
Carpenter, R., 112, 114
cat and dog, 4, 6, 10, 11, 12–13
caught out, 42
Central Youth Employment Executive, 179–80
Chamberlayne, John, 51
Chappell, G. S., 189
character formation, cricket and, 86–7, 140–2
Charles II, King of England, 41
Charterhouse School, 105
Chatham, 25, 47
Chelsea, 36
Chertsey, 55
Chislehurst, 53, 54
Churchill, Charles, 88
Clackmannanshire, 136
Clapham Common, 25
Clarke, 69

Clarke, William, 101–8, 110, 116, 139, 188
club-ball, 6, 13
clykett, 16
Coleridge, Samuel, 84
Compton, Dennis, 161
Compton Verney, 145
The Connoisseur, 62
Corbett, 92
Cornhill Insurance Company, 188
Cotswold Games, 19
country-house cricket matches, 145
County Championship: 1873–1894, 120–37; eligibility, 123–4, 156; founding of, 92, 93; MCC recognition, 128, 130, 134, 137, 156; post-war, 155–8; reorganization, 157–8; rise in popularity, 116; suspension during World War II, 162; teething troubles, 130, 135–7
county cricket: amateur *v.* professional players, 138–45; attitude to MCC, 128, 136; consolidation, 145–6; criticisms of at beginning of century, 142–5; decline in attendance, 155–6, 170–1; eligibility, 123–4, 156; finances, 178–9; formation, 96–100; growing support for, 115, 116; post-war, 155–9; post-war 'golden age', 169–70; present-day, 169–86
Coventry, 69
Coventry Mercury, 69
Cowdrey, Colin, 170
Coxheath, 47, 48
Craute, 61
creag, 14–15
crease, etymology, 15
cricket: etymology, 14–15; historiography, 1–8
'The Cricket Industry', 2
Cricketers' Association, 156, 188
Cricketers' Fund, 109, 114, 115
Cromwell, Oliver, 22
Croxteth, 145
Cumberland, Duke of, 36
Cutbush, 62

Daft, Richard, 102, 107, 139, 149
Dakin, Samuel, 104–5
Dark, James, 70, 73, 88, 90, 102
Darnley, Earls of, 60, 99
Dartford, 48, 53, 54, 55, 62
Dartford Heath, 35
Dean, John, 108
Deede family, 98
Defoe, Daniel, 51–2
Denbighshire, 136
Denison, William, 92, 94, 103, 105
Derby, Earl of, 27
Derbyshire: County Championship, 120, 121; finances, 179; and the formation of county cricket, 96
Derrick, John, 16
The Devil and the Peers, 75
Dexter, Ted, 185
Dickens, Charles, 2
Dicker, 24
Dingate, Stephen, 61
Disraeli, Benjamin, 127
Diver, Ducky, 112
Dollery, Tom, 153–4
Donegal, County, 136
Dorset, Dukes of, 40, 46, 47, 53, 56, 60, 61, 64, 65
Dorset Fields, 68, 74
Dover, Robert, 19
Downing, 70
Dublin, 102
Dugdale, Sir William, 22
Dulwich, 48

Eastham, George, 188
Edgbaston, 154
Edinburgh, 118
Edward I, King of England, 14–15
Edward III, King of England, 17
Egerton, 47
Elizabeth I, Queen of England, 25–6, 27
Eltham, 19, 62
Elyot, Sir Thomas, 22
England: dismissal of Greig as captain, 177; first 'tests' *v.* Australia, 124; *v.* Hampshire, 40; *v.* Kent, 50, 62, 63, 98, 99–100; *v.* Middlesex,

England—*contd.*
115; *v.* Nottingham, 78; regain
Ashes (1953), 169; *v.* Sussex, 94
Escrick, 145
Essex, early 'county' matches, 68;
finances, 165
Eton, 86; *v.* Harrow, 71, 72, 90, 91;
v. Westminster School, 71–2
etymological derivations, cricketing
terms, 14–15

Farnham, 59
Mr Farrar's Club, 47
Fennex, William, 79
Fitzgerald, R. A., 114, 132
Flowers, W., 148
folk-game, cricket as a, 5–8, 9–23,
60
follow-on, 125
football, 5, 9–10, 17, 22
Foreign Post, 24
Forest Ground, Nottingham, 106
Fox, Charles, 38
Francis, C. K., 145
Frederick, Prince of Wales, 36, 44,
48, 49, 50
Freemantle, Andrew, 64
Freemantle, John, 64
Frittenden, 47
Fry, C. B., 130, 170
Fulham, 36

Gage, Sir William, 34–5, 39, 45
Gale, Frederick, 98
gambling on cricket, 25, 33, 40–1,
42–3, 44, 55, 76–8
Gamelin, M., 74
The Gentleman's Magazine, 46, 76
Gentlemen *v.* Players, 71, 72–3, 90,
131, 132, 136–7, 155
Gentlemen of London, 35, 36
Gentlemen of Middlesex, 35
George, 61
George IV, King of England, 67
Gilbert, 89
Gillette Cup, 156, 157
Gladstone, William, 126

Glamorgan, County Championship,
124
Gloucestershire: County Champion-
ship, 120, 121; early cricket in, 34;
finances, 179; and the formation of
county cricket, 96; stob-ball, 15
goff, 11
Goldwin, William, 41–2
Goodwood, 34, 61
Grace, W. G., 110–11, 123, 125–6,
131, 132, 149
Grandserre, John Joseph, 74
Gray, Thomas, 188
Green, 61
Green, C. E., 143
Green Man and Still, 78
Greenwood, Job, 107, 118
Greenwood, Luke, 118
Gregory IX, Pope, 13
Greig, Tony, 177, 188
Grimston, R., 140
Grundy, J., 112, 114
Guildford Royal Grammar School,
16
Gunn, William, 147

Hadlow, 54
Hambledon: aristocracy and match
organization, 45, 54; *v.* England,
56, 57; history, 55–60; introduction of the third stump, 43–4;
as the mecca of cricket, 67;
occupations of the players, 63–4;
standard bat kept by, 43
Hampshire: County Championship,
123, 160; dialects, 15; early
'county' matches, 35, 40, 49, 68,
97; early cricket in, 34, 55;
finances, 179
handball, 10
Harris, David, 59, 64
Harris, Lord, 48, 97, 100, 147
Harrison, Sir William, 52
Harrow, Eton *v.*, 71, 72, 90, 91
Hartley, Edmund, 21
Hartley, Edward, 21
Hawke, Lord, 139, 143, 146, 156
Haygarth, Arthur, 3, 6, 48

Hayward, Tom, 112, 151
Haywood, 130
Hazelrigg, Sir Arthur, 142
Hendren, Patsy, 154
Henry VII, King of England, 26
Henry VIII, King of England, 26-7
Hertfordshire: early 'county' matches, 70; v. MCC, 123
Hillyer, W. R., 100
Hirst, G. H., 130, 151
hit-wicket rule, 43
Hobbs, Sir Jack, 151, 153
Hodswell, 62, 63
Holmes, Revd R. S., 136-7
Horningtoft, 105
Horsmonden, 53, 54, 62-3
Hothfield, 145
Howard, T. C., 77
Hughes, Thomas, 86
Hull, 107
Humphrey, Lawrence, 22
hurling, 5, 10
Hutton, Len, 156

Iddison, R., 112
Imperial Cricket Conference, 125
Incogniti, 100
'independent' players, 61-3, 66
Industrial and Professional Careers Research Organization, 180-1
Ingleby-Mackenzie, Colin, 160
International Cricket Conference, 187
Ipswich, 118
Isle of Thanet, 47

Jackson, F. S., 170
Jackson, John, 112, 118-19, 130, 139, 147
Jamieson, John, 12-13
Je-ne-sais-quoi Club, 67, 74
Jenner-Fust, Herbert, 72, 96-7
Jessop, 130
John Player Sunday League, 157, 158
Johnson, Samuel, 37
Jones, Evan B., 121

Keate, Dr, 72
Kennington Common, 35, 48
Kennington Oval, see Oval
Kent: bowling style, 93; challenge to MCC's supremacy, 111; County Championship, 120, 121, 141; dialects, 15; early matches in, 24, 34, 47-8, 53, 96-7; v. England, 50, 62, 63, 98, 99-100; and the formation of county cricket, 96; Silver Cup competition (1873), 122
King, Gregory, 37, 51
Kingscote Club, 105
Kipps, 62
knappan, 4
Knatchbull family, 98
Knatchbull-Hugessen, W. W., 99
Knight family, 98
Knight, G. T., 87, 93, 94, 96
Knox, Ronald, 126

Lamb, Squire, 56
Lambarde, William, 52
Lambert, William, 63, 65-6, 72, 77, 78, 79
Lancashire: County Championship, 120, 121, 150; and the formation of county cricket, 96
laws: effect of aristocracy on, 41-4; 1727 Articles, 41-2, 43; 1744 rules, 43, 44, 49; MCC's first code, 44; MCC's early influence on, 68-70, 74, 87; MCC's 1884 revisions, 125
LBW, 43
Lee, George, 63
Leek, John, 14
Lees Court, 145
Leg-before-wicket (LBW), 43
'legs', 78
Leicester, 69, 74, 103
Leicester Journal, 69, 74
Leicestershire: early 'county' matches, 98; finances, 179; Hazelrigg's captaincy, 142; professional players from, 103
Leigh-Pemberton, Edward, 99
Lennox, Duke of, 56
Lewes, 35

Lillywhite, James, 134, 148–9, 150
Lillywhite, John, 109, 112
Lillywhite, William, 72, 93, 94–5, 105–6
Linton, 47
Littleboy, Mr, 52, 53
Lloyd, David, 187
Lockyer, T., 112
London, 45, 46, 48–9, 53–4, 60, 71, 74, 78, 88–90
London Club, 44, 48–9
London Society of Antiquaries, 14
London Spy, 41
Lord, Thomas, 68, 70, 73, 77, 87
Lord's Cricket Ground (first), 68, 73
Lord's Cricket Ground (second), 68, 72, 73–4
Lord's Cricket Ground (third), 80, 105, 107; disappearance of amateur status at, 154; drop in standard of play at, 131; first professionals at, 91–2; first Varsity match, 72; Gentlemen v. Players, 155; introduction of round-arm bowling, 95; James Dark purchases, 88, 90–1; Lillywhite at, 105–6; Lord sells, 87; MCC at, 68, 70, 73, 87, 88; MCC purchases, 88; Middlesex's first match at, 133–4; Northern players refuse to play at, 113–14; origin, 68; players coming late to the ground at, 108; Silver Cup competition, 122; William Lambert barred from, 78
Mr Louch's Club, 47
Love, James, 63
Ludford, Roger, 17–18
Lynn, 70
Lyttleton, C. G., 109

MacLaren, A. C., 130, 170
Maidstone, 21, 62, 99, 102
Maltus, Simon, 17
Manchester, 115
Mann, Sir Horatio, 40, 46–8, 56, 60, 61, 65
Mann, Noah, 64, 65
Marshall, William, 36

Martin, Richard, 21
Martin, William, 21
Martingbell, 97
Martyn, Nicholas, 17–18
Marx, Karl, 82
Mary I, Queen of England, 27
Marylebone Cricket Club (MCC): aristocracy and, 87; attempt to replace its authority, 110–11; changes in cricketing laws, 69–70, 74, 87–8; and the County Championship, 120, 121, 122, 124, 128, 130, 134, 135–6, 137, 156; and county cricket, 126–8; deterioration and rejuvenation, 130–7; disputes with professionals, 108–9, 113–15; early years, 67–80; 1884 rule revisions, 125; founding, 48, 60, 67, 73; Lillywhite employed by, 105–6, 109; membership, 132–3, 134–5; and over-arm bowling, 95–6, 109; professional players and, 91–2, 93; and round-arm bowling, 93–6; Samuel Dakin employed by, 105; and the superiority of London cricket, 88–9
Matthews, 95
May, Peter, 170
Melton Mowbray, 69–70
Merrow Down, 35
middle classes, take up cricket, 51–3
Middlesex: County Championship, 96, 120, 121; early 'county' matches, 35, 68, 97, 99; v. England (1867), 115; started playing at Lord's, 133–4
Middlesex, Earl of, 36
Middleton, Lord, 35
Miller, 61
Milles, G. W., 99
Mills, John, 62
Mills of Bromley, 62
Minor Counties Cricket Association, 125
Minshull, 61
Mitchell, R. A. H., 131, 132
Mitford, J., 79
Mitford, Mary, 81
Montford, Lord, 36, 48

Morley, F., 148
Morning Post, 40
Moulden, 25
Moulsey Hurst, 36
Mynn, Alfred, 99, 100, 105

National Review, 100, 141
Needham, 69
new ball rule, 125
New Romney, 47
Newark, 118
Newbolt, Sir Henry, 141
Newland, Richard, 54, 55
'no-ball' rule, 43, 87, 95–6
Norfolk, early 'county' games, 70, 96–7
Norfolk Chronicle, 70
Norman family, 98
North, Lord, 28
North *v.* South, 114, 136
Northamptonshire, County Championship, 124
Northernwood, 145
Northumberland, Duke of, 28
Norton family, 98
Norton, W. South, 111
Norwich, 105
notches, 42
Nottingham, 78, 79, 89–90, 106, 107
Nottingham Journal, 89
Nottinghamshire: County Championship, 120, 121; dispute with Surrey, 112, 113, 115; early 'county' matches, 98; England players from, 103; finances, 179; and the formation of county cricket, 96; John Jackson plays for, 118; lack of matches in 1840s, 106–7
'Nottinghamshire Schism' (1881), 148–50
Nutfield, 79
Nyren, John, 43–4, 56–8, 59, 64–5
Nyren, Richard, 56, 58, 63, 64–5

Oakham, 69–70
Old Etonians, 71

Oldham, 102
one-day matches, 157, 158
Onslow, Lord, 35
Osbaldeston, Squire, 71, 77
Oval, 111, 112, 113, 121, 132
overs, rules, 125
overseas tours, 112
Oxford, 105
Oxford, Lord, 40, 53
Oxford University *v.* Cambridge University, 71, 90, 91

Packer, Kerry, 187–9
Palairet, 130
pale-maille, 11
Parr, George, 111, 112, 113, 139
Parvishe, John, 16
Paterson, W. H., 147
Patshill, 145
Penshurst, 35, 61
Perkins, H. A., 133
Perkins, William, 19
Phillips, Edward, *The Mysteries of Love and Eloquence*, 22–3
Pilch, 92, 97, 99, 100, 102, 105
pitches: improvement, 125; twenty-three yard pitch, 43
Players, 88; Gentlemen *v.* Players, 71, 72–3, 90, 131, 132, 136–7, 155
Political and Economic Planning (PEP), 2, 171, 172
Pope, Alexander, 75
popping crease, 42
popping hole, 42
Porter, John, 16, 18
Post Boy, 24–5
Postman, 25
Powlett, Charles, 55–6
Powlett, William, 60
Preston Hall, 145
Proctor, M. J., 189
professional players: county cricket, 138–45, 146; disputes amongst (1860s), 112–13; 1846–1870, 101–19; 1873–1962, 138–54; the first, 40, 45; loyalty, 164–5; MCC's dispute with, 93–6, 108–10, 113–15; MCC engages first, 91–3;

professional players—*contd.*
  'Nottinghamshire Schism', 148–
  50; pay and other benefits, 91–
  2, 107–8, 150–1; post-war, 154,
  155, 162–9; pre-war, 159–63;
  'retained' players, 61, 62, 63, 66,
  79; retirement, 66, 79–80, 118–19,
  152–3, 166–9; and the rise of
  county cricket, 115–18
Prudential World Cup and Trophy,
  157
Purchase, Richard, 64
Puritanism, and cricket, 19–21, 75
Pycroft, Revd J., 79–80, 102
Pye, 61
The Pyed Horse, Chiswell Street, 50

Quidnunc, 100

Rait-Kerr, R. S., 68–9
The Ram, Smithfield, 50
Ranjitsinhji, Prince K. S., 130, 139–
  40, 146, 170
retained players, 61, 62, 63, 66, 79
retirement, professional players, 66,
  79–80, 118–19, 152–3, 166–9
Rhodes, W., 130, 151
Richards, I. V. A., 189
Richmond, 62
Richmond, Duke of, 34–5, 39, 40–3,
  45, 54, 55, 61, 66
Ring, John, 61
Robert of Malden, 18
Robertson, Jack, 162, 176
Robin, Long, 62
Rockingham, Lord, 40
Romney, 62, 63
Rood Ashton, 145
Root, Fred, 151–2, 153
Rowbotham, 112
rules, *see* laws
run-out, 42
runs, 42

Sackville, Lord John, 36, 39, 40, 61,
  62

St Austell, 95
St Helens, 102
St James Chronicle, 76
Sandwich, Earl of, 38, 115
Saturday Review, 144–5
Sawyer, 62
Scarborough, 145
school matches, 71–2, 86, 90, 144
Schweppes County Championship,
  157
Scotton, W. H., 148
Selby, J., 148
Selby, Thomas, 97
Sevenoaks, 48
Shaftesbury, Lord, 83
Shaw, Alfred, 148, 149, 150
Sheffield, 97, 102, 105
Sheppard, David, 170
short-runs, 43
Shrewsbury, A., 147, 148, 150
Sileby, 104
Silver Cup competition (1873), 120,
  122–3
Sir Horatio Mann's Club, 47
Sissinghurst, 47
Slaughter, Richard, 21
Slindon, 54–5
Small, John, 63
Smith, George, 50
Snow, John, 174–5
Soame, Sir Peter, 35
Somerset: County Championship,
  123; finances, 179; stoolball, 15
la soule, 10
South Derbyshire Club, 105
Southgate, 99, 145
Southwark, 52
Southwell, 118
Spiers and Pond, Messrs, 112
sponsored cricket, 156–8, 171, 188–9
Spooner, R. H., 130
The Sporting Magazine, 87, 93
Squire, Dr H., 3–4
Star and Garter Club, 67
Stead, Edwin, 35, 36, 39
Steel, D. C., 147
Stephenson, H. H., 112, 113
Stewart, Peter, 63
stob-ball, 15

Stoddart, A. E., 147
Stoneyhurst School, 15
stoolball, 6, 10, 11, 13, 15, 21
Stow, John, 22
Strathavon, Lord, 48
Strutt, Joseph, 11, 12, 14
stumps: etymology, 15; introduction of the third, 43–4; specifications, 43
substitutes, use of, 43
Sueter, Thomas, 63
Suffolk, early 'county' games, 97
Sunday observance, 20, 75
Surrey: v. All-England (1858), 111; challenge to MCC's supremacy, 111–12; County Championship, 120, 121; dispute with Notts, 112, 113, 115; early 'county' matches, 35, 36, 49, 54, 97; early cricket in, 24, 34; England players from, 112; first professional players, 92; and the formation of county cricket, 96; Hobbs's desire to play for, 151; v. Sussex (1859), 111–12
Sussex: County Championship, 120, 121; dialects, 15; early 'county' matches, 35, 49, 97; early cricket in, 24, 34; v. England (1828), 94; England players from, 112; and the formation of county cricket, 96; Silver Cup competition (1873), 122; stoolball, 15; v. Surrey (1859), 111–12
Sussex, Earl of, 24
Sutherland, Duke of, 118
Swinfield, 47

Tankerville, Earl of, 46, 56, 60
test cricket, 183, 189–90, 224–5
Thirsk, Joan, 30
Thomas, Percy, *Old English Cricket*, 4
tip-cat, 4, 6, 11, 12, 13
Tonbridge, 53
Town Malling Club, 97, 98, 105
trap-ball, 4, 10, 11–12, 13
Trent Bridge Ground, 106
Trevelyan, G. M., 37–8

Truro, 102
Turvey, Richard, 17–18

umpires, powers of, 43
United XI of England, 108, 110, 112, 113–15, 189
United South of England XI, 112
United States of America, tours of, 112

Verulam, Earl of, 128–9
Vice Regal Lodge, 145
village cricket, 7–8, 34, 45, 46, 53

Waldegrave, Lord, 36, 48
Walker, Harry, 59, 64
Walker, J., 99
Walker, Tom, 59, 64
Walker, V. E., 109
Walpole, Horace, 40
Ward, Thomas, 21
Ward, William, 68, 71, 77, 87, 88
Warner, Sir Pelham, 71
Warwickshire: player transfers, 165; pre-war conditions, 153–4
Waugh, Alec, 145
Waymark, Thomas, 61, 63, 66
Wells, H. G., 126
Wells, James, 59
Wells, John, 59, 64
Wenman, Edward, 99, 100, 105
West, Ralph, 21
West Kent Club, 96–7
Westminster School, 71–2
White, 'Shock', 43
White Conduit Club, 67–8, 80, 73, 74
whites, 125
wicket, etymology, 15
wickets, post-war, 164
Willes, John, 93
Willoughby, 132
Willsher, Edgar, 100, 109, 111
Wilton, 145

Wiltshire, stoolball, 15
Winchester College, 106
Winchilsea, Earl of, 68, 74
Wisden, John, 108, 112
Woodward, 89
Wootton, 114
Worcestershire: County Championship, 124; finances, 178–9; professionals' pay, 151–2
Wordsworth, 72
World War II, 155, 162–3

The Worlds Work, 142
Wye, 47

Yorkshire: collective professional protests, 150; County Championship, 120, 121, 155; early 'county' matches, 97–8; and the formation of county cricket, 96

I Zingari, 100